Louis D. Brandeis, Felix Frankfurter, and the New Deal

LOUIS D. BRANDEIS, FELIX FRANKFURTER, AND THE NEW DEAL

By

Nelson Lloyd Dawson

1980

Archon Books

First published 1980 as an Archon Book,
an imprint of The Shoe String Press, Inc.,
Hamden, Connecticut 06514

Library of Congress Cataloging in Publication Date

Dawson, Nelson L
Louis D. Brandeis, Felix Frankfurter, and the New Deal.

Bibliography: p. 251
Includes index.
1. Brandeis, Louis Dembitz, 1856-1941. 2. Frankfurter, Felix, 1882-1965. 3. Law—United States—History and criticism. 4. United States—Politics and government—1933-1945. 5. Judges—United States—Biography. I. Title.
KF8744.D38   973.917'092'2   80-18409
ISBN 0-208-01817-4

CONTENTS

ACKNOWLEDGMENTS

I wish to acknowledge the valuable assistance given by the staffs of the Franklin D. Roosevelt Library, the Manuscript Division of the Library of Congress, and Manuscript Library at Princeton University. I am grateful to Louis Starr, director of the Columbia Oral History Research Office of Columbia University, for permission to quote from some of the reminiscences of the Columbia Oral History Collection. A special debt of gratitude is due the late Pearl Von Allmen, former law librarian at the University of Louisville, who permitted me to examine the Brandeis papers and graciously provided me the space to do so.

I am happy to acknowledge the invaluable aid given by Dr. Richard Lowitt, who directed the preparation of my dissertation. He was always ready with suggestions, guidance, and encouragement. He has remained a valued friend and adviser since my graduate school days.

A particular debt of gratitude is due my family. My wife Susan has been patient and encouraging throughout my academic career. My parents, Mr. and Mrs. P. Lloyd Dawson, gave me much help and support while I was in graduate school. I deeply regret that my mother, who was very interested in my researches, did not live to see the completion of this book.

INTRODUCTION

The New Deal was not an ideological monolith, but a composite of various, often competing, social philosophies. For this reason, the concept of two New Deals is an oversimplification. Recovery and reform were not mutually exclusive concepts. They were seen in various ways by different New Deal advisers (whose name was legion), and the resulting situation was considerably more complex than that presented by the model of two New Deals.[1]

The significance of various strategies was enhanced by the president's lack of a consistent philosophy. Roosevelt did not have such a philosophy when he entered the White House, and there is no evidence that he ever developed one.[2] Presidential advisers often had the disconcerting experience of having Roosevelt agree to some measure they urged only to discover later that their advice had been superseded by another suggestion from someone else.[3] Roosevelt did not have a consistent philosophy, but he did have a set of attitudes. He wanted to help people and to pull the country out of the depression. He was willing to use governmental power on a hitherto unprecedented scale to do so. He was willing to try a variety of experiments because he had no clear idea of what would work. This flexibility made the convictions of his advisers more important than would have been the case with a president, such as Woodrow Wilson, who entered the White House with his program already developed.

New Deal policy, therefore, cannot be understood simply as the legislative embodiment of a clearly defined program, but can be understood only as the result of a complex process of discussion, disagreement, struggle, and compromise between the president, his advisers, and Congress. This means that any adequate study of New Deal policy must give considerable attention to Roosevelt's advisers. Even in the early days of the New Deal, the names of Felix Frankfurter and Louis D. Brandeis appeared in the writings of knowledgeable observers. Opinion varied as to the role of these men in the evolution of policy, but commentators agreed that they exerted significant influence.[4] Further analysis has strengthened this conclusion.

The secondary literature of the New Deal also contains many references to Brandeis and Frankfurter. Much has been written about their socioeconomic philosophy and their circle of friends, acquaintances, and protégés in and out of government. There has been no detailed discussion, however, of their ideas in relation to the New Deal and no sustained analysis of their efforts to translate ideas into policy. This study discusses the Brandeis-Frankfurter philosophy and traces its influence on the evolution of New Deal policy.[5] It is an analysis of how ideas influenced policy through a complex network of personal relationships.

CHAPTER I

Brandeis, Frankfurter, and Roosevelt:
The Background of Their New Deal Relationship

Felix Frankfurter first encountered Brandeis when, as a student at the Harvard Law School, he heard the well-known "People's Attorney" deliver his famous lecture "The Opportunity in the Law" to the Harvard Ethical Society. The lecture presented two themes basic to Brandeis's philosophy: the danger of class warfare caused by economic injustice, and the role lawyers should play in averting the crisis. This meeting occurred on 4 May 1905.[1]

When Frankfurter left Harvard in 1906, he served as an assistant district attorney under Henry L. Stimson in the Southern District of New York. Stimson obtained Frankfurter through his old friend Prof. James B. Ames of the Harvard Law School.[2] After helping Stimson in his unsuccessful gubernatorial bid in New York in 1910, Frankfurter followed him to Washington when Stimson became secretary of war. Frankfurter served as a law officer in the Bureau of Insular Affairs.[3]

In a letter to William O. Douglas in 1934, Frankfurter recalled that he was a "hot Hamiltonian" when he went to Washington.[4] This Hamiltonianism led him to vote for Theodore Roosevelt in 1912.[5] Frankfurter, a young New Nationalist progressive, tried to persuade Brandeis to vote for Roosevelt.[6] This appeal failed, and Brandeis became one of Wilson's most important advisers and an architect of the New Freedom.[7] Had Frankfurter never grown close to Brandeis, his Hamiltonianism might have persisted so that by

1

1933 his philosophy would have been similar to that of such men as Adolf Berle, Jr., Rexford Tugwell, and Raymond Moley.[8] Brandeis exerted a strong influence on Frankfurter's intellectual development. In 1916 Frankfurter stated that he had come into "intimate personal contact" with Brandeis "beginning with 1910 and particularly after I went to Washington."[9] Brandeis's first letter to Frankfurter was probably the one written 14 June 1910 in response to Frankfurter's request the day before for a copy of the brief in the Ballinger-Pinchot case. In sending the brief, Brandeis congratulated Frankfurter for his work in an Illinois case upholding a ten-hour law for women.[10] By the summer of 1912, the "Dear Mr. Frankfurter" address had become "My Dear Frankfurter" and the closing salutation had become "Most Cordially."[11]

During Frankfurter's stay in Washington, he lived with other bright young men in an establishment known as the "House of Truth."[12] Brandeis was a frequent visitor to this house in 1913 during his trips to the capital.[13] Herbert B. Ehrmann recalled that Frankfurter was also a dinner guest of Brandeis's during this period.[14] By 1914 Brandeis thought of Frankfurter as a promising young man. He suggested that Frankfurter join the faculty of the Harvard Law School, believing that he could best serve the cause of reform by educating future leaders.[15] Even while Brandeis was urging Frankfurter to join the Harvard faculty, he was working behind the scenes for the appointment. He wrote his friend Winfred T. Denison suggesting that Roscoe Pound, a professor at the school who became dean in 1916, urge Stimson to smooth the way with influential men in New York. He observed realistically that his own "recent clashes with the capitalistic world seem to disqualify me for that task."[16] Brandeis also wrote Pound directly, assuring him that Stimson "will not hesitate to give all possible assistance since he now definitely knows that it is Frankfurter's desire to come to the School."[17] Brandeis's interest in Frankfurter did not wane after the appointment. He helped Pound raise an endowment for a professorship in administrative law and was, according to Dean James B. Thayer, influential in getting Frankfurter named to the post.[18]

Frankfurter, in turn, admired Brandeis. In 1915 he wrote to the

Cosmos Club in Washington urging Brandeis's admission, stating that he was "one of the few thinkers in the profession concerned with the fundamental problem of legal education." He concluded by saying that Brandeis was affecting the thought of the nation as only two or three others had done.[19] Frankfurter urged Elihu Root to support Brandeis's nomination to the Supreme Court in 1916. He attributed his own standards and purposes "in professional and public matters" to two men, Brandeis and Stimson, adding that he saw Brandeis "frequently" and considered with him "various professional problems at close range."[20]

Brandeis's elevation to the Supreme Court did not interfere with his deepening friendship with Frankfurter. Indeed, Frankfurter took over some of the projects Brandeis had to drop after his confirmation. Archibald MacLeish asserted that Brandeis's greatest influence on Frankfurter was in converting him to the "Brandeis brief" method of arguing socially significant cases.[21] Frankfurter successfully argued the case of *Bunting* v. *Oregon* (1917) before the Supreme Court as an unpaid counsel for the National Consumers League after Brandeis's appointment.[22]

The Brandeis-Frankfurter partnership was influencing national political events as early as 1917. In September 1917 Frankfurter urged Newton D. Baker, Wilson's secretary of war, to send someone west to investigate the causes of labor unrest. He suggested Sidney Hillman and added that "the foregoing views have the support of Mr. Justice Brandeis."[23] In December 1917 Frankfurter recommended that the secretary of war create "a single-headed manager to direct the industrial energies of War." Wilson received the same suggestion from Brandeis.[24]

Zionism provided another link between the two during these years, and this remained an enduring concern. In 1919 Oliver Wendell Holmes, Jr., wrote Harold Laski, the English socialist, that when Brandeis called on him after his visit to Europe and Palestine in 1919, he seemed "transfigured by his experiences."[25] Brandeis's interest in Zionism developed some six years earlier, and Frankfurter became his lieutenant in Zionist affairs. He was Brandeis's "eyes, ears, and spokesman" at the Paris Peace Conference.[26] When Brandeis resigned from the Zionist organization in 1921, Frankfurter followed suit.[27]

By the beginning of the 1920s, Brandeis and Frankfurter were close friends. Their correspondence covered a wide range of topics, including politics, law, and Zionism. The letters reflected little involvement in national political affairs simply because small opportunity existed in the 1920s for progressives in their particular situation. As their friendship grew, their expressions of esteem grew more generous. As early as 1916 Brandeis wrote Emma Frankfurter, Felix's mother, that her son "has won so large a place in our hearts and brought so much joy and interest into our lives that we feel very near to you who are nearest to him."[28] In 1925 Brandeis wrote appreciatively to Harold Laski of Frankfurter's "rare qualities" and predicted that if he could teach for twenty years "he will have profoundly affected American Life."[29] At the end of the decade Frankfurter seemed to him "clearly the most useful lawyer in the United States."[30]

One measure of their growing intimacy was Brandeis's willingness to confide in Frankfurter about Supreme Court matters, for Brandeis's reticence about judicial affairs was proverbial. Years later in a letter to Alpheus T. Mason, Brandeis's biographer, Frankfurter quoted Norman Hapgood, one of the justice's closest friends, as saying:

> I wish Louis would get off the Court. Before he was on the bench I used to be able to talk with him about the Supreme Court with the utmost freedom. Now that he is on it, he will not talk with me about it at all, no matter how I tackle him.

Frankfurter concluded that as far as he knew "I was the only person to whom he talked about these matters."[31]

Brandeis also expressed his appreciation of Frankfurter by means of direct financial assistance. In 1934 he told Judge Julian W. Mack of New York that he had "for years" made Frankfurter an allowance of $3,500 a year "for public purposes."[32] This practice seems to have begun in 1916 when Brandeis gave Frankfurter $250 for expenses incurred at his suggestion for activity in "public matters."[33] Brandeis was also willing to give extra amounts for special projects. In 1929, for example, he agreed to provide $2,500 to help Frankfurter publish a casebook.[34] Brandeis's aid was not rigidly confined to "public purposes." On at least one occasion, Frankfurter mentioned financial troubles resulting from his wife's illness, saying that he could get the money "through odd jobs for some of my N.Y. lawyer friends" but that he begrudged the time involved.[35] In a later letter Frankfurter wrote warmly of Brandeis's assistance, concluding "You know my affectionate gratitude."[36]

Brandeis's willingness to help Frankfurter economically demonstrates the roles each played in the relationship. Brandeis was helping Frankfurter do what he could no longer do because of his position on the Court. Frankfurter played the more active role as befitted his relative youth, his friendship with Roosevelt, and his lack of a constraining public position. Brandeis was the elder statesman whose ideas provided the strategy of reform and whose prestige fired its idealism with the strength of moral example.

These roles emerged distinctly during Roosevelt's gubernatorial career in New York. Roosevelt's victory in 1928 gave Frankfurter and Brandeis something the years of Republican ascendency had long denied them—a leader and a political environment receptive to their ideas.[37] It was no coincidence that the Frankfurter-Roosevelt correspondence, which had slowed to a standstill in the early 1920s, began to pick up sharply in 1928. Brandeis, however, maintained a distance from Roosevelt during his gubernatorial years. The justice apparently did not have many suggestions, and whenever he did have advice to offer Frankfurter acted as the bearer of his views to Roosevelt.

Shortly before Roosevelt's election in 1928, Brandeis expressed concern for a good counsel to represent New York State before the Supreme Court, and he also asked for an attack on the notorious "third degree."[38] Frankfurter quickly communicated these concerns to Roosevelt and, despite Brandeis's statement that it was "entirely unnecessary" for him to see Roosevelt, suggested to the governor that he meet with Brandeis in Washington.[39] Brandeis expressed confidence in Frankfurter's influence with Roosevelt by saying that he was sure that "the request from you will accomplish what is desired."[40] He also expressed belief in Frankfurter's importance to

the "resuscitated Democratic Party" by observing that he had
earned "a position as thinker which should enable you to exert
much influence hereafter."[41] Frankfurter, for his part, kept
Brandeis informed of events during Roosevelt's Albany years.[42] By
the beginning of the New Deal, therefore, the relationship between
Brandeis and Frankfurter had grown into "the utmost intimacy."[43]
A triangular relationship between Brandeis, Frankfurter, and
Roosevelt had also been formed. By 1933, Frankfurter was already
acting as the mediator between Brandeis and Roosevelt.

There clearly was trust, respect, and affection between Brandeis
and Frankfurter, and yet it was not a relationship of colleagues. The
differences in age and station made that impossible. In 1933
Brandeis was a seventy-seven-year-old Supreme Court Justice
and Frankfurter a fifty-one-year-old law professor. And yet it was
not a paternal relationship either. Perhaps the teacher-student or
master-disciple model is best. There is a hint of deference in
Frankfurter, and a note of guidance on the part of Brandeis.

Harold Laski believed that Brandeis dominated Frankfurter. He
alluded to Brandeis's "strange hold over Felix" during the course of
some Zionist negotiations, observing that "Felix is clay in his
hands."[44] This picture is overdrawn. Frankfurter was never at a
loss for words, but there is nothing negative about Brandeis in his
extensive correspondence. There are only expressions of appreciation, admiration, and affection.[45] The relationship was not based on
power but on affection. At most there was only the willing
deference of Frankfurter to the wisdom of an older, more
experienced mentor and friend. The two men shared a warm
friendship which endured, though not without testing, the stress of
a severe crisis in American history.

Frankfurter and Roosevelt were introduced by Grenville Clark at
the Harvard Club in New York City in 1906.[46] This meeting,
Frankfurter recalled, produced only a casual acquaintance.[47]
Although they saw each other sporadically after 1906, their
relationship remained casual until World War I. Both were part of
the Wilson administration, served together on the War Labor
Policies Board, and saw each other frequently.[48] Even during these
early years, the irrepressible Frankfurter was full of suggestions.

He urged Roosevelt to adopt Frederick Taylor's system of scientific management at the Charlestown Navy Yard. Roosevelt demurred, expressing doubt that any such move "should be imposed from above on an unwilling working force."[49]

Frankfurter "lost sight" of Roosevelt during the decade 1918-1928.[50] There was only a brief exchange of letters and a visit during Roosevelt's illness throughout this period.[51] The contact was renewed after Roosevelt's victory in 1928, and the next four years were crucial in the relationship. In late 1928 Frankfurter wrote Roosevelt and mentioned the "good talk" he had had with him. He assured Roosevelt that he was always at his disposal and was "most eager" for the success of his administration.[52] During Roosevelt's gubernatorial years, he and Frankfurter

> were in frequent touch by phone and letter. Frankfurter made occasional trips to Albany and Hyde Park . . . Frankfurter was helpful, but not to the exclusion of Roosevelt's other advisers, nor was his advice always acted on.[53]

There were several areas of concern: the judicial system, public utilities, and politics. Political advice became more frequent in 1932.

Frankfurter was active in recruiting competent men for Roosevelt, for he believed that an expert civil service was the key to good government. When his book *The Public & Its Government* appeared in 1930, Frankfurter quickly dispatched a copy to Roosevelt, and about six months later he offered to read him the last chapter.[54] When Roosevelt established a Commission of Revision of the Public Service Commission Law, his appointees "consulted with him frequently and also with Felix Frankfurter."[55] Frankfurter was quick to congratulate Roosevelt when he made a good appointment.[56] Frankfurter maintained that he rarely made unsolicited personnel suggestions, but his definition of "unsolicited' had a scholastic subtlety.[57] His suggestions were not always accepted, for Roosevelt sometimes had inescapable obligations, but Frankfurter did enjoy considerable success. As "one of Roosevelt's most influential advisers outside of the small

coterie in Albany and New York," he bombarded the governor
with personnel recommendations, "many of which Roosevelt
accepted."[58] Frankfurter's tactics were similar to those used by
Brandeis during Wilson's administration. Brandeis suggested
many people for a variety of positions, but insisted that he
"carefully refrained from recommending anybody to any office
except where my advice has been asked."[59] His notion of
"unsolicited" was as flexible as Frankfurter's, however, since he
would arrange his social life to enhance his opportunities to meet
and influence important people.[60]

Frankfurter was deeply involved in power policy during
Roosevelt's New York years. Immediately after Roosevelt's
election Frankfurter told him that hydroelectric power raised
"the most far-reaching social and economic issues before the
American people, certainly for the next decade."[61] Roosevelt
consulted Frankfurter about power policy on several occasions.[62]
Frankfurter adopted the Brandeis "prudent investment" basis
for determining utility rates, and he urged Roosevelt to resist a
utility-sponsored voluntary approach to the question. Roosevelt
took his advice.[63]

Frankfurter also gave Roosevelt political advice which at times
transcended New York State concerns. Sometimes the impetus
came from Brandeis. In the middle of April 1930, Brandeis wrote to
Frankfurter that Roosevelt should "be prepared to pounce upon
Hoover" at the end of the sixty-day period which Hoover had
predicted would see the end of unemployment problems.[64] Two
days later Frankfurter passed this suggestion along to Roosevelt.[65]
The governor apparently welcomed such advice, for he often
expressed a desire to talk to Frankfurter and sometimes invited him
to Albany.[66] In the summer of 1932, Roosevelt wrote Frankfurter:
"It was grand to see you both [Felix and Marion Frankfurter] last
week. You stimulate me enormously. Repeat the dose again."[67]

Frankfurter, for his part, recalled that during the gubernatorial
years he and Roosevelt formed "rather easy, I might say
intellectually intimate ties."[68] Yet he had reservations about
Roosevelt. In late 1931, he wrote the historian Walter Notestein:
"Were I God, of course, I should want more of a fellow to guide our

destinies during the next four years than is Roosevelt."[69] As late as the summer of 1932, he admitted to Samuel Eliot Morison that Roosevelt's dealings with Tammany Hall showed a lack of "both courage and political calculation."[70] In the fall of 1932 Frankfurter wrote Al Smith that "no one was ever more ardent than I to have you in the White House," and went on to say that life would be better for all Americans "if that great human quality which you generate would radiate from the White House."[71]

At almost the same time, however, Frankfurter wrote to Roosevelt: "No predecessor of yours, not even T.R. . . . brought to the Presidency so extensive and intimate a knowledge of his countrymen as you have."[72] This was generous sentiment, yet it came in the same month in which he wrote a nearly apologetic letter to the Harvard epidemiologist Hans Zinsser who had described Roosevelt as a shallow and ambitious young man. Frankfurter's reply had the irritated tone of someone on the defensive. He came close to saying that Roosevelt was the lesser of two evils.[73] It is impossible to reconcile these statements. Frankfurter could be devious and opportunitistic. He was a master at cultivating potentially useful people by stressing their "virtue" in the hope that compliance with his aims could be elicited as a response. One biographer described this method as "friendship by expectation."[74] This is putting a good face on something other observers might describe in less kindly terms.

It is clear that four years of working with Roosevelt had not given Frankfurter great confidence in his ability. Strong reservations remained. Yet Frankfurter saw Roosevelt as the only practical progressive choice in 1932. Before the Democratic convention he preferred Smith, but believing that Smith could not be elected, he supported Roosevelt as an acceptable alternative.[75] It is difficult to determine what Roosevelt thought of Frankfurter, or of anybody, because the former's reserve was so great.[76] In the context of his personal interactions in general, however, it seems that Roosevelt and Frankfurter enjoyed a good relationship which deepened throughout the 1930s during the stress of political struggles. Although the two grew closer as the years passed, theirs began as an intellectual relationship. Indeed, Frankfurter seems to have thought of himself as Roosevelt's mentor. He reported to Brandeis Marion's comment after a meeting with Roosevelt that he had talked to him "as though he might be one of my students."[77] Roosevelt, needless to say, would not have shared this estimate. By 1932 the Brandeis-Frankfurter relationship was fully developed, but this was not true of the link between Frankfurter and Roosevelt. Their friendship, however, provided the basis for future development during the New Deal years.

CHAPTER II

The Social Philosophies of
Brandeis and Frankfurter

The social philosophies of Brandeis and Frankfurter are important for this study because they provide the general framework for an understanding of the goals the two men pursued during the New Deal. Their philosophies, particularly Brandeis's, have been widely discussed, so this chapter will focus on those aspects of their thought most directly related to their New Deal recovery program.

Brandeis's social philosophy was based on firmly held moral convictions which determined his attitude to specific issues. Charles Wyzanski argued that the basis of Brandeis's morality was economics.[1] Frankfurter, on the other hand, asserted that "the basis of his economics was morality."[2] Brandeis's morality was not based on metaphysics. He was indeed a worldly philosopher. David Riesman, Brandeis's law clerk for the 1935-36 term, said that Brandeis once observed that he "had no time for metaphysics." For Riesman, who confessed to a strong interest in the subject, this was one of the justice's "severe self-limitations."[3] Fanny Brandeis, one of the justice's nieces, recorded a conversation she had with him in 1940 near the end of his long life. He had expressed an unwillingness to worry about specific projects and when Fanny asked him what he did worry about, Brandeis replied, "I always went on the principle of 'Do what you can and hope for the best'—I worked on the problem at

hand."[4] This approach, while not satisfactory to the David
Riesmans of the world, enabled Brandeis to work with serenity.

Whatever Brandeis's self-limitations in metaphysics, however,
his moral convictions were deeply held and vigorously defended.
Dean Acheson told how he, somewhat mischievously, enticed
Harvard law professor Manley Hudson to assert in Brandeis's
presence that "moral priniciples were no more than general-
izations from the mores or accepted notions of a particular time
or place." The eruption was "even more spectacular" than
Acheson had anticipated. Brandeis began to "prophesy." He
asserted that morality was truth, and truth "had been revealed to
men in an unbroken, continuous, and consistent flow by the
great prophets and poets of all time." It was, Acheson
commented, "an impressive, almost frightening, glimpse of an
elemental force." A short time later Hudson was standing on the
street "shaking with emotion." So much, Acheson concluded,
for the concept of Brandeis as the morally neutral scientist of the
law![5] Not without reason did Roosevelt call Brandeis "Isaiah,"
partly in jest and partly, one suspects, with awe.[6]

Brandeis consistently related politics to morality. In 1920 he
interpreted the rise of Harding and Coolidge as evidence of America's "unworthiness."[7] He complained that the United States had
"slipped back badly in 25 years, in order—security to life and
property; in liberty of speech, action and assembly; in culture;
and in many respects in morality."[8] Brandeis saw the 1920s as an
era of American moral decline. The prosperity of the decade was a
threat to the integrity of the American people. "Nothing is more
difficult to endure wisely," Brandeis remarked, quoting Goethe,
"than a succession of beautiful days."[9] Perhaps the most
revealing indication of his perspective is found in a letter
Josepheus Daniels wrote to William Jennings Bryan. Daniels told
Bryan that he:

> had a long talk yesterday with Mr. Brandeis. I mean Mr.
> Justice Brandeis. The great need of the hour, he said, is for a
> righteous leader to preach "the fear of God." He wanted me
> to write you and urge you, for the time, to let everything go,

and wage a crusade for decency and righteousness. He has seen the debauchery in Washington, he feels the moral obloquy and fears the people are aroused. "Bryan is the preacher of righteousness, urge him to quit all else and turn his powers towards arousing the nation to repentance and cleansing."[10]

That Brandeis the agnostic should urge the fundamentalist Bryan to a moral crusade is vivid testimony to the intensity of his moral commitment.

But Brandeis combined empirical flexibility with moral firmness. His conviction about what ought to be did not blur his perception of what was. Facts were Brandeis's sovereigns, not catchwords.[11] Brandeis himself once remarked that his famous "Brandeis Brief" should have been entitled "What Every Fool Knows."[12] He asserted that "nobody can form a judgment that is worth having without a fairly detailed and intimate knowledge of the facts."[13] Brandeis's chief impact on jurisprudence was to insist that law and life were interrelated and that only a fool would wish them kept apart. Some of his most trenchant criticisms were reserved for members of his own profession who preferred orthodoxy to fact. As a philosopher of the law, Oliver Wendell Holmes preferred theory to fact. Brandeis disapproved of this Olympian detachment and told Holmes that he "knew nothing about the evils that one who had been much in affairs had seen and known." Holmes ruefully observed to Laski, "He bullies me a little on that from time to time."[14]

Brandeis had an insatiable thirst for detail. Holmes confided to Laski that "the way that cuss is loaded with facts on all manner of subjects leaves me gawping."[15] He urged others to devote themselves to a similar mastery of detail. On one occasion he "drove a harpoon" into Holmes by suggesting that he devote his next leisure "to the study of some domain of fact—suggesting the textile industry which, after reading many reports, I could make living to myself by a visit to Lawrence."[16] Brandeis practiced what he preached. His correspondence contains innumerable requests for information from a wide variety of sources. In 1934

Brandeis received a letter from Edwin B. George, an official in the
Commerce Department, which began:

> In response to your request of March 13 for retail sales for
> 1933 in Massachusetts of boots and shoes and food there are
> no actual figures available, but using the figures of the U.S.
> Census of Distribution covering the year 1929 as a base, we
> are able to make estimates for 1933 as follows.... [17]

A maze of statistics followed. The Brandeis Papers include many
similar letters in response to the justice's inquiries.

Brandeis's expression "the curse of bigness" provides an
excellent introduction to his philosophy. There is more involved
in this phrase than belief in the desirability of small business
enterprise. Indeed, this opposition is based on Brandeis's
conviction that people are limited in their ability to control
institutions and events. Herbert Aptheker summarized Brandeis's
position (derived from a conversation he had had with him along
with some other students) thus:

> You started out by saying that in considering a way of life
> for mankind one must always remember that one was
> dealing with human beings. One must always keep in mind,
> you said, the humbleness of man's mind. Man's mind has
> not developed or developed very minutely in, say, the last
> five thousand years, but the conditions of man's life have
> changed, have become more and more complex. [18]

This belief in the "humbleness of man's mind" explains
Brandeis's conviction that bigness is a curse. Aptheker provides
the connection:

> We may compare (as you did) the tremendous corporation
> with "a fifty ton truck in a California side-street." You went
> on to say ... that man could not properly and intelligently
> run that truck. You went on to speak of an administrator or
> director of a tremendous corporation who simply was

unable to understand and digest all the facts concerning the manifold problems of his business.... You say these corporations cannot be regulated, cannot be controlled ... So they must be destroyed. Man must go back to "honest individualism."[19]

So Brandeis opposed Leviathan in all its forms. Milo Perkins recalled that Brandeis had spoken to him "philosophically on the horrors of bigness and the sanctity of littleness in *all* fields of human activity." Brandeis's opposition to bigness "was not limited to industrial corporations!"[20] But this position, which seemed so astonishing to Perkins, is the only one consistent with his sense of human limitation. Brandeis's aversion to bigness also applied to big government. The strength of his feeling was illustrated by his uneasiness, even during the New Deal, when Congress was not in session. In the fall of 1933 he wrote Frankfurter: "There is some comfort in the thought that each day brings Congress's convening nearer. It was a terrible thing to leave absolute power in the hands of one man—and adjourn for so long a period."[21]

Brandeis's fear of the federal Leviathan led him to believe that state and local governments were indispensable to democracy. In 1928 he advocated restoring to the states "the taxing power of which they have been robbed by extreme government instrumentalities decisions & interstate commerce decisions of recent years."[22] In 1933, along with justices Benjamin Cardozo and Harlan Stone, he dissented in the case of *Liggett Company* v. *Lee*. Justice Owen Roberts wrote the majority opinion which asserted that a Florida tax on chain stores was unconstitutional because it discriminated between chain stores and local businesses.[23] Brandeis, however, argued that the Constitution "does not confer upon either domestic or foreign corporations the right to engage in interstate commerce in Florida."[24] He argued that the people of Florida may have been acting solely to help small business because of their belief that the chain stores were thwarting American ideals by encouraging inequality of opportunity, and sapping the resources and vigor of local communities.[25]

Brandeis concluded by citing the "widespread belief" that the true prosperity of America's past came from the courage and resourcefulness of small businessmen.[26]

Brandeis dealt with a different aspect of state-federal relations in the case of the *New State Ice Comany* v. *Liebmann*. In the early 1930s, the state of Oklahoma acted to prevent ruinous competition among ice companies by prohibiting the establishment of any new firms. This law was ruled unconstitutional by the Supreme Court.[27] Once again Brandeis wrote a powerful dissent. As in the Liggett case, he argued for the legislative freedom of the states, asserting that this freedom has important social implications because it permits economic experimentation which federal legislation alone could not duplicate. Such experimentation was all the more important in a time of national emergency. "If we would be guided by the light of reason," he concluded in a widely quoted passage, "we must let our minds be bold."[28]

This stress on the states led Brandeis to urge bright young men to build their careers on the local level. He encouraged this even during the New Deal when a greatly expanded federal bureaucracy absorbed large numbers of public servants. For Brandeis the basic resource was trained people, and he did not wish to see all the capable leaders in Washington.[29] He believed that local government must be maintained if democracy is to survive. In 1925 he wrote to his brother:

> History teaches ... that the present tendency toward centralization must be arrested—if we are to attain the American idea—and that for it must be substituted intense development of life through activities within the several states and localities.[30]

Brandeis believed that a diffusion of power among different levels of government would reduce the danger of a political Leviathan.

Of course, Brandeis saw an equal if not greater threat from the corporate Leviathan. He believed that the Sherman Act was inadequate, and that taxation was the best weapon. Emmanual

Goldenweiser, former director of the Federal Reserve Board, recalled that Brandeis told him he was in favor of taxing heavily "any corporation that has a charter from a State different from the one in which its business is situated."[31] To Frederic Howe, who had written asking how he would limit corporate size, Brandeis replied that he would levy

> an annual excise tax rapidly progressing in the rate as the total capitalization of the Corporation rises, the amount of capitalization to be measured by the aggregate face value of a) its stock, bonds and similar securities ... plus b) the aggregate value of the stocks, bonds and other securities of all subsidiary or other corporations of which it holds as much as twenty percent of the outstanding stock and/or bonds or other securities.[32]

Another of Brandeis's concerns was financial oligarchy, which he considered a threat to the freedom and economic well-being of Americans. His view of financial oligarchy is summed up in his book *Other People's Money*.[33] Brandeis argued that banks and insurance companies are parasites because they make no essential contribution to the economy but prey on it, using other people's money to do so. He had an almost instinctive distrust of bankers. He told Goldenweiser that as a boy he had seen the sign "First National Bank—United States Depositary," but he had not learned until fifty years later that the sign meant simply that the government had the first mortgage on the bank while the depositors had only the second mortgage.[34]

Rigorous taxation was also Brandeis's way of limiting the power of the financial oligarchy. He would eliminate virtually all holding companies, prevent interlocking directorates, and separate commercial banking from savings banks.[35] He believed that this method could significantly reduce the power of finance and restore the people's economic independence. Brandeis also supported economic options, particularly in the field of insurance. His concern over insurance abuses led him to advocate competition, and he was active in the Massachusetts

Savings Bank Insurance League.[36] Brandeis was willing to use government agencies, as when he favored postal savings as a means of providing an alternative to banks. Indeed, he advocated having the post offices take on the functions of savings banks.[37]

Brandeis was a good deal more concerned about capital than about labor. Nevertheless his approach to unions is best understood in the context of his concern about the abuse of power. He supported labor unions at a time when most people opposed them. This stance, mild as it seems today, contributed to his reputation for radicalism. Yet he was also concerned about the power of unions and favored their incorporaton as a way of keeping them under control. He argued that the immunity unions enjoyed only encouraged the courts to "apply freely, perhaps too freely, the writ of injunction."[38]

Brandeis's concern about the power of industry led him to oppose the open shop. Americans, he asserted, have come to realize that "unions and collective bargaining are essential to industrial liberty and social justice."[39] But, on the other hand, he argued that

> the American people should not, and will not accept unionism if it involves the closed shop. They will not consent to the exchange of the tyranny of the employer for the tyranny of the employee. Unionism therefore cannot make a great advance until it abandons the closed shop; and it cannot accept the open shop as an alternative.[40]

The middle way, which Brandeis advocated during a stint as unpaid mediator in a garment workers' strike in 1910, was the preferential union shop. The basic feature of this type of shop is that the manufacturers "should, in the employment of labor . . . give the preference to union men, where the union men are equal in efficiency to any non-union men. . . . "[41] Brandeis would concede to the employers the right to decide on the fitness of the workers, but he suggested that obvious cases of discrimination be dealt with by an "appropriate board."[42] While Brandeis denied that the preferential union shop was a perfect solution, he clearly saw it as a prudent middle way between the dangers of big industry and big labor.[43]

Brandeis's view of the role of the judiciary is also consistent with the rest of his philosophy. He was a firm believer in judicial restraint. One of his most revered teachers at the Harvard Law School, James Bradley Thayer, had been a powerful advocate of this doctrine.[44] In a closely reasoned historical analysis of the doctrine of judicial review, Thayer argued that the Court should not even consider the constitutionality of legislation unless "those who have the right to make laws have not merely made a mistake, but have made a very clear one,—so clear that is is not open to rational discussion."[45] In discussing the relationship of the courts to the legislatures, Thayer argued that the people should realize

> the great range of possible harm and evil that our system leaves open, and must leave open, to the legislatures, and of the clear limits of judicial power; so that responsibility may be brought sharply home where it belongs.... Under no system can the power of courts go far to save a people from ruin; our chief protection lies elsewhere.[46]

Frankfurter observed that no member of the Court "invokes more rigorously the traditional limits of its jurisdiction than Brandeis."[47] Although Brandeis usually differed with fellow justice George Sutherland, he appreciated Sutherland's great knowledge of jurisdiction.[48] Brandeis's performance in the case of *Ashwander* v. *Tennessee Valley Authority* is significant. TVA, in Brandeis's opinion, was one of the most productive of the New Deal agencies.[49] Nevertheless, when its constitutionality was challenged, Brandeis refrained from upholding it directly, arguing in a concurring opinion that the Court should simply have affirmed the favorable judgment of the circuit court. The stockholders had never shown "fraud, oppression, or gross negligence," and judicial review should be limited to "actual cases and controversies."[50]

Brandeis also advocated restricting the jurisdiction of the lower courts. He wrote Frankfurter that

> the great movement against federal courts—high & low— should be diverted from its present objections and ... canalized on reducing the jurisdiction of the district courts,—not only should the diversity jurisdiction be abolished ... but most of the jurisdiction added in 1875 & later should be abrogated, but in no case practically should the appellate federal courts have to pass on the construction of state statutes.[51]

Brandeis did not approve of recalling judges, arguing that as a remedy it was "crudely radical and inartistically bad."[52] His solution to the crises caused by intransigent courts was to limit their jurisdiction. Only this limitation could effectively prevent usurpation of power by judicial legislators.

Paul Freund has asserted that Brandeis was dedicated to helping create and maintain "the structures and processes of a working democratic federalism."[53] He was committed to making the existing system work more effectively and was not at all inclined to abandon it in despair.[54] An effective democratic federalism must be based on moral values and guided by social experimentation if it is to endure. And if it is to be truly democratic and federal, it must be free of the curse of bigness in both the economic and political arenas. Every aspect of Brandeis's thought fits consistently into a structure designed to produce this end. His mind was truly "of one piece."[55]

It is difficult to analyze Brandeis's philosophy using the traditional categories of liberal and conservative. Although he was widely regarded as a liberal (even as a radical) in his own time, some recent scholars have stressed the conservative elements in his thought.[56] He attempted "to deal with the dilemma of modern society, the latent tensions between the need of the state to act and the resulting restrictions on individual freedoms."[57] Brandeis took the middle road between the liberals' excessive reliance on governmental power and the conservatives' distrust of political activism. Both extremes "lacked that sense of balance which Brandeis valued so highly."[58] If one were forced to reduce the complex blend of liberal and conservative elements in Brandeis's thought to a formula, one could say that he advocated the use of liberal means to obtain conservative ends. He was willing to use the power of the state, sometimes in surprising ways, to secure and guard the traditional values of Jeffersonian democracy.[59]

In a 1963 letter to Arthur M. Schlesinger, Jr., Frankfurter repudiated certain emphases found in New Deal monographs. He asserted that Schlesinger and others had been wrong "in assuming that I saw completely eye to eye with Brandeis on socio-economic matters, any more than it is true that I was an echo of his outlook on the law, particularly constitutional law." Frankfurter acknowledged a debt to Holmes and Thayer as well as to Brandeis.[60] The key words in this statement are "completely" and "echo." Seldom do any two people agree "completely" on an area as vast as "socio-economic matters." No one would suppose that Frankfurter was merely an "echo" on anything, particularly on something as encompassing as constitutional law. But while Frankfurter denied that he was a doctrinaire Brandeis disciple, he did not deny Brandeis's profound influence on his thought.

Frankfurter clearly accepted Brandeis's belief in the "curse of bigness." He wrote Walter Lippmann that

the crux of the business is not the wickedness of the Mitchells but the power which is wielded by concentration of financial power which they are wholly unworthy ... to wield because of the obfuscations and the arrogances which power almost invariably generates. Again I say the Lord hasn't created anybody competent to rule wisely the kind of a thing the Chase bank was ... Brandeis saw it all with a seer's discernment more than twenty years ago, and everything that he prophesied since has been vindicated with an almost tragic uncanniness.[61]

On the same subject he wrote Brain Truster Raymond Moley that

"Neither you nor I are doctrinaire either about the curse of bigness or the blessing of smallness. Like most things that matter in this world, it's a question of more or less, of degree, of when big is too big and when little is too little."[62] This statement, taken out of context, could indicate that Frankfurter differed significantly with Brandeis. In fact, he was no more dogmatic on this question than Brandeis, who preferred to examine each case separately instead of contenting himself with sterile abstractions.

Frankfurter's acceptance of Brandeis's philosophy is also indicated by his enthusiastic promotion of Brandeis's books. Commenting on the edition of *The Curse of Bigness* in 1934, Frankfurter observed that the publication is "a truly important event . . . on several counts" and went on to say: "If you do not feel inclined to send a copy of The Curse to F.D.R., I should like to do."[63] He was also enthusiastic about Brandeis's *Other People's Money*. From England during his stay at Oxford in 1934, he wrote: "Also I rejoice to see 'Other People's Money' . . . I ordered a lot and am distributing them here."[64] Shortly before Brandeis was to see Roosevelt early in the first term, Frankfurter exhorted him to "let him have a full dose of bigness, bankers, & regularity of employment. Also—the proper pursuit of public works program."[65] But while Frankfurter accepted Brandeis's outlook on the curse of bigness, he approached the problem from a somewhat different perspective. Indeed, the moral tone is stronger in Frankfurter than in Brandeis. The heart of the problem in Frankfurter's view was "the conscience of the rich."[66]

Frankfurter divided society into two active groups: the grasping rich who subvert democratic institutions, and the virtuous citizens dedicated to their preservation.[67] The bulk of the population was usually indifferent but capable of action when aroused by bold leadership. For Frankfurter, it was essential to be committed. There was no room in his view for fence straddling. In 1931 he wrote editor Norman Hapgood:

We ought to stop this nonsense of thinking everybody in this country a liberal because he says he is a liberal. I know you have a slight tendency to think yourself above these warring views and to consider yourself an exponent of a comprehensive eclecticism.... The fact is, there are conservative forces in society and there are democratizing forces in society.[68]

Frankfurter called himself "not an ideologue but a stark empiricist," but when questions of fundamental loyalty were concerned there was no room for mere eclecticism, however comprehensive.[69]

This conviction helps account for the intensity of Frankfurter's hostility to conservatives. He asserted to Roosevelt:

Some things need to be killed not merely scotched. That was especially true of the mean and meretricious conception of "the American way of life" with which the Hearsts and the Hamiltons and the minor fry tried to fool and frighten the American people. For the country's welfare and for the fate of western democracy, it was essential to destroy the synthetic concoction which was offered by a poisonous press and a blind plutocracy.[70]

Yet Frankfurter's aim was no more revolutionary than Brandeis's. He took great delight in repeating what his Harvard Law School colleague Thomas R. Powell said about his conservatism: Powell said that Frankfurter, far from being a radical, was wearing himself out trying to get capitalists to live up to their pretensions.[71] Although Frankfurter could speak eloquently of the failure of capitalism, in his opinion the basic problem was not the system but the capitalists. He expected the worst from the rich and anticipated their constant opposition to reform. His contacts with the affluent were not extensive, and his correspondence with Brandeis and Roosevelt is full of invidious references to them.

Frankfurter observed to Brandeis that "the rich & the old crowd are beginning to open up on F.D. Their 'patriotism' has retired as they are coming out of the storm cellar."[72] In October

1933 he wrote to Roosevelt that "business, financial and political forces" are "stirring beneath the surface, ready to become overt as soon as they think they dare encounter the unparalleled tide of popular favor now running in your direction."[73] This was the most consistent theme in Frankfurter's correspondence with Roosevelt, and he also pressed it on the president in private conversations. In the spring of 1935, Frankfurter wrote to Brandeis that Roosevelt

> seems keenly aware of the intentions of Big Business & Finance and so when I told him, very frankly, your views re 'irrepressible conflict' he said "he's got his finger on the crux of the situation." He then went on to tell me his political dilemma—to baby them along for the present & wait for a fight or fight now. . . . I replied that you wouldn't have him declare war, but recognize that here *is* war & act on that assumption.[74]

Frankfurter continually confronted Roosevelt with the necessity of resisting the wealthy, and Brandeis's use of William H. Seward's "irrepressible conflict" phrase demonstrates approval of this tactic. Brandeis and Frankfurter believed that they were fighting the battle for American democracy and not merely indulging in antibusiness rhetoric for political advantage.

Brandeis spoke about the curse of bigness while Frankfurter emphasized the conscience of the rich. Does this indicate a difference in philosophy? Although Frankfurter accepted Brandeis's thesis about bigness, he may have been less committed to it than his mentor. But it is more likely that the difference was tactical rather than philosophical. The antibusiness rhetoric was strongest in the Frankfurter-Roosevelt correspondence. Frankfurter might well have believed that Roosevelt responded better to personal rather than to institutional challenges. Frankfurter commented:

> If only Business could become still more articulate in its true feelings toward F.D.R. so that even his genial habits

would see the futility of hoping anything from Business in
'36, so that he would act more on "irrepressible conflict."[75]

How did Frankfurter propose to fight this battle against bigness
and for democracy? He shared Brandeis's skepticism about the
Sherman Act, commenting that in 1890 the Act "began its career of
futile resistence to the power of economic monopoly."[76] Like
Brandeis, Frankfurter believed that taxation was the most
important weapon against wealth and power, and that the
"systematically inculcated hostility to the taxation of wealth" was
the greatest barrier to an equitable economic system.[77] His view on
decentralization was similar to Brandeis's. He wrote Brandeis in
1935 that

> Princeton went very well. I really stirred interest in the
> opportunities for state action & the indispensability under
> our democratic scheme—if it is to survive—of state &
> regional action & restricted federal action.[78]

Frankfurter's commitment to decentralization was such that he
opposed turning the child labor question over to Washington,
arguing that there were many important subjects which should not
be relegated to the federal government "because such concentration
would be self-defeating in its execution and make for a
corresponding paralysis of local responsibility."[79] In *The Public &
Its Government*, Frankfurter promoted such regional solutions as
governor's conferences and interstate agreements which are
"outside the Constitution but not forbidden by it." Regional
problems call for regional solutions and "control by the nation
would be ill-conceived and intrusive."[80]

The ultimate weapon in the battle for good government,
however, was people. Frankfurter placed great stress on the
importance of the expert. Many in the nineteenth century naively
believed that democracy could work almost automatically but in
actuality, Frankfurter asserted, it "is dependent on knowledge and
wisdom beyond all other forms of government."[81] His awareness of
the inherent fragility of democracy led Frankfurter to emphasize

the need for "men of skill and wisdom for public administration."[82] The expert in government is linked with the governmental commission, a "relatively new phenomenon." Frankfurter asserted that it is "idle to feel either blind resentment against 'government by commission' or a sterile longing for a golden past that never was."[83] He recommended a "physiological study of administrative law in action" instead of vain regrets. Frankfurter was aware of dangers in this approach, and warned against an elitist view of government. The expert, he was fond of saying, should "be on tap, but not on top."[84] Administrative power must be "properly circumscribed and zealously scrutinized."[85] Procedural regularity, public scrutiny, and criticism—especially by "an informed and spirited bar"—could help minimize abuses.[86]

It was important that public administrators be experts because the special interests have experts at their disposal.[87] In 1937 Frankfurter wrote to Roosevelt:

> You know that there is no single aspect of public affairs with which I have been more deeply concerned than the promotion of public service as a permanent career for the nation's best abilities. That, in a way, has been my predominant interest in the School here.[88]

Yet important as intelligence was, it was not enough:

> Nothing brought home to me more poignantly the post-war materialism and the debasing influence of the so-called leaders of the bar than the standards of worldly success by which youngsters of generous impulse were so often deflected from public service.[89]

So the ideal public servant must not only possess brains, but "disinterestedness and social purpose."[90] For Frankfurter the problem of effective and responsive government was a problem of personnel. The strength of this conviction explains the zeal with which Frankfurter acted as a governmental recruitment officer during the New Deal.

Although Frankfurter denied that he was an "echo" of Brandeis on constitutional matters, his view of the role of the courts was similar to Brandeis's. Frankfurter was an articulate exponent of judicial restraint, believing that the due process clause had been abused by the courts so that, by means of the fifth and fourteenth amendments, "federal and state legislation now has to meet the increasingly unknown and unknowable terrors of 'due process.' "[91] He paid tribute to retired Justice John Clarke for the fidelity with which he had adhered "to those standards of constitutional restraint without which our democracy cannot function, and departure from which has caused such grave difficulties . . . to the Court."[92] In the case of *Dennis* v. *United States*, Frankfurter discussed judicial restraint in terms reminiscent of James B. Thayer:

> Our duty to abstain from confounding policy with constitutionality demands perceptive humility as well as self-restraint in not declaring unconstitutional what in a judge's private judgment is deemed unwise and even dangerous.[93]

But while Frankfurter was aware of judicial abuses, he put no faith in any "mechanical device" like the recall of judges to achieve judicial reform.

> It is idle to abuse abuses, and equally futile to fall back upon mechanical contrivances when dealing with a process where mechanics can play but a very small part. The remedy does not lie in panaceas like the recall of judges . . . the ultimate determinant is the quality of the Justices.[94]

Frankfurter's view of the place of the courts in America's constitutional system reflected his distrust of concentrated power, and his conviction that the only dependable resource in the struggle for democracy is dedicated public servants. It is necessary to pursue this line of thought one step further. Frankfurter rejected elitism. In a democracy government cannot be isolated from the people. Speaking of the democratic faith, Frankfurter warned:

The real battles of liberalism are not won in the Supreme
Court. To a large extent the Supreme Court, under the guise
of Constitutional interpretation of words whose contents are
derived from the disposition of the Justices, is the reflector of
that impalpable but controlling thing, the general drift of
public opinion. Only a persistent, positive translation of the
liberal faith into the thoughts and acts of the community is
the real reliance against the unabated temptation to straight-
jacket the human mind.[95]

What Frankfurter said here about the courts applies equally to the
other branches of government. "Everything turns on men,"[96] and
ultimately the men in question are not governmental officials only,
but the citizens of the nation whose collective opinion is that
"impalpable but controlling thing" which determines the direction
of policy and the strength of democracy.

This survey of Frankfurter's social thought has led to a modest
result, for his philosophy is neither systematic nor theoretical. It is
more a set of attitudes than a philosophy as such. One looks in vain
for those abstractions and constructs which could ensure his place
among the major social thinkers of American intellectual history.
And yet despite these limitations, Frankfurter's insights remain
valuable. His stress on the importance of good people in public
service is as pertinent today as it was during the New Deal era. It is
easy for system builders and theoreticians to brush aside this
emphasis as naive. But society is not some vast machine which
needs only a bit of fine tuning by social engineers to be put right.
Committees, bureaucracies, and governments are only as good as
the individuals who compose them. And for all the manipulations
of institutional reformers, it remains true that everything turns on
human beings.

Brandeis's social philosophy, the product of years of reflection,
was recorded for the public in a large number of essays, lectures,
interviews, and, ultimately, books. This philosophy, while com-
phrensive and flexible, was not designed to cope with the
depression. And so while Brandeis's social ideas shaped his
attitudes to many New Deal policies and issues, his specific

response to the economic crisis was a bold, innovative recovery program. This program was not a detailed legislative proposal but, rather, a generalized strategic overview. Since it was not formulated until well after his elevation to the Court, Brandeis's sense of judicial propriety precluded open advocacy. Instead, these ideas were informally presented to acquaintances in letters and private conversations.

The result is that Brandeis's recovery program was not widely known by either his contemporary critics or more recent historians. So it is necessary, first of all, to describe this program, which, all the evidence suggests, Frankfurter wholeheartedly supported. Brandeis's philosophy, presented sympathetically here, has not always been treated so kindly. His views have been vigorously attacked by both liberals and conservatives, though not, obviously, for the same reasons. It is only fair that these critics be permitted to present their objections. And yet giving Brandeis's opponents their day in court serves another motive besides simple justice; it also makes possible a sharper focus on a basic historiographical issue.

The lack of knowledge of Brandeis's recovery program has made it difficult to assess accurately his role in the evolution of New Deal policymaking. Most of the criticism and analysis of Brandeis's response to the depression focuses on his social philosophy in general, and ignores his recovery program. And so while the criticisms of his philosophy may be well taken, knowledge of his response to the emergency has been strangely incomplete. Both contemporary critics and more recent scholars have had a firm idea about what it takes to be a "Brandeisian." The curious thing is that by a more complete understanding of his thought, Brandeis himself does not qualify.

While Brandeis's recovery program was a response to a particular emergency, it was also a logical extension of many elements already present in his social philosophy. Brandeis assured his daughter Elizabeth Raushenbush that unless people understand "the curse of bigness" and the principle of "nothing too much," there will be no "working 'new deal.'" And, he added gloomily, "we are apt to get Fascist manifestations."[97] Bigness resulted in "the extreme mal-distribution of wealth" which could be remedied only by a vigorous tax system, not for revenue only but "to eliminate the great inequalities between our people. . . ."[98] The targets were wealthy individuals and giant corporations. Brandeis advocated a "confiscatory inheritance tax." The ultimate purpose was to tax great wealth "out of existence through income and inheritance taxes."[99] So confident was Brandeis of the efficacy of this course that he told Frankfurter the government should spend the money in advance for needed projects "in anticipation of the large tax returns which will come in when our super-rich die."[100] The large corporations were also objects of attack. When Sen. Burton K. Wheeler asked Frankfurter about Brandeis's views on the taxation of "the bigness of corporations,"[101] Frankfurter suggested that corporation taxes should be augmented with a profits tax so that

> all corporations with gross assets of $1,000.000 or more shall pay an annual franchise tax of one fourth (¼) of one percent of such assets held at the end of the preceding year and providing that no deduction of amount should be made for holdings of, or in, a subsidiary or other corporation.

Frankfurter also suggested that corporation taxes be increased.[102]

Quite apart from the revenue generated, Brandeis's tax program was a reform measure designed to combat the curse of bigness. But this program was also essential in Brandeis's recovery strategy, for it alone could produce the money necessary to end the depression. Economic recovery, Brandeis observed, required "a comprehensive program of great magnitude" in which a massive governmental venture into public works was essential. But he was not content simply to urge great expenditure because the nature of the projects was of great importance. He advocated permanent investments for projects of lasting social value. Although he did not describe the projects in detail, he mentioned such things as afforestation, flood control, soil erosion control, irrigation efforts, navigation improvements, and the creation of lakes and ponds. He also showed interest in slum clearance, adult education, and a variety of other social programs.[103]

Brandeis advocated quick action to put two million men to work within six months along with "another million or two indirectly." This massive commitment "would turn many a wheel now inert."[104] Such an effort would help other New Deal programs because "it will so hearten folks everywhere and particularly on the Hill that it will make it possible for Roosevelt to put through his other measures."[105] Most of the projects would not arouse hostility because business and property values would not be threatened. Strong opposition would come only from the "super-rich."[106] Although he did not spell it out in detail, Brandeis seems to have envisioned a kind of revenue sharing. He wrote Frankfurter that the program could be financed by loans initially and then "by high estate & income taxes with share to the States."[107]

Even before the inauguration, Brandeis questioned Roosevelt's willingness to embark on such a thoroughgoing program. He criticized Roosevelt's position on public works as "fine in quality—but deficient in quantity for this exigency," observing that this was one of those cases where "difference in degree is difference in kind. We must have the whole-sale proposition." Still, Brandeis did not give up hope, for "perhaps R. intends this; & merely put out a trial balloon."[108] Yet Roosevelt's statement was deficient on two other counts. He had indicated that only self-liquidating projects should be considered, while Brandeis held out for permanent investments. He was also troubled because Roosevelt did not mention tax reform. Once more Brandeis expressed the hope that this merely reflected Roosevelt's "good politics."[109]

Frankfurter, however, not only accepted Brandeis's program, but acted as an effective propagandist for it. In the March 1933 issue of the *Survey Graphic*, Frankfurter presented the idea to the public, arguing for a public works program "even larger and more ambitious than the one [Senator Robert F.] Wagner sponsored." Frankfurter used Brandeis's figures, asserting that a good public works program could create two million direct, and two million more indirect, jobs. He linked this massive spending with a "socially sound taxing system" of high estate and income taxes, and concluded by quoting the British economist John Maynard Keynes's statement that the West had the ability to solve its economic problems with intelligence and resolution.[110]

It was appropriate that Frankfurter concluded his summary of Brandeis's program by quoting Keynes, for both he and Brandeis admired him. Frankfurter was instrumental in introducing Keynes to American scholars. The two had become friends at the Paris Peace Conference in 1919, and Frankfurter took a copy of Keynes's *Economic Consequences of the Peace* back to the United States with him. He showed it to Brandeis and Graham Wallas who praised it highly.[111] Frankfurter gave a copy to Walter Lippmann who was with the new publishing firm of Harcourt, Brace and Company. The book became a best-seller and contributed significantly to the success of the firm. Frankfurter also arranged to have extracts of the book published in the *New Republic*, with which he was associated, and "for many years thereafter this journal provided an important outlet in the United States for Keynes's views."[112]

Brandeis and Frankfurter became enthusiastic advocates of Keynes's ideas. In 1931 Brandeis sent Frankfurter a clipping which dealt with Keynes's views on loan sharks.[113] He wrote to Frankfurter: "As to imposts and the tariff, I agree entirely with Keynes—also as to deflation of the pound sterling."[114] By early 1932 Brandeis was characterizing Keynes as "a real fellow" and "an extraordinary economic mind."[115] Frankfurter occasionally sent Brandeis articles and other material by Keynes. Brandeis commented that he found Keynes's position on debts "powerfully illuminating."[116] Frankfurter urged Keynes to write Roosevelt his famous open letter of 31 December 1933. He told Keynes there was "considerable sentiment" in Congress for "heavy increases in public works appropriations," and said that he thought Roosevelt would be receptive:

I write because I think that a letter from you with your independent arguments and indications would greatly acceler-ate the momentum of forces now at work in the right direction.[117]

When the letter appeared, Brandeis said it was "superb."[118] Brandeis and Frankfurter were Keynesians who believed that massive public works spending financed by rigorous, progressive taxation could end the depression.

But despite the importance Brandeis attached to his recovery program, his critics ignored it almost completely and focused their attack on his social philosophy in general. His belief in the curse of bigness aroused the opposition of many liberals during the New Deal when planning and consolidation seemed dominant. David Riesman wrote to Frankfurter that his friends treated Brandeis's views with disdain, and even his former law clerks "adopt the shallow philosophy of the Nation."[119] Max Lerner observed that Brandeis was not "the prophet come finally into honor in his country," but rather

> still in the opposition. . . . If anything he is now more solitary and even more tragic. For a long time he fought the "curse of bigness" in business, and the industrial collapse seems to have justified him. . . . He finds now that it has been transferred to government. And he is still fighting it, which may make him, in the eyes of many, another Don Quixote—a gaunt and gallant but essentially helpless figure out of another era, earnestly tilting at windmills.[120]

This characterization of Brandeis as an out-of-date thinker peddling the old-fashioned ideal of atomization in a new era of consolidation and extolling a nineteenth-century kind of laissez-faire in an age which demanded planning was the major thrust of the liberal criticism.[121] Harold Laski, for example, observed that *The Curse of Bigness*, while the expression of a "noble passion," was "like the pronouncement of a believer in the Ptolemaic astronomy that the new Copernican world will not do."[122]

The members of the Brain Trust, that coterie of Roosevelt's advisers chiefly responsible for the planning and consolidation phase of the New Deal, were particularly outspoken in their criticisms, probably because of the keenness of the competition. A. A. Berle, Jr., dealt superciliously with Brandeis's philosophy in a

letter to Roosevelt in which he summed up his opposition to
bigness, but concluded that "as long as people want Ford cars they
are likely to have Ford factories and finance to match."[123] Berle
criticized Brandeis's tax policy by pointing out, rather cryptically,
that decentralization through taxation is not as simple as it looks
because the real problem is not concentrated wealth, but
concentrated power.[124] In the introduction to *The Modern
Corporation and Private Property*, Berle discussed the "inevitable"
trend toward bigness and accused Brandeis of trying "to turn the
clock backward."[125]

Tugwell and Moley's criticism of Brandeis's philosophy was
similar to that of Berle, though Tugwell, even in retrospect, showed
greater animosity.[126] Tugwell was convinced that Brandeis and
Frankfurter were exerting a profound influence on Roosevelt even
during the campaign.[127] As an advocate of large-scale planning, he
feared their power over Roosevelt because it would mean "the
completion of the long-delayed Wilsonian agenda of reforms."[128]
Tugwell recalled telling Roosevelt that planning "was a serious
departure from the principles of Brandeis and his supporters. They
could be expected to object and rally the old Wilsonian forces."[129]
Moley, Tugwell recalled, agreed that Brandeis was a dangerous
influence, saying that he been Wilson's "dark angel" and that he
was "hovering again in our neighborhood, only he was a Justice
now, and he had to have deputies."[130]

The Brandeis philosophy, as Tugwell viewed it, was that
"collectivism must be abandoned. . . . The only safe business was a
little one: make them all little and all would be safe."[131] Moley's
analysis was similar. He rejected "the traditional Wilson-Brandeis
philosophy that if America could once more become a nation of
small proprietors, of corner grocers and smithies under spreading
chestnut trees, we should have solved the problems of American
life."[132] For both men, and for Berle as well, Brandeis's philosophy
was anachronistic. Looking back to an idyllic Jeffersonian
simplicity, Brandeis was, they argued, essentially unreconciled to
the reality of the modern business evolution toward consolidation
which requires, as a necessary alternative to chaos, large-scale
government planning. Brandeis was resisting an evolution toward

greater efficiency. Tugwell accused Brandeis of inconsistency because he supported Frederick Taylor's scientific management, while continuing to use "all his influence for atomization."[133]

These criticisms of the Brain Trusters are representative of the views of the liberals who opposed Brandeis's ideas.[134] But there is nothing in this analysis which shows awareness of Brandeis's recovery program. Indeed, only Moley acknowledged that the program existed, and he dealt with it summarily in a later work by characterizing it as "frivolous to the point of absurdity."[135] The evidence clearly shows that Moley was aware of the program at the time, and if Moley knew of it, Tugwell and Berle must have heard of it from him since, in the early New Deal, he conferred with them frequently. Yet they did not criticize the program at the time. Their silence on this point, whatever the cause, has helped prevent a complete understanding of Brandeis's role in the New Deal policy debate.[136] For whatever one may think of Brandeis's recovery program, it was surely a more ambitious undertaking than some nostalgic effort to rehabilitate corner grocers and village smithies.

CHAPTER III

The Interregnum

Neither Brandeis nor Frankfurter were primarily political advisers, and their correspondence shows that their role during the 1932 campaign was limited. Frankfurter's correspondence with Roosevelt during the period from the convention to the inauguration was meager, although he saw him several times during the summer of 1932 and talked with him on the telephone at least once.[1] Frankfurter did give some political advice. He was concerned about Roosevelt's problems with Governor Ely of Massachusetts and with Al Smith, urging Roosevelt to seek reconcilation with both men.[2] He advised Roosevelt to balance his views on relief with an open oppositon to the Bonus Bill.[3] Such advice shows that Frankfurter was aware of the need for political expediency. But Frankfurter and Brandeis were in the background during the swirl of political calculation and campaigning in 1932. They were willing to let others get Roosevelt elected. Their concern was with the policies to be pursued after the election.

Roosevelt relied on associates like Louis Howe and Jim Farley to handle political matters.[4] There was also the Brain Trust which consisted primarily of Tugwell, Berle, and Moley.[5] Although Frankfurter and Brandeis objected to what they considered Farley's excessive concern with political calculation, they felt no great rivalry with him during the campaign.[6] Relations with the

Brain Trust, however, were strained from the beginning. Tension was attributable to both policy differences and personality clashes.

Frankfurter's relationship with Berle was particularly difficult. Berle had spent 1916 in Brandeis's law office, and his father had been one of Brandeis's friends, but these ties did not ensure an amiable relationship.[7] Berle's difficulties with Frankfurter stemmed from his student days at Harvard where he seems to have set himself the task of challenging Frankfurter at every opportunity.[8] Frankfurter admitted that he and Berle disliked each other. He wrote Max Lerner:

> As to Berle, I cannot think what eats him in relation to me. I can't think of a single reason for his hating preoccupation of me, unless it be that when he was a student ... I paid no attention whatever to him, having realized in the course of one short talk ... that he was a boringly humorless creature with too much ego in his cosmos.[9]

There were also tensions with Tugwell.[10] Neither Brandeis nor Frankfurter trusted him. Brandeis noted that Tugwell's view on planning "does not augur well for the future of American Democracy."[11] Frankfurter characterized Tugwell and Berle as "greedy for power and sure of their own wisdom to control it wisely."[12]

Of the three major figures in the Brain Trust, Frankfurter and Brandeis had the best relationship with Moley, the one man in the Brain Trust who felt some sympathy for their ideas. Frankfurter conducted a brisk correspondence with him through the spring of 1935. In a memorandum dated 19 May 1932 Moley advocated large-scale public works, welfare measures, taxation of undistributed surplus corporate income, heavier taxation of the wealthy to redistribute income, along with holding company regulation, and banking and securities exchange reforms.[13] Despite Moley's occasional irritation with Frankfurter, he cooperated with him closely for some time.[14]

When Brandeis discussed his recovery program with Frank-

furter at the end of January 1933, he commented he was
"particularly anxious to see Moley," for he was "eager" to talk to
Moley about recovery.[15] Frankfurter then wrote Moley telling
him that Brandeis was anxious to talk to him "about a public
works program which seems to him ... indispensable for
recovery."[16] He enclosed a copy of Brandeis's recovery plan.
Frankfurter and Brandeis hoped that Moley would serve as an
effective transmitter of their views to Roosevelt.[17] As late as April
1934, Frankfurter protégé Tom Corcoran acknowledged the
value of Moley's assistance and suggested that Brandeis and
Frankfurter's allies reorganize "under the unofficial direction of
Ray Moley who can practically make his office here after his
Columbia classes are through."[18]

Moley, however, soon revealed some conservative instincts. In
May 1934 Corcoran reported Moley's criticism of Brandeis's
commitment to an "Indian war" against bankers.[19] Frankfurter,
who was aware of Moley's second thoughts, characterized him as
"mercurial."[20] When Moley began working full time for *Today*
magazine in 1935, the relationship with Frankfurter became
tenuous. Moley observed that when he severed relations with
Roosevelt in 1936, he "could provide no further means for the
transmission of Frankfurter's suggestions": Frankfurter was
"one of the considerable number of old friends who terminated
their relations with me at that time."[21]

Because of disagreements with the Brain Trust, particularly
with Tugwell and Berle, Frankfurter and Brandeis valued direct
communication with Roosevelt. Frankfurter saw him in August
1932 and recorded his impressions for Brandeis. It is clear that
they had already agreed to make some personnel suggestions.
Frankfurter stressed Roosevelt's need for "a critical, skeptical,
informed person at his side—one also with real knowledge of
Washington during the last few years."[22] He suggested Max
Lowenthal.[23] He also mentioned that Donald Richberg and
Joseph Eastman were reliable experts on railroad problems, and
that Bernard Flexner was knowledgeable about utilities.[24]
Personnel matters dominated. The meeting showed the pattern of
Frankfurter's dealing with Roosevelt.

Though Frankfurter and Brandeis did not have close contact with Roosevelt during the campaign, Tugwell already imagined them to be sinister powers behind the throne:

> What I did not know in 1932, and never gave enough weight to when I did know, was that there was one old man in the shadows to whom the awe and reverence of sonship went without reserve. This, of course, was Brandeis. And Frankfurter was his prophet.... Berle and I were not so innocent that we did not recognize our great opponent.[25]

Tugwell overrated Frankfurter's influence with Roosevelt, and he also exaggerated Roosevelt's reverence for Brandeis. Indeed, even Tugwell admitted that Frankfurter was an infrequent guest of Roosevelt's during this period, but he also recalled that "he never joined in our discussions; but we heard of him and sensed his influence."[26]

Alienation between Frankfurter and the Brain Trust surfaced in an exchange of letters between him and Berle regarding the behavior of Lowenthal. Berle complained to Frankfurter that Lowenthal had attended a Brain Trust session and taken an opposing position on an issue already "settled" by the group. He asked Frankfurter to keep Lowenthal in line.[27] Frankfurter's response was blunt: "I am troubled that the judgment of a man so wise ... as is Lowenthal should be deemed irrelevant simply because the issue had been previously discussed by your group."[28]

Despite such tensions, Tugwell recounted that the Brain Trust felt complacent early in the campaign:

> He [FDR] went with us toward a comprehension of large-scale technology, the forces it had created and the consequences of allowing it to escape regulation—or rather of allowing its management to be gathered into a few privately controlled ganglia.... That, essentially, was our explanation of the current trouble. It was one he seemed to accept.[29]

This position was argued in Roosevelt's speech at Oglethorpe University which was written by Ernest K. Lindley of the New York *Herald Tribune*. It represented the "high tide of collectivism."[30] Brain Trust smugness did not last long, however. Near the end of August, Roosevelt delivered a speech at Columbus, Ohio, which criticized Hoover's efforts at planning and focused on federal regulation of banks, security exchanges, and holding companies. Roosevelt stressed the evils of economic centralization and the concentration of wealth.[31] The Brain Trust was aghast. The speech represented "a retreat from Oglethorpe." It was the result of Brandeis's influence, and Tugwell was "impressed, not to say dismayed."[32] By the time of the Pittsburgh speech in October "collectivism was no longer mentioned; Oglethorpe was forgotten, and we were pushed to one side" with only Brandeis and Bernard Baruch "still in the field."[33]

This assessment was unduly pessimistic. Collectivism was not out of consideration; otherwise there is no satisfactory explanation for the National Recovery Administration or the Agricultural Adjustment Administration. Nobody had gained control of Roosevelt either during the campaign or thereafter. In fact, the early New Deal was closer to the Brain Trust ideal than to the Brandeis-Frankfurter approach. Tugwell was not always a reliable observer. He was correct in seeing that Frankfurter and Brandeis were his opponents, and that Frankfurter was active in transmitting Brandeis's views to Roosevelt. However, he also spoke of Brandeis's "mysterious channels" because he could not refrain from projecting a sinister aura around the activities of his two formidable opponents.

But the truth was that, far from being in a strong position, Brandeis and Frankfurter had serious handicaps. They had no political strength. They did not represent any interest group or voting bloc. They did not have the force of the business community behind them. They held no official positions which gave them regular access to Roosevelt, or even quasi-official positions such as those held by members of the Brain Trust. But they did have two significant advantages. The relationship between Frankfurter and Roosevelt, while not yet fully developed, was a strong asset as was Brandeis's prestige in liberal circles. Their strength lay in personal connections and influence. Frankfurter was well fitted for this kind of role. His persuasiveness, tact, and charm made him almost irresistible. Brandeis provided the philosophical framework, but it was Frankfurter who had the vital job of personal contact. Despite Tugwell's lamentations, however, Brandeis and Frankfurter were not in control of Roosevelt by the end of the campaign although Frankfurter continued to pepper him with advice right down to election day.[34] The campaign interval had done little more than reveal where the lines of battle lay. Issues had been raised but not resolved. Roosevelt's victory in November was not a triumph for any faction within his circle of advisers. The battle had only begun.

The "lame duck" period after a presidential election was always an awkward and potentially dangerous period even in the best of times, and in periods of crisis the danger was intensified. The time from November 1932 to March 1933 was particularly crucial because of the depression. Significant cooperation between Hoover and Roosevelt seemed unlikely due to bad feeling resulting from the campaign.[35] Nevertheless, because cooperation was important in diplomacy, Hoover proposed a conference with Roosevelt to deal with the foreign debt.[36] Both men opposed cancellation of the debt, but this area of agreement was overshadowed by other differences. Hoover believed the cause of the depression lay overseas and thought its cure must come from international measures. Roosevelt, on the other hand, had no faith in the efficacy of an international approach and looked to domestic policy for solutions.[37] Their meeting, which occurred in Washington on 22 November 1932, did not ease tensions. If anything, distrust increased. Hoover was convinced that Roosevelt did not understand his position, and Roosevelt went away resenting what he thought was Hoover's attempt to bring him to heel. The rest of November and most of December was spent in uneasy maneuvering with Hoover pushing Roosevelt for commitments the president-elect was unwilling to make.[38] Things had apparently reached an impasse.

At this point Frankfurter intervened successfully. On 22 December he called Henry Stimson, Hoover's secretary of state, and reported that Roosevelt had asked him, "Why doesn't Harry Stimson come up here and talk with me and settle this damn thing that nobody else seems to be able to?"[39] Stimson discussed the possibility of a meeting with Ogden Mills, Hoover's secretary of the treasury, but he received no encouragement. Stimson reported this to Frankfurter, and matters seemed to have bogged down again. But on 23 December Stimson received a message from Roosevelt by way of Frankfurter and Herbert Feis.[40] Feis later reported that he received four telephone messages from Frankfurter conveying information Roosevelt wanted passed on to Stimson.[41] The next day Frankfurter relayed Roosevelt's offer to meet Stimson within several days. Stimson told him that he would have to wait until Hoover returned to Washington.[42]

Moley, meanwhile, had been watching these contacts uneasily. Both he and Tugwell were nationalists who believed that Stimson was trying to lure Roosevelt astray. They had been relieved at the breakdown of talks in late December, and viewed these initiatives with alarm.[43] Tugwell reported that he had seen Moley, who was upset "at the kind of advice F.D.R. seemed to be accepting" and "cursed Frankfurter heartily."[44] But matters progressed while the Brain Trust watched helplessly. Stimson recorded the wide range of topics which he wished to discuss with the president-elect.[45] Hoover did not return until after the first of the year, but in the meantime Frankfurter tried to improve Stimson's opinion of Roosevelt, and he briefed Roosevelt on Stimson's personality.[46]

Stimson saw Hoover on 3 January and urged a meeting with Roosevelt. Hoover agreed on the condition that Roosevelt request a meeting in writing. When Stimson relayed this message to Roosevelt, Frankfurter remarked that it was like "an eighteenth century minuet."[47] In any case, Roosevelt complied, and the meeting finally occurred on 4 January.[48] This encounter produced substantial agreement, and Stimson was particularly gratified by Roosevelt's approval of his Manchurian policy. They met again in Washington on 19 January. These meetings led to another meeting with Hoover which produced agreement on the procedure for opening debt discussions with the British. Later, Roosevelt's secretary of state designate Cordell Hull conferred with Stimson. Stimson left office believing that the transition had been accomplished smoothly.[49]

The impetus for Frankfurter's part in this rapprochement came from Roosevelt although Frankfurter was a master at encouraging people, in one way or another, to act "spontaneously." In any case, Roosevelt used Frankfurter's relationship with Stimson to break through a baffling impasse, and Frankfurter was certainly willing to serve as a mediator. He would probably have done so whatever the issues because of his ties with the principals. The key issue was a smooth transition of administrations. The fears of the Brain Trust were exaggerated. There was little danger that Roosevelt would have accepted Hoover's explanation of the depression, and it was naive for the Brain Trust to entertain this suspicion. While the Frankfurter-Brandeis correspondence does not contain any references to Frankfurter's mediation, there is no reason to think that Brandeis did not approve if only for the wider possibilities it foreshadowed.

In fact both Brandeis and Frankfurter were eagerly involved in preparing for the advent of the new administration. After the election Brandeis commented that the job "had been thoroughly done," but added that "now comes FDR's real test."[50] Brandeis helped prepare Roosevelt for the test by assuring him in person on 23 November that he was willing to help in any way he could.[51] Roosevelt did most of the talking at this meeting, and Brandeis found his comments reassuring, for he seemed "well versed in most fundamental facets of the situation" and had assured the justice that his administration must be innovative. Brandeis noted with satisfaction that Roosevelt was "against the bankers," and he took the opportunity to stress to Roosevelt the value of estate taxes to finance public works programs.[52] Brandeis, who was not easy to please, seemed impressed with the president-elect. Brandeis was busy with other interviews during this period. Huston Thompson saw him in late November about security legislation, and he reported to Roosevelt that Brandeis had suggested the best way to control holding companies would be by taxing their dividends.[53] Brandeis stressed to Frankfurter the importance of getting good lawyers for governmental agencies, suggested a thoroughgoing investigation of banks, and proposed a limitation on attorneys' fees in tax proceedings against the government.[54]

Frankfurter was also active during this period. From the beginning of 1933 to the inauguration, Frankfurter's busy correspondence with Moley was filled with suggestions about legislation and personnel. He passed on a memorandum by James Rosenberg on the Reconstruction Finance Corporation.[55] He recommended Nicholas Kelley for a post in the Treasury Department.[56] He suggested such men as Joseph Eastman, Milo Matbie, Frank McNinch, and David Lilienthal to serve along with Adolf Berle on a committee to draft utility control legislation, and urged that Moley encourage the president-elect to deal with this topic in his first message to Congress.[57]

By the beginning of the New Deal, Brandeis and Frankfurter had a well-defined recovery program which they were convinced could work, and which they were determined to urge upon Roosevelt. They also understood the importance of personal contact with Roosevelt, with those close to him, and with those whom they could place in various positions within the burgeoning governmental agencies. Their mode of operation was set. What remained was to exploit as effectively as possible the opportunity provided by Roosevelt's election.

CHAPTER IV

Launching the New Deal:
Recruitment and Personnel

Roosevelt's victory, coming after many years of Republican control, meant a vast changeover in the governmental bureaucracy. Brandeis and Frankfurter grasped this opportunity to bring competent, dedicated people into the new administration and from the beginning were deeply involved with recruitment and placement. Never again would personnel issues be as pressing as they were in the first months of the new administration. Frankfurter, operating from Harvard, combined with Brandeis in Washington to form a New Deal recruiting agency.

It was fitting that Frankfurter himself was among the first Roosevelt asked to join the new administration. On 8 March 1933, Roosevelt offered him the position of solicitor general. Frankfurter was swept

> completely off my feet. It was the first reference, directly or obliquely, that Roosevelt had ever made to me about my holding any office although at Albany and over the phone he had discussed with me and very intimately, questions of personnel for the Cabinet and other places in the Government.[1]

Roosevelt assured Frankfurter that Homer Cummings, the new attorney general, "knows all about you and admires you greatly and is most enthusiastic about having you as Solicitor General."[2]

Frankfurter told Roosevelt that the office was so demanding that it "would preclude participation" in advising on administration policy. He could not be solicitor general and "have anything to do on any matters on which you want my help." Roosevelt suggested that the position would be a springboard for the Supreme Court and advised Frankfurter to seek advice from Chief Justice Hughes and Brandeis.[3] Brandeis, however, told him that it would be "absurd" to take the post. Frankfurter told Roosevelt that he was grateful "for such an impressive manifestation of confidence and for such generous friendship," but after discussing the matter with Brandeis, Holmes, and his wife Marion, he had decided that he could be "of more use to the public and to you by not becoming Solicitor General."[4]

Frankfurter decided to stay at Harvard where he could serve Roosevelt as an unofficial adviser, without being bound to the inexorable demands of an exacting office. While Frankfurter envisioned his own role clearly, it took conviction to refuse Roosevelt even with the moral support of such men as Brandeis and Holmes. Although Roosevelt called Frankfurter "an independent pig" concealing, perhaps, a bit of irritation beneath a mask of playfulness, there is no evidence that the refusal damaged their relationship.[5] Frankfurter's decision did keep him from time-consuming, exacting duties and enabled him to play a broader advisory role.

Frankfurter and Brandeis were not content to maintain a close relationship only with the president. They believed that it was important to place talented people in the executive departments and to establish good relationships with Cabinet officers. Frankfurter recalled that Roosevelt had discussed Cabinet personnel with him.[6] He congratulated Roosevelt "on the ensemble of your Cabinet—and to achieve the right ensemble was ... the most important and difficult of your tasks." He was particularly pleased with the appointments of Cordell Hull, William Woodin, Thomas Walsh, Frances Perkins, and Henry Wallace.[7] However, he disliked Henry Morgenthau, Jr., who replaced the ailing Woodin in the Treasury Department, and he was lukewarm about Homer Cummings who succeeded Walsh in the Justice Department.[8]

Frankfurter and Brandeis got along best with the temperamental Harold Ickes, secretary of the interior. After Frankfurter sent him a brief congratulatory note, Ickes responded warmly by saying that he wanted to have a "real talk" with him.[9] When Ickes learned that Frankfurter was in Washington, he contacted him at the Cosmos Club and "went over later for a minutes' talk about the legal setup of the Department." Ickes had "a most delightful talk" with Brandeis (arranged by Frankfurter) "on government policies, particularly with relation to my own Department." The secretary felt as though he had been "sitting at the feet of one of the fine old prophets."[10] Brandeis reported to Frankfurter that Ickes had agreed to appoint Nathan Margold as his solicitor.[11] Frankfurter was delighted with the news.[12]

Soon after Margold's appointment, Frankfurter wrote to Ickes:

> I promise not to make a nuisance of myself, and as time goes
> on the stream of my letters will become more sluggish. But I
> venture once more to act as a conduit, this time to send on
> the enclosed from Norman Hapgood.

Hapgood recommended Louis Glavis for a position in the department, and Frankfurter cited Glavis's "implacable devotion."[13] Ickes quickly replied that he remembered Glavis very well and hoped to use him in some capacity.[14] Several days later Margold wired Frankfurter:

> Considering Louis Glavis for important investigation ... if
> you know him wire me collect marked personal . . his
> qualifications and whether there is any basis for attacking
> his record effectively.[15]

Evidently Ickes had begun the investigation of Glavis and then had turned the job over to Margold without telling him that the suggestion had been transmitted by Frankfurter in the first place. In any case Glavis was hired, and he served as the department's director of investigations from 1933 to 1936.

Margold's appointment expanded Frankfurter and Brandeis's influence because he turned to his mentors for advice. In late March he told Frankfurter that he had had a long talk with Brandeis, who had given him "some invaluable suggestions as to how to conduct myself in my new and very trying position." Margold also said he hoped to see Frankfurter soon.[16] Brandeis had several personnel suggestions which Frankfurter quickly passed on to Margold. Near the end of March Brandeis wrote to Frankfurter that "if Glavis or Slattery are not taken, possibly you may think Gardner J. [Jackson] the man for Ickes."[17] Frankfurter passed these suggestions along to Margold, and he also asked him to "outline the substance of his talk with Brandeis" so that he could then "put out of my mind some matters that I have been storing up against the day when I can talk or write to you."[18]

In early April Frankfurter suggested Erwin Griswold for a position in the department.[19] Margold was surprised that Frankfurter knew that Slattery was being considered for a position. He reported that he had mentioned Jackson to Ickes but his reply "was noncommittal for the present."[20] In mid-April Frankfurter referred Margold to Corcoran for some possible appointments and recommended Alger Hiss who was, Frankfurter asserted, "first-rate in every way."[21] When the intensive period of recruitment ended in the spring of 1933, the correspondence between Margold and Frankfurter thinned out considerably. Most letters were brief exchanges about departmental legal business, while matters of personnel and larger policy were rarely discussed. Ickes was difficult to work for but Margold remained his solicitor until 1942, and Ickes wrote a vigorous letter of defense when Sen. Pat McCarran of Nevada raised objections to Margold's confirmation as a federal judge in 1947.[22]

Frankfurter did not concern himself only with personnel matters but attempted to influence policy as well. He observed that Ickes's appointment as public works administrator

lifts not a little anxiety that has been generated in me by press reports regarding the public works program. It gives

assurance that that program will be pursued with that
boldness which Mr. Justice Brandeis deems so indispensable
in dealing with the problems of our time—boldness guided,
as it is in your case, by complete disinterestedness and
wisdom.[23]

This is another example of Frankfurter's "friendship by
expectation" method.[24] Frankfurter also congratulated Ickes on
a speech he had given. Ickes thanked Frankfurter for his kind
words about the speech but ignored public works.[25] In fact, Ickes
acted with excessive caution, agonizing interminably over each
project before reaching a decision.[26] By late September Brandeis
was already complaining about Ickes's "dilatoriness."[27] The
Public Works Administration completely failed to stimulate the
economy. So much for "friendship by expectation" in this case.
But although Brandeis and Frankfurter were not able to
influence Ickes's policy, they maintained good relations with
him, soothed his frequently ruffled feelings, and urged him in his
bad moments to stay on the job.[28]

Frankfurter and Brandeis approved of the appointment of
Frances Perkins as secretary of labor. They had known her
previously as a valuable member of Roosevelt's gubernatorial
staff. In the summer of 1932 Frankfurter asked her for
documented details "regarding Governor Roosevelt's achieve-
ments and efforts as Governor."[29] In February 1933 Frankfurter
set up an appointment with Perkins to discuss the proposed New
York state minimum wage law.[30] Brandeis asserted that the
Cabinet was "on the whole reassuring," and singled Perkins out
for special praise as "the best the U.S. affords; & it is a distinct
advance to have selected a woman for the Cabinet."[31] Frankfurter
quickly began making unsolicited personnel recommendations,
writing her about "a number of key posts that I am sure give you
concern."[32] Three days later Perkins asked Frankfurter for a
memorandum on the use of the government's purchasing power
to set industrial standards for wages and hours.[33] Frankfurter
assured her that this use of the purchasing power was
constitutional, and promised to send a detailed analysis.[34]

Perkins herself returned to the subject of personnel, writing to Frankfurter: "I want to follow your advice with regard to a Solicitor. Can you recommend a good one?"[35] This comes close to being a silly question. Frankfurter responded: "Of course all the advice I have is yours ... I have I believe some admirable suggestions for you."[36] Brandeis suggested that Paul Freund "would probably make just the kind of Solicitor Frances Perkins says she needs," and shortly thereafter he suggested that if Freund was not selected, "possibly Ray Stevens is worthy of consideration."[37]

Frankfurter saw Perkins on 25 March and later wrote to her appreciatively that he left "with an invigorated sense of what this Administration purposes and how many of those hopes will be realized by you."[38] Frankfurter also discussed public works with Perkins.

> Am I wrong in feeling that there is considerable uncertainty and indecision in regard to a large public works program? At all events ... I know you are convinced that such a policy is basic and must be pushed ahead. I suggest that Brandeis would give you considerable reinforcement particularly on the financial side. I suggest you see him this week when he is not sitting.[39]

Perkins replied tersely: "I am to see Brandeis tonight. Your feeling is correct."[40]

In the middle of April Frankfurter began his effort to get Charles Wyzanski appointed solicitor of the Labor Department.[41] Brandeis, aware of this goal, inquired, "Did you get Wyzanski through?"[42] Frankfurter, however, not only had to sell Perkins on Wyzanski, he also had to sell Wyzanski on the job, assuring him that he was "just the man for the job."[43] It is likely that Brandeis, who saw Wyzanski on 24 April, also urged him to accept.[44] Frankfurter kept up his efforts and in early May was able to report to Perkins that he had had "a good talk" with Wyzanski and predicted that she will find "no further deflection of energy into the channel of undue modesty."[45] Once Wyzanski had been persuaded, opposition developed in the Senate, particularly from Pat McCarran, the conservative Nevada Democrat. Frankfurter appealed to Sen. Robert Wagner of New York, who assured him he would do anything he could to help Wyzanski.[46] Frankfurter also asked Corcoran to urge Donald Richberg to mobilize his friends in the Senate.[47] McCarran's opposition was weak, and Wyzanski was confirmed easily.[48]

Frankfurter and Brandeis continued to consult with Perkins after Wyzanski's appointment. Brandeis saw her about the Black Bill on 10 May and reported to Frankfurter that she "feared it greatly and came in ... to get my advice."[49] Frankfurter continued to stress the importance of public works and urged Perkins to be "unrelenting in insisting upon your convictions, because I think they are the convictions of wisdom."[50] Frankfurter recommended Oliver Sprague, one of his colleagues at Harvard, as "one of the few fiscal economists who realizes that finance is an instrument of social policy."[51] Frankfurter wanted Perkins to meet Sprague, and Brandeis arranged a dinner gathering on 25 May which included Sprague and Perkins.[52]

By the fall of 1933, Frankfurter's correspondence with Perkins tapered off, though their friendship continued. Frankfurter's first critical statement about her occurred in early 1934 when he commented: "As to heavy matters F. Perkins is too naive. But the wonder is she is as good as she is & so one is grateful."[53] In May 1935 Frankfurter reported to Brandeis a conversation he had had with Perkins, observing that she is "sensitive to criticism" and simply wanted to "pour out her heart." Frankfurter commented that Perkins "needed mostly reassurance of spirit" but added "I felt mostly sorry for F. D. when I left her."[54] The portrait drawn is that of a basically well-intentioned woman who was overwhelmed by her responsibilities. Their relationship, however, remained a friendly and mutually helpful one.[55]

Frankfurter maintained a more consistent relationship with Wyzanski. In the summer of 1933 Frankfurter suggested some possible labor mediators, concluding "if the foregoing names are of the kind that interest the Secretary, I shall be glad from time to time, if others occur to me, to send them on."[56] Wyzanski must have replied quickly because three days later, Frankfurter sent him a list of 147 names![57] Later in the year Frankfurter requested that Wyzanski turn historian for a time and tell "something of what has been happening in your own immediate concerns and something of your responses to them."[58] In February 1934 Frankfurter warned Wyzanski against federal incorporation of business on the grounds that incorporation would mean ineffective centralization.[59] When Wyzanski took a new post in the Justice Department, Frankfurter wrote him a congratulatory letter.[60]

It is difficult to be specific about the influence of Brandeis and Frankfurter in the Labor Department. They were able to place a number of men in various posts, but their ability to shape policy was limited. Perkins had a progressive record in her own right dating back many years and thus was already in favor of many things Frankfurter and Brandeis advocated. Their impact on the department seems to have been limited largely to the contributions of the people they placed in it.

While Frankfurter and Brandeis got along well with Ickes and Perkins, they were not so fortunate with Attorney General Homer Cummings. This was frustrating for them because they naturally had a special interest in the Justice Department. In late July 1933 Harold Stephens, an assistant attorney general, replied to a Frankfurter letter saying: "I much appreciate your expression of interest in the work of the Department of Justice and your belief that ultimately Justice is the most significant aspect of the Government. I fully agree with you."[61]

Brandeis and Frankfurter were pained by their realization that things were unsatisfactory in the department. As early as May 1933, Brandeis complained that Solicitor General J. Crawford Biggs was making a bad impression.[62] Frankfurter wrote to Roosevelt of Justice Harlan Stone's concern about the quality of personnel in the solicitor general's office.[63] In mid-June Brandeis again complained about incompetence in the department.[64] The response of Brandeis and Frankfurter to this situation followed a familiar pattern. The attorney general himself, a presidential appointee, was invulnerable, but there were other positions within the department which Frankfurter and Brandeis quickly moved to fill.[65]

They were interested in placing Dean Acheson in the Justice Department. In fact, Brandeis had initially suggested that he might become solicitor general.[66] Acheson himself recalled that Frankfurter had recommended him to Roosevelt for the position. Roosevelt consulted Cummings about the possibility, but the reaction "being immediate, violent, and adverse, the proposal was withdrawn."[67] Frankfurter's influence was hardly strong enough to induce Roosevelt to override a Cabinet officer on a departmental personnel matter.[68]

In May Brandeis examined loopholes in tax legislation with William A. Sutherland, and discussed the possibility of his becoming an assistant attorney general.[69] In early July Sutherland wrote to Frankfurter that he had been asked by Lilienthal to work as a counsel for TVA, reporting that Lilienthal had told him he had been recommended by Corcoran.[70] Sutherland had already met Arthur E. Morgan of the TVA at Brandeis's residence on 20 May, and "had the opportunity of talking with him twenty or thirty minutes at that time."[71] Brandeis and Frankfurter wanted Sutherland in public service, preferably in the Justice Department. Frankfurter suggested to Roosevelt that Sutherland be drawn into tax work and urged that Erwin Griswold and Paul D. Miller be retained in the solicitor general's office because of their skill in tax cases.[72]

In mid-July Cummings rejected Sutherland, who then pursued his contacts with Lilienthal.[73] Roosevelt had evidently passed Frankfurter's suggestions directly on to Cummings, who agreed that Miller and Griswold should remain in the department. He went on to say, however, that Sutherland "would not meet the situation at all and it is rather too bad that this is so because, within certain limits, he is a man of very excellent attainments."[74] Cummings never bothered to say why Sutherland would not do, but Sutherland told Frankfurter that the attorney general resented the efforts made on his behalf.[75]

Frankfurter's best contact in the department until 1935 was Harold Stephens. In July Stephens wrote to Frankfurter that he was

> delighted to find in my Division of the Department of Justice a number of men from the Harvard Law School, including several who had their training specially under you ... they have proved able assistants indeed.[76]

Several months later Stephens assured Frankfurter that

> Mr. Cummings holds your judgment in high respect, and, as you know, I do also, and we are both, of course, cognizant of the great confidence that the President has in you.[77]

Subsequent correspondence indicates that Frankfurter made several personnel suggestions which were accepted, but by this time only subordinate positions were still open. After the fall of 1933, Frankfurter's correspondence with Stephens became sporadic.

This contact with Stephens, however, did not ease Frankfurter's fears about the Justice Department. Indeed, the weaknesses of the department were apparent to others, including Harold Ickes who observed that it was "simply loaded with political appointees and hardly anyone has any respect for the standing and ability of the lawyers over there." While Cummings was a man of "considerable ability," he "apparently delivered himself into the hands of the place hunters."[78]

Ickes recorded that Frankfurter saw Roosevelt on 16 December and talked with him about the Justice Department, with the result that the president "now thoroughly understands the weakness of that Department."[79] In late 1934 a glimmer of hope appeared. Frankfurter reported to Brandeis: "I had a good talk with Stanley Reed. He is a very fine Kentuckian."[80] But it was not until March 1935 that Frankfurter could rejoice that Biggs had been replaced by Reed, who was "a modest man" with "the great faculty of getting good men about him."[81] But while

Brandeis and Frankfurter were able to work with Reed, Cummings remained a formidable barrier. Ironically, the department most directly related to Frankfurter and Brandeis's professional competence was almost impervious to their influence.

The Treasury Department was also important to Frankfurter and Brandeis because of the place of taxation in their recovery program, but while they had a keen interest in the department, they exerted almost no influence, and their correspondence contains a litany of complaints about its problems. The basic difficulty was the relationship between Frankfurter, Brandeis, and Secretary of the Treasury Henry M. Morgenthau, Jr. Although in one letter Morgenthau mentioned visiting Brandeis and saying that he was "very dear & generous" in his friendship, correspondence between the two was sparse, and Brandeis deplored Morgenthau's performance as secretary.[82]

There were more letters between Frankfurter and Morgenthau, but these were brief and perfunctory. Frankfurter was more bitterly critical of Morgenthau than of anyone else in New Deal circles. He felt Morgenthau was "small-minded" and "really a disgrace."[83] Perhaps one reason for their antagonism can be seen in Frankfurter's comment about Morgenthau's "anxiety not to be tarred by my stick & More generally not to be declared one of the 'liberal Jews.'"[84] Frankfurter reserved special enmity for people he considered pseudoliberals, and he put Morgenthau in this category. Ethnic kinship only embittered matters. So Morgenthau was ignorant, arrogant, and "a stupid bootlick."[85] This bitterness frustrated any attempt on the part of Frankfurter to exert significant influence in the Treasury Department.

Frankfurter and Brandeis were unable to compensate for this alienation from Morgenthau by cultivating any important subordinates. The director of the budget, Lewis Douglas, was a fiscally orthodox, conservative Democrat whose wife expressed deep resentment of Frankfurter.[86] In 1934 Douglas was succeeded by Daniel W. Bell, who was a Morgenthau man.[87] Morgenthau's most knowledgeable and influential assistant was Herman Oliphant, a well-known legal theorist. Frankfurter had little contact with him. He was, in Frankfurter's view, a man who

"liked servitors" and who was "meanly jealous."[88] Rosewell
Magill, the department's tax expert, was "a bland, pleasant
fellow, who will offend no one, but he is fundamentally a
conventional, conservative mind."[89]

The Treasury's monetary advisers in the early days were
George Warren of Cornell and James Harvey Rogers of Yale.
Enthusiastic advocates of the commodity dollar, both believed
that recovery could be attained through the right fiscal policy.[90]
Frankfurter's only helpful contacts in the department were with
subordinates. In late 1933 Corcoran occupied a minor post in the
Treasury, and was able to give Frankfurter and Brandeis some
inside details of the administration's fiscal policy and some
insight into interdepartmental struggles. He reported disagreement over the president's gold-buying decision. There was a
"legal duel between the law departments of the yes-men led by
Oliphant ... and ... my little gang led by Dean" Acheson.[91]

Corcoran and his "little gang" did not fare well. They soon
came "under suspicion" and Corcoran planned a return to the
Reconstruction Finance Corporation.[92] After his departure,
however, he retained an interest in the Treasury. He reported
that Oliphant had asked him for a "loan" of personnel from time
to time and that he was planting other men in the Treasury
"whom Oliphant doesn't know are ours."[93] But while Corcoran
had informants within the department, he was unable to
influence policy.

Frankfurter's other important contact in the department was
Dean Acheson. This is interesting in itself since Acheson,
according to Corcoran, "thoroughly despises the President as a
political trimmer, a skimper of problems, and an arrogant bully
from the first clashes of the London Conference."[94] This shows
that Frankfurter did not demand absolute ideological loyalty in
his proteges. Indeed, Corcoran indicated that Acheson was trying
to maintain a certain distance from Frankfurter himself by asking
him for personnel suggestions instead of Frankfurter.[95] Nevertheless when Acheson left the Treasury Department in November
1933 during the dispute over gold buying, Frankfurter and
Brandeis lost another of their fragile links with the department.[96]

It is hardly surprising that Frankfurter and Brandeis were unable to influence the course of fiscal policy by their contacts in the Treasury Department. Indeed, this impotence existed even before Morgenthau became secretary. In March Lowenthal wrote to Brandeis:

> As for the larger steps you outlined—so far is one from opportunity to urge them effectively, that one cannot even urge steps to effectuate the program adopted by the Treasury officials themselves. . . . Woodin is Secretary and has taken a shine, apparently, to the staff which functioned under Mills.[97]

Morgenthau's appointment only made a bad situation worse. Frankfurter had at least expressed a fondness for Woodin which transcended ideology.[98] Frankfurter's inability to influence events within the Treasury Department was summed up in his complaint to Brandeis: "the Treasury I can do nothing with."[99] Frankfurter and Brandeis lacked support for their recovery program from the Cabinet department most relevant to its implementation. This was a serious and enduring disadvantage.

Frankfurter and Brandeis were never very interested in the Commerce Department. Secretary of Commerce Daniel Roper was rarely mentioned in their correspondence.[100] John Dickinson, one of Frankfurter's former students, was the assistant secretary of commerce, but the correspondence between Dickinson and Frankfurter was slight.[101] Frankfurter came to distrust Dickinson because he was opposed to massive public works and was an advocate of recovery through industrial control.[102] Frankfurter warned Roosevelt that Dickinson was not the man to serve as assistant attorney general in charge of antitrust matters, informing the president that Dickinson had publicly criticized the Sherman Act and that therefore it would be "embarrassing" to place him in the position.[103] On other occasions Frankfurter expressed misgivings about Dickinson's probusiness attitude.[104] So there was no important contact with the Department of Commerce. Perhaps Brandeis and Frankfurter believed that the department was not important to their recovery program. They were undoubtedly discouraged by its long history of subordination to business interests.

Little need be said about the relation of Frankfurter and Brandeis to the other Cabinet departments. Roosevelt's appointments to War, Navy, and the Post Office reflected political considerations, and in any case these departments were remote from their concerns.[105] There was little contact with the Department of State. Secretary of State Cordell Hull played an important role at the London Economic Conference which had domestic repercussions, but his main concern was foreign affairs.

CHAPTER V

Launching the New Deal:
Legislation and the Administrative Agencies

Roosevelt was inaugurated in the middle of a banking crisis which threatened to paralyze the nation's economy. The Emergency Banking Relief Act of 9 March 1933 contained little substantive reform, but Roosevelt's continuation of the bank holiday halted the panic and permitted orderly reconstruction.[1] The administration then turned to the question of substantive reform of the nation's banking structure. Of all businessmen, bankers were the chief villains in the view of Frankfurter and Brandeis. With other people's money, bankers dominated the nation's economy for their own selfish purposes.

Yet neither Frankfurter nor Brandeis said much about banking legislation, and neither showed enthusiasm over the banking acts of 1933 and 1935. They were not indifferent to flaws in the system, but they did not think that legislation was the remedy. Brandeis commented in early March that while improvements could be made in banking, "the chief evil is banking practices. Until we can get honest, fearless bankers—no improvement of the system will avail much."[2] This is not to say that Brandeis and Frankfurter were content simply to wait for the appearance of honest bankers. Brandeis had some remedies for banking problems, but the legislation of 1933 and 1935 did not come to grips with what he believed to be the fundamental issues.

In March 1933 Brandeis called for the government to "open

wide" postal savings, and later that month, without even
commenting on the Banking Act of 1933, he warned that no one
should be misled "by the prospect of central bank or all-in-the-
reserve system remedies or branch bank talk. The evidence shows
that lack of these things was not the real cause of our trouble."[3]
In May Brandeis wrote to Frankfurter that he favored a thorough
investigation of the reasons for bank failure, believing that bank
bigness would prove to be the most important factor.[4] Brandeis
accused bankers of trying to get Roosevelt to "let up" on
securities legislation. "A little money," he observed, "lent with
discretion to little fellows would do infinitely more good than
'security issues' galore."[5] Although Brandeis commented more
than Frankfurter on banking matters, Frankfurter expounded
Brandeis's position to others. He wrote to Colorado Sen. Edward
Costigan:

> The air is full these days of talk that our difficulties are due
> to the many small units in our financial system and that we
> need concentration of financial power—a few big powerful
> or one central bank. Maybe we do and maybe we don't. But
> in any event let's not embark on such a policy on the
> assumption that it was the small banks as against the big
> ones which got us into trouble . . . the important thing . . . is
> that we do not know . . . the truth of the relation of the big
> banks to the collapse of our banking system until scrutiny of
> bank assets reveals how much of the load of the small banks
> consists of securities foisted on them by the big.[6]

Harry Shulman recalled that Brandeis said he would "take
the Government out of the hands of the banker" by making the
post offices available for saving (with no limitation on amount)
and checking. He would also make them agencies for issuing
securities. Brandeis suggested splitting up the banking business
by prohibiting "any bank from doing any more than one kind of
banking business."[7] Brandeis called for an autopsy of the banking
system, and asserted that

commercial banking as such is safe and that it is only the long-time loans, mortgages, and security loans that caused the collapse, as well as loans to officers and directors or their interests.[8]

Brandeis's approach to the banking problem was of a piece with his ideas about the curse of bigness in all areas of American economic life, and the solution was the same. Therefore Frankfurter and Brandeis had little interest in the Banking Act of 1933. The Banking Act of 1935 strengthened the Federal Reserve Board,[9] giving the Board power over open market operations and the authority to determine the nature of sound assets on which reserve requirements were to be met.[10] None of the men responsible for the act, with the exception of Goldenweiser, had any significant contact with Brandeis or Frankfurter.[11]

Goldenweiser saw Brandeis in May 1935, when the act was under consideration, and reported that Brandeis's interest in the measure was "primarily centered on the question of whether it would do anything to prevent directors and officers of the banks having any personal interest in the character of their loans and investments." He also asked whether the bill would "improve the contact between the lending officers of the banks and the borrowers." Goldenweiser had to concede that the bill did not bear on either of these concerns.[12] Frankfurter observed to Roosevelt that Marriner Eccles's arguments in its favor seemed to him "very persuasive," but he did not elaborate as he usually did on subjects where he felt genuine enthusiasm.[13] Brandeis and Frankfurter remained uninterested in the act and aloof from the men who administered it. While Brandeis later conceded that Eccles "sounds hopeful," he admitted that he had never met him or any of his close friends and that "no one has ever suggested inviting him in."[14]

Banking legislation was generally regarded as helpful, but few people believed it would produce recovery. The two pillars of the early New Deal recovery effort were the NRA and the AAA. The myth of Brandeis-Frankfurter control of Roosevelt is dispelled by the existence of the NRA, since this agency with its concept of a government-business planning "partnership" was alien to their philosophy. Moley observed that by adopting the NRA, Roosevelt was abandoning "the atomistic competitive solution of Wilson and Brandeis."[15] Tugwell also disapproved of the NRA. He asserted that the agency "became the medium of a back to work movement. . . . But its use as the central balancing mechanism of the economy was never developed. Indeed no attempt was made to develop it."[16] Tugwell criticized the NRA for not going far enough, while Brandeis and Frankfurter believed it went too far.

Many people had a hand in shaping the National Industrial Recovery Act. Paul Douglas, Senator Wagner, Donald Richberg, and Hugh Johnson all played important roles. Perkins, Tugwell, and John Dickinson helped initially but dropped out because of the pressure of other duties.[17] Hugh Johnson, the first administrator of the agency, explained the program at a New York meeting, attended by Frankfurter, of several important labor leaders and industrialists. Johnson later reported that the group "went over the fundamentals" of the NRA program and "were in general agreement."[18] But this was not true, at least in Frankfurter's case. Frankfurter later said that the meeting focused on the necessity of a bottom level for wages and prices and the need for industrial stability, standards for wages and hours, and reemployment.[19] These goals did not deal with those aspects of the NRA which Brandeis and Frankfurter distrusted, and Frankfurter insisted that he "had nothing whatever to do with the legislation, with drafting its form, or with administering its provisions."[20]

Frankfurter did contact Johnson in the early days of the NRA. In May he invited Johnson to Cambridge "for quiet planning," saying that "if I am of any use to you, you could up here get out of me all there is in me."[21] In June he congratulated Johnson on a speech, and Johnson replied cordially, telling Frankfurter that his telegram meant more than all the others he received.[22] In July Frankfurter congratulated Johnson on the textile code and asked to be put on the mailing list for all the agency's publications.[23] In September Frankfurter wrote to Johnson that the coal code was "a great achievement."[24]

Correspondence between the two, however, soon ceased. Frankfurter, undoubtedly with Brandeis's approval, stressed the reforming provisions of the NRA as opposed to its planning features.[25] Brandeis and Frankfurter praised some of these provisions, but Johnson was committed to the planning approach.[26] As early as July, Brandeis said that the problems of the NRA were "inescapable."[27] Writing from England in October, Frankfurter observed to Brandeis that "NRA is going as badly as you had feared it would."[28] In a memorandum about the NRA Frankfurter noted that the agency could be useful only if it served "to increase the interchange of goods and services in this country," while a reduction of production and price increases could have only a temporary and limited benefit. Demand would have to be stimulated for recovery to occur. Large-scale public works projects were essential, and the labor clauses "at once assume a commanding importance" because they also would stimulate demand.[29]

Brandeis and Frankfurter hoped that something could be salvaged from the NRA labor provisions. Frankfurter wrote to Donald Richberg, who was second in command in the NRA, urging him to avoid wage differentiations based on sex.[30] He later dealt with the labor question in broader terms. Alluding to some industrialists' "intransigent attitude against collective bargaining," he urged Johnson and Richberg to take the lead in promulgating codes for reluctant industries, with particular attention given to "appropriate limitations of hours at appropriate minimum wages." Wages and hours provisions were the "two crucial features for recovery."[31] Brandeis's estimate of the NRA remained pessimistic. In August he observed that the agency was having "troubles galore."[32] He had urged Johnson by telephone to protect "real labor organizations," and emphasized that "without regularity of employment—the New Deal is impossible."[33] Brandeis later noted that the NRA had "a terrible record in putting men back to work," and implied that the agency was retarding recovery.[34]

In September 1934 Johnson announced that he had been in

"constant touch" with Brandeis during the NRA's early days, but Brandeis denied this vigorously.[35] Brandeis recalled that he had seen Johnson in May and told him that the proposed National Industrial Recovery Act was bad because of "the impossibility of enforcement, the dangers to the small industries, the inefficiency of the big unit, be it governmental or private."[36] Johnson seemed to Brandeis "a crushed man" later, when the difficulties of the agency had become apparent. But Brandeis admitted that he

> was much touched by the brief talk. I felt that he had showed manliness in coming to me, who had predicted failure, instead of avoiding me as most men would have done, when the predicted failure was apparent. Since then I have heard nothing from him in any way.[37]

Although Frankfurter had written to Roosevelt about the "very serious situation Johnson's outburst had created," Brandeis made no public refutation.[38] After Johnson resigned in September 1934, Brandeis wrote to Frankfurter that the "NRA general set-up should result in early liquidation of nearly all except the labor provisions."[39] This statement summarizes their evaluation of the agency. They saw hope only in its labor provisions which could promote recovery by increasing demand and therefore employment.

Brandeis and Frankfurter never expected much from Johnson, believing that his outlook, administrative failures, and personality were all undesirable. But they did have hopes for Donald Richberg, who succeeded Johnson as head of the NRA. Richberg, a 1904 graduate of the Harvard Law School, was an expert in labor law who had obtained a reputation as a liberal in the 1920s.[40] Frankfurter had known Richberg for some time and had persuaded him to take David Lilienthal into his law practice. Later Richberg recommended Lilienthal for the Wisconsin Public Service Commission.[41]

Brandeis and Frankfurter thought Richberg would be influential in public service. Brandeis believed that Richberg would be wasted even as solicitor general. In October 1932 Lilienthal noted that Frankfurter had told him that he had spoken to Roosevelt about Richberg, and that a meeting between them had occurred. Frankfurter told Lilienthal that the president "took quite a shine" to Richberg.[42]

Frankfurter recommended Richberg to Johnson, and he became the second most powerful man in the NRA. His accession was one way in which Frankfurter and Brandeis hoped to influence the direction of the agency. Frankfurter's correspondence with Richberg was cordial during the spring and summer of 1933, but it faded quickly after that.[43] Richberg and Brandeis never exchanged many letters. In the summer of 1933 Mrs. Brandeis wrote him a letter of encouragement,[44] and Brandeis later wrote to him that "with you, Ickes, and Lilienthal in seats of power, it really looks like a New Deal."[45] Brandeis also attempted to influence Richberg through common acquaintances. In early September Lincoln Filene, a liberal Massachusetts businessman, wrote to Richberg: "Following talk with our mutual friend the Justice at Chatham today on certain phases of the labor situation, he earnestly suggests I talk over same with you. . . . I will meet you anywhere you desire."[46]

In early 1934 Richberg wrote to Brandeis that he had recently seen Roosevelt and "reviewed all your suggestions concerning taxes—and he *took notes* on all of them which was a strong indication of real interest."[47] Disillusionment set in quickly, however. In early 1934 Frankfurter said that he had read some "ominous things" about Richberg.[48] In the fall he noted that Richberg was "becoming more calculating" and conceding too much to business interests.[49] Finally in November Frankfurter wrote to Brandeis that Richberg "really is . . . irreclaimable." He attributed Richberg's decline to his wife's greed and his own ambition.[50]

In late April 1935, when the possibility of rewriting the NRA act was being discussed, Richberg wrote to Roosevelt that if the legislation

is sufficiently devitalized to conform to the anti-monopoly ideas of Senators Borah and Nye, it will in my opinion be

made so ineffective and unworkable that it would be worse
than nothing ... I am asking an opportunity to discuss this
with you before any concessions are made to the defeatist
position which some of your friends are sincerely urging
because of their lack of information and experience.[51]

But an unworkable law was precisely what Brandeis and
Frankfurter wanted. In August 1934 Frankfurter and Roosevelt
discussed the NRA and Frankfurter reported that the president
wanted to keep only the wages, hours, and child labor
provisions.[52] If this is correct Roosevelt was leaning to the
Brandeis-Frankfurter evaluation of the agency.

In May 1935 the Supreme Court ruled the NRA unconstitutional in the case of *Schechter* v. *United States* (295 U.S. 528) with
Brandeis concurring.[53] There is no doubt that Frankfurter
disapproved of the NRA, but since the decision irritated
Roosevelt, he found himself in an awkward position. Frankfurter
felt that as the agency was failing anyway, it should be allowed to
fall of its own weight. He knew that if the issue went to the Court,
Brandeis would vote against the administration. The irony was
that this tension was generated by an agency which was about to
disappear.[54]

Frankfurter tried to prevent a Court test, but Richberg pushed
for an appeal.[55] Alarmed, Frankfurter wrote to the president that
he had

had a talk with Stanley Reed, particularly about the Belcher
case. Made clear to him what seemed to me the decisive
reasons for dismissing this appeal. ... He, himself, believes
the case should be dismissed but wondered whether the
views of the NRA people were not a reflection of yours. I
assured him that if he were convinced, as he is, of the
wisdom of dismissing the appeal, he would have your
support.[56]

First Frankfurter helped persuade Stanley Reed to dismiss the

Belcher case and then brought in Roosevelt's influence at the crucial moment. It is impossible to determine exactly what occurred between Reed and Roosevelt, but the observation that Frankfurter "endorsed" Reed's decision seems an understatement.[57] Frankfurter also tried to prevent the *Schechter* case from getting to the Court. On 4 April 1935 Corcoran sent Roosevelt a telegram advising him to "hold whole situation on NRA appeals in abeyance" because the "fundamental situation on Court not changed." Frankfurter urged a "thorough discussion by all concerned."[58] He succeeded in persuading Roosevelt to wait, but the president's telegram to Attorney General Cummings arrived too late. Frankfurter believed that someone within the administration deliberately delayed it.[59]

Frankfurter was not able to avoid the tension created by Brandeis's opposition to the administration, but he quickly moved to salvage what he could. Soon after the *Schechter* decision, he wrote Roosevelt about its consequences. Frankfurter recommended that fair labor clauses be attached "to contracts for Government loans and grants."[60] He also suggested that the "administrative mechanism of the NRA be extended to provide a vehicle for the exchange of information" and as "an aid and stimulant to appropriate action by the States." He urged the passage of the Wagner bill, and recommended that the principle behind the Webb-Kenyon Act be used to protect the "decent labor policies of the several States by Federal legislation."[61]

Frankfurter worked to disassociate the NRA from the administration. In a memorandum to Roosevelt, he observed that the NRA had been "undertaken in response to the demands of industry obsessed with the idea that it was hobbled by the limitations of the Sherman Law and could not get on its feet without the removal of these limitations."[62] Frankfurter concluded that there were some things "no one would disagree about with the NRA" such as limitations on hours, minimum wage, and control of child labor.[63] Two days after the *Schechter* decision Frankfurter wrote to Roosevelt outlining his thoughts "on the issue of the Supreme Court v. the President." He asserted, rather paradoxically, that more antiadministration decisions by the Court would help the New Deal:

> That is why I think it so fortunate that the Administration has pending before Congress measures like the Social Security bill, the Holding Company bill, the Wagner bill, the Guffey bill. Put *them* up to the Supreme Court. Let the Court strike down any or all of them.... *Then* propose a Constitutional amendment giving the national Government adequate power to cope with national economic and industrial problems.

Frankfurter argued that this would give the president "an overwhelming issue of a positive character" for the 1936 campaign.[64]

This argument, though plausible, was disingenous. Would Frankfurter, who had diligently tried to avert a clash with Court, view its escalation with such equanimity?[65] "Put them up to the Supreme Court" meant, in Frankfurter's oblique idiom, "push these bills through Congress." Frankfurter had tried to avert judicial repudiation of the NRA. But once it had occurred, he used it as a way of urging the president to push more reform legislation through Congress.[66]

The other pillar of the early New Deal's planning phase was the AAA. Frankfurter's background was strictly urban; he wrote to Roosevelt in 1933 that "opinion on the merits of Agriculture Bill is beyond my competence." He made the valid but rather banal observation that the bill could be valuable for its experimental approach to national problems.[67] It was rare for the opinionated Frankfurter to be so reticent, but apparently he made no effort to educate himself about agricultural matters. In 1935 Norman Thomas asked Frankfurter to speak to Roosevelt about the plight of Southern sharecroppers. Frankfurter replied that he "did not know anything about agriculture" and that it would not "be proper for him to raise the matter with Roosevelt."[68] Frankfurter's ignorance of agriculture was indeed a standing joke between the president and himself.[69]

Brandeis also had nothing to do with the framing of the AAA measure, but he was not without ideas about the nation's agricultural problems. Throughout the 1920s he had been aware of the depression of agriculture and the plight of the farmer. He frequently referred to agricultural problems, such as the disparity between retail and wholesale prices for farm products, and the inadequacy of rural credit.[70] He believed that farmers could free themselves from monopolies through cooperative efforts. He told his brother Alfred that "the only escape from the Packing monopoly has seemed to me to lie in many packing plants distributed, through cooperatives like the Danish, over the farming region."[71] In agriculture, as elsewhere, there was no substitute for the traditional virtues of thrift and industry. Brandeis spoke admiringly of Italian farmers in Alabama who, welcomed as tenant farmers, quickly saved enough money to buy their own land.[72]

But virtue alone was not enough. More credit for farmers was crucial. Throughout the 1920s Brandeis complained that federal lending agencies were supporting the banks more than the farmers. He denounced the "pretty terrible" record of the Farm Loan Board and the banks, which revealed "much pettifogging political corruption, particularly employing incompetents and also financial corruption in many places." Brandeis blamed the banks for boosting farm values artificially, unwisely foreclosing on farmers, and then selling the land to speculators. These actions depressed the market for farm land and made a bad situation worse.[73] Brandeis continued to advocate greater farm credit. In the summer of 1933 he asked Frederic Howe, head of the AAA's Consumers Council, about how the agency could expand farm credit.[74] Brandeis also knew how badly much of the nation's farm land needed reclamation. He pointed out the ravages of soil erosion. Lilienthal wrote to Brandeis in 1936 that he had first heard of such problems from him in the summer of 1932, and recalled that Brandeis had suggested that soil conservation was "a problem for public agencies, of urgent necessity, and which was adapted to a problem of public works."[75]

Brandeis was deeply concerned about the rural poor, particularly Southern tenant farmers. He supported Commonwealth College, a radical labor college in western Arkansas which had begun as a socialist colony in California.[76] Gardner Jackson, whom Brandeis introduced to the college and its work, recalled that "the justice several times during those first months sent me cheques to help finance the effort."[77] Brandeis approved of the Resettlement Administration and the establishment of cooperative enterprises in its communities.[78] He gave "sizeable contributions" to the Southern Tenant Farmers' Union.[79] His interest in the small farmers led him to urge Gardner Jackson to press the sharecroppers' case with Henry Wallace and Chester Davis.[80] As a means of limiting the curse of bigness in agriculture, Brandeis suggested that the government retain title to the land it acquired so that it could then be leased to small operators.[81]

Brandeis linked agricultural recovery with the recovery of society as a whole. Agricultural projects were prominent in the massive public works effort he advocated. But there was no provision in his agricultural program for the sweeping production controls of the AAA. His program comprised three elements: extension of credit, public works, and a variety of programs to help small farmers and sharecroppers. Brandeis was as dubious about the AAA as he was about the NRA. Even before the AAA measure was passed by Congress, Brandeis was "worried as thunder about it."[82] He feared that it would only accentuate the trend toward agricultural bigness and lead to an increase in absentee ownership and the number of sharecroppers. Gardner Jackson reported that Brandeis "went into the whole business, as a prophecy—the increase in corporate farming."[83] He urged Jackson to tell his friends "that these are my thoughts before this act is acted upon."[84]

The performance of the AAA gave substance to his misgivings. By August 1933 Brandeis was "increasingly skeptical of the agricultural performance,[85] and by 1935 his opinion of the AAA was completely negative. He was "convinced that this whole AAA production curtailment policy will prove disastrous."[86] For Brandeis it was obvious that the AAA, as well as the NRA, was having "the effect of retarding recovery."[87] Brandeis also denied that the AAA was democratic even when referendums were used because "the program was imposed from above, and did not arise locally out of understanding from below."[88] Brandeis's criticism of the AAA, therefore, paralleled his reaction to the NRA.

In contrast to Brandeis, Frankfurter was ambiguous in his attitude to the AAA. He observed that Stanley Reed's brief in appealing the *Butler* decision (which had invalidated the AAA) was "an altogether admirable brief" for the agency.[89] He advised Roosevelt to give a long talk to the nation about agriculture, observing that it was "extremely important to review with great particularity the extraordinarily powerful story of the terrible conditions that led to the AAA and the equally extraordinary results of it."[90] Moley, however, asserted that while Frankfurter knew very little about agriculture, he had a "deep antipathy" to the AAA.[91] His testimony is significant since he was closely associated with Frankfurter during the AAA's formative period.

Brandeis, who had strong convictions about agriculture, openly disapproved of the AAA. Frankfurter's relationship with Roosevelt made his position more difficult. He handled the president tactfully, talking to him a great deal about things he approved and ignoring unpleasant subjects. It seems likely that Frankfurter also disapproved of the AAA, though perhaps less strongly than Brandeis (acknowledged ignorance can lessen the intensity of convictions), but he could not say so without the risk of offending Roosevelt. This kind of tightrope act put Frankfurter in an awkward position on several occasions. Norman Thomas pressed Frankfurter on the sharecropper issue, and Frankfurter pled ignorance as a defense.[92] Oswald Villard wrote to him in 1936:

> I insist that the worst failure of our friend F.D.R. is that he is not speaking out on subjects like this and civil liberties. Although Norman Thomas appealed to him for the sharecroppers, he has done nothing. ... So we are drifting straight into Fascism by this easy route of the repeal of our constitutional liberties.[93]

Frankfurter's reply was a vague refutation of the doctrine of historical determinism which made no effort to defend the administration's agricultural policy.[94]

While Frankfurter and Brandeis admired Secretary of Agriculture Henry Wallace, neither was very close to him.[95] In the early days of the AAA, however, the Frankfurter charm was directed even to the recalcitrant Tugwell. Frankfurter wrote him that "the two of you [Wallace and Tugwell] are an admirable team and I left the Department of Agriculture with a real sense of elation."[96] Frankfurter recommended Lowenthal, William O. Douglas, and Acheson for positions in AAA.[97] But this correspondence did not last beyond May 1933. George N. Peek, the first administrator of the AAA, was also unsympathetic to Frankfurter. In 1936 Peek recalled that

> a plague of young lawyers settled on Washington. They all claimed to be friends of somebody or other and mostly of Felix Frankfurter and Jerome Frank. They floated airily into offices, took desks, asked for papers and found no end of things to be busy about. I never found out why they came, what they did, or why they left.[98]

The second head of the AAA was Chester C. Davis, a Montana farmer and journalist, who had been the state's first commissioner of agriculture. Brandeis and Frankfurter did not know him well. The economic advisers for the AAA were not close to them either. Louis H. Bean was not in their camp, and Mordecai Ezekiel did not even meet Brandeis until 1936.[99] In the opinion of Frankfurter, Gardiner Means had produced the best parts of *The Modern Corporation and Private Property* which he wrote with A. A. Berle, but Means was an apologist for bigness.[100]

Brandeis and Frankfurter exerted their greatest influence in the legal department. Frankfurter had initially recommended the AAA's general counsel Jerome Frank as counsel for the Department of Agriculture, but when Jim Farley raised political objections, Frank was shifted to the AAA. Frank had first met Frankfurter through Judge Julian Mack in 1930. He approached

Frankfurter about a government job in the summer of 1932, and Frankfurter told him to be ready for a "curious offer." Later he got a call from Tugwell.[101] Harold Stephens wrote to Frankfurter that Wallace had a high opinion of Frank and that "his selection was made because of your high opinion of him."[102] Once Frank was appointed he recruited a staff, and this broadened Frankfurter's influence. For a time, Tugwell and Frank lived together and "invited in to live with them, gratis, a shifting pattern of Felix Frankfurter's young lawyers."[103] With Frankfurter's help, Frank succeeded in recruiting perhaps the most controversial group of young men to be found anywhere in the New Deal ranks.

Nathan Witt, who had studied under Frankfurter and James Landis, was one such recruit.[104] In June 1933 Witt wrote to Frankfurter that he had had an interview with Frank: "I have met with a kind reception everywhere, and I feel vastly encouraged. I know that for you I need make no attempt to put into words my appreciation of what you have done."[105] Before sending this letter along to Landis, Frankfurter wrote in the margin: "Jim, what a beautifully solid & serene lad this."[106]

Lee Pressman had also been a student of Frankfurter's and joined Frank in Washington. Pressman and Witt, in turn, approached Gardner Jackson.[107] Frankfurter recommended Jackson to Nathan Margold as "a very dear friend of mine."[108] In making this suggestion, Frankfurter was repeating what Brandeis had said to him about the value of placing Jackson.[109] Jackson eventually became an aide to Frederic Howe, who headed the Consumers' Council of the AAA.[110]

Another of the controversial young recruits was Alger Hiss, who had attended the Harvard Law School from 1926 to 1929 and had attracted Frankfurter's attention there. Frankfurter sent him off to serve as Holmes's law clerk for the 1929-30 term.[111] Frankfurter had recommended him to Margold as "first rate in every way."[112] Like Jackson, Hiss was rejected by Ickes but hired by the AAA. The relationship of these men to Frankfurter and Brandeis varied. The connection with Witt and Pressman was tenuous.[113] Brandeis had the closest relationship with Jackson, with whom he worked on the sharecropper problem after Jackson left the AAA.[114]

Tension developed within the AAA as the young reformers attempted to implement their ideas. Although Chester Davis, whom Wallace had appointed to replace Peek, was a man of broad sympathies, he felt he had no choice but "to work with all the forces in the agricultural picture" including the big distributors. For the reformers, however, the AAA was not merely a means of restoring farm income, but also "an opportunity to revise the distribution of income within the agricultural community."[115] Conflict was inevitable.

The reformers' hostility to the big distributors, particularly in dairy production, generated tension. Jackson was active in this fight and took the matter directly to Wallace. Wallace, after listening "in reverie," replied:

> I don't understand you—you and your friend Justice Brandeis. When you see something you think is wrong, you want to do something about it right away. I'm not like that. I'd rather sit under a tree and let the cycle of time help heal the situation.

Wallace also observed that Tugwell and Davis were "two illmatched horses," and that one of them would probably have to go eventually.[116] This did not satisfy the reformers who were hardly content to leave things to the "cycle of time."

Another controversial issue was the role of the consumers' counsel of the AAA. In late 1934 Gardner Jackson wrote to Brandeis that

> the abolition or serious crippling of the activities of the Consumers' Counsel of the Agricultural Adjustment Administration ... would, in effect, give the interests in what you described as our "unequal fight" a virtual carte blanche.

Jackson also praised the consumer agencies of the NRA and the National Emergency Council. He relayed to Brandeis Frank's opinion that his office depended on data provided by the consumers' counsel because "the economic data is not thoroughly developed by the other sections."[117]

But it was the sharecropper issue, basic to the reformers, which finally led to the purge of the AAA. When Alger Hiss wrote a directive in early 1935 which adopted the Southern Tenant Farmers' Union position that every tenant had the right to continue in his place during the life of the contract, Davis determined to eliminate the reformers. He demanded that Wallace permit him to fire the dissidents, and Wallace, who had tried to avoid the decision, finally agreed.[118] Tugwell, who was out of Washington when the purge occurred, labelled the action "part of a studied plan to drive all liberals out of the Department." He remained in Agriculture a little longer only as a personal favor to Roosevelt.[119]

Brandeis and Frankfurter disapproved of the purge. Brandeis observed that "AAA developments are very regrettable."[120] Frankfurter said that Wallace "seems to be obfuscated."[121] Yet despite regret over the turn of events, they reacted with surprising mildness. Neither had much hope for AAA. They did not think that a small number of reformers scattered in the legal counsel's office and the consumers' counsel could accomplish much. Brandeis and Frankfurter were not close to the reformers; indeed, they shared reservations about some of them. The closest relationship was that between Jackson and Brandeis, and there is no evidence that Witt, Hiss, or Pressman had much contact with either Brandeis or Frankfurter.[122]

Though Brandeis and Frankfurter did not question the goals of the reformers, they were doubtful of their wisdom and their behavior. Frankfurter noted:

Our liberal friends have not been the wisest in temperament & actions. They are not long-headed campaigners, talk too much both publicly & privately & exercise bad judgment as to men & measures.

Even Jackson, while "lovable," was a "very indiscreet fellow" who occasionally leaked information to the press.[123] Frankfurter's relationship to Frank was never very good. In his summary of "our liberal friends" Frankfurter commented:

> And Jerome Frank—well that's a long long story, which I've had for a long time from Frank Shea & other reliable friends of Jerry Frank's—hadn't much sense.[124]

Frankfurter did not spell out what he meant, but his correspondence with Frank is illuminating.

In the summer of 1935 Frankfurter wrote to Frank that he shared Frank's doubts about the worth of his "continuance in Washington" under the existing circumstances of "trench warfare" for which he was not temperamentally suited.[125] He questioned Frank's legal realism by reminding him that "the essence ... of 'realism' in advocacy is to win a case and not to vindicate new philosophic insights or even to expose the bunk of old arguments or old slogans."[126] Frankfurter's criticism of Frank's legal philosophy was coupled with the assertion that he lacked discretion. Referring to Frank's "gratuitous candor," he asked:

> Will it surprise you to hear that friendly talk even when made to friends by an official in an administration which outrages established interests is likely to be misused?[127]

Although Brandeis and Frankfurter disapproved of the basic strategy of the early New Deal, they did support some of its reform legislation. They were both interested in the regulation of securities. The collapse of the stock market and the election of a reformer made some attempt to regulate the securities market likely. Roosevelt, wasting little time after the election, turned the matter over to Secretary of Commerce Daniel Roper who, in turn, called in experts including Huston Thompson.[128]

In March Thompson presented a draft to Roosevelt which Landis characterized as unworkable because it did not exempt the sale of outstanding securities, and made the issuer responsible for their soundness. Landis observed that this would have "held an incalculable threat over the sellers of securities."[129] The Thompson bill, sponsored initially by representatives Sam Rayburn of Texas and Henry Ashurst of Arizona, quickly came under heavy congressional attack. The hearing was a "complete debacle."[130] Seeing that the bill was in trouble, Rayburn asked Moley to help him get a better bill.[131]

Moley recalled that he had asked Frankfurter to help with securities legislation, and Frankfurter reported that he went to Washington on 6 April "as a result of a telephone request from the President communicated through Assistant Secretary [of State] Moley."[132] Frankfurter took Landis along to help with details, thinking it would be a valuable experience for a professor of legislation, and Ben Cohen also accompanied him.[133]

Frankfurter, Cohen, and Landis decided to use the English Companies Act as a model. Then Cohen, Landis, and Corcoran, whose role was less important, went to work while Frankfurter attended to other duties in Washington.[134] The bill was drafted over the weekend and was ready by 9 April. In accordance with Roosevelt's request, the bill did not confer authority to pass upon the soundness of securities.[135] Cohen, Landis, and Frankfurter then met with the House Commerce Committee to discuss the draft. Although Frankfurter was familiar with the outline of the bill, he had received a copy of it only the night before. Nevertheless, he

> took the lead in the exposition of our draft. It was a brilliant performance ... he handled the main structure of the bill magnificently.[136]

During the rest of April the bill was further refined by Landis and Cohen. Corcoran also worked with them, but only in the evenings.[137]

While the Thompson bill was still under consideration, the Cohen-Landis draft was introduced by Rayburn. Frankfurter

brought presidential influence to bear. Rayburn's dissatisfaction
with the Thompson bill was probably the result of Roosevelt's
intervention. On 17 April Frankfurter sent the president his

> warmest thanks for your intervention with Rayburn on the
> Securities Bill. . . . I am keeping in close telephonic touch
> with the situation. . . . I don't have to tell you that the
> subject is very complicated, with many ramifications,
> raising a number of difficult drafting problems.[138]

The House considered the Cohen-Landis bill while the Senate was
still dealing with the Thompson proposal sponsored by Duncan
Fletcher, chairman of the Finance Committee.

On 8 May, Frankfurter informed Roosevelt that Fletcher was
willing to withdraw the Thompson bill. Frankfurter hoped that
Roosevelt would

> deem it appropriate to encourage Senator Fletcher in his
> intention in interest of speedy enactment of your proposal.
> You may have noticed uniform comment in House debate as
> to great care with which Rayburn bill was drawn to
> effectuate your proposals.[139]

And yet as late as 17 May Thompson was still asking advice from
Brandeis about his version.[140] The Senate finally agreed to delay
voting on the Thompson version until the House passed the
Cohen-Landis bill. The subsequent conference debate was
acrimonious, but, except for a few minor changes, the bill was
unchanged. It passed easily and was signed by Roosevelt on 27
May.[141] Cohen wrote to Landis wryly:

> I am afraid it is a little unfortunate for us that the Act passed
> so nearly as we drafted it. That gives us too much of a
> parental interest in the darned thing. The rules and
> regulations and the decisions of the Courts have as much
> chance of satisfying us as the clothes that strangers might
> choose for our babies.[142]

Frankfurter was gratified, and he characterized the act as a "belated and conservative attempt" to correct long-standing abuses. He gave Brandeis credit for preparing the climate of opinion for the act by his "impressive analysis of the workings of our financial forces, of the traps and pitfalls that beset the investor."[143] Henry L. Stimson had opposed the act as an obstacle to the flotation of new capital, and he accused Frankfurter of being influenced by "an excess of crusader's zeal."[144] But Frankfurter defended the act by arguing that it was a conservative measure. He argued that he had exerted "a moderating influence" on the reformers by comparing the Thompson draft (with its rigid "let the seller beware" approach) to the Cohen-Landis bill.[145]

Brandeis was not directly involved in the drafting of the measure.[146] In mid-April Thompson came to him "much disturbed" by complications connected with the "Frankfurter-Landis re-drafting of the bill," and Brandeis told him to see Landis or Frankfurter.[147] Brandeis saw Landis and Cohen later while they were still working on the bill, but unfortunately he gave no details of their conversation.[148] It is clear, however, that Brandeis approved of the Securities Act since it embodied some of his earlier suggestions. In early August he observed that the act was not preventing new investment, as had been predicted by the enemies of reform.[149] Brandeis and Frankfurter regarded the act as beneficial but not indispensable. It was a desirable reform measure, but by itself it was unable to speed recovery.

Brandeis and Frankfurter were also enthusiastic about the TVA. They did not take the initiative since the agency resulted from a meeting of minds between Roosevelt and Sen. George W. Norris of Nebraska.[150] Nor were Brandeis and Frankfurter involved in drafting the TVA legislation. Indeed neither knew much about the technical problems involved, though they applauded the venture. Willard Hurst, one of Brandeis's law clerks, recalled that

Brandeis regarded TVA as a great achievement in human inventiveness and regional decentralization. The Justice was particularly interested in the "grass-roots" phase of the enterprise.[151]

In the summer of 1933 Brandeis told Frankfurter that "Arthur Morgan & Dave Lilienthal have gotten the most alluring job in Gvt," and later when Brandeis drew a balance sheet on the New Deal, the TVA appeared on the positive side of the ledger.[152]

Although Frankfurter and Brandeis did not influence the legislation which created the TVA, they helped place Lilienthal on its board of directors. Lilienthal had been a student of Frankfurter's in 1921, and Frankfurter persuaded Donald Richberg to accept him as a law partner in 1923. In 1931 Richberg recommended Lilienthal to Gov. Philip LaFollette for service with the Wisconsin Public Service Commission.[153] Lilienthal served on the commission until early in 1933. Brandeis wrote to Frankfurter that it seemed doubtful that Lilienthal would be reappointed after LaFollette's defeat at the polls and concluded: "I suppose FDR will snatch him if he doesn't—perhaps if he does."[154] In the winter and spring of 1933 Frankfurter corresponded frequently with Lilienthal about employment possibilities in government.[155] Brandeis recommended him to Arthur Morgan after the latter was appointed TVA board chairman in May 1933, and Morgan passed the recommendation on to Roosevelt.[156] When Lilienthal's appointment was announced, Frankfurter wrote to Roosevelt that it was "a truly great appointment."[157]

Lilienthal quickly became uneasy over what he thought were Morgan's concessions to the power companies, and turned to Frankfurter for advice. Frankfurter reported to Brandeis that

Dave Lilienthal was here overnight—full of Tennessee V. matters. Arthur Morgan is incredibly naive—and defensive and worse. Happily, the other Morgan has been educated & he & Dave are two to one for the right things & effective methods. Dave is showing a wise head, patience and technical capacity.[158]

Brandeis commented succinctly that "Dave Lilienthal has quite a job on his hands."[159] Lilienthal kept Frankfurter and Brandeis informed of affairs within the agency. They supported and advised him as he fought to keep the cost of power low, and resist the encroachments of the utility companies.[160] Lilienthal also was an effective voice in favor of decentralization. He used Brandeisian language in arguing that excessive centralization was "perhaps the most disturbing characteristic of our time. For in the scene of general bigness, men continue to come about the same size."[161] But although Brandeis and Frankfurter approved of the TVA and were involved in its struggles, they knew that, like the Securities Act and other reforms, it could not cure the underlying malaise that afflicted the economy.

The first phase of the New Deal ended in the summer of 1933. For Brandeis and Frankfurter it was a mixed performance. They regarded some of the legislation favorably. Banking and securities reform and the TVA were desirable, but not central to recovery. The twin pillars of the administration's recovery program were inconsistent with their philosophy. The NRA and the AAA were valued only for their reform potential, but the potential was never fulfilled. Brandeis and Frankfurter were not uncritical admirers of Roosevelt, and as the first phase of the New Deal blended into a period of vacillation, their criticisms grew more intense.

CHAPTER VI

The New Deal in the Doldrums

Roosevelt's first term had two periods of reform separated by a lull. While the first reform period, comprising chiefly the legislation of the first hundred days, enjoyed some success, the depression proved intractable. Uncertain what to do next, the president wavered before moving forward again. This period from late 1933 to the spring of 1935 was difficult for Brandeis and Frankfurter. They became increasingly impatient, and their distress bordered on a loss of faith in Roosevelt. While Roosevelt did nothing, Brandeis and Frankfurter waited uneasily. Yet when he acted, they often believed he was mistaken. The lull in reform activity was dominated by fiscal policy. Roosevelt probably never really believed that monetary legerdemain would cure the depression but he was so desperate for recovery that he was willing to try it despite the opposition of some of his advisers.[1]

Roosevelt had inherited plans for the London Economic Conference from Hoover, who believed that the depression was a global event which had led to the American collapse.[2] From this perspective an international conference seemed desirable, and Roosevelt was interested initially.[3] But the Brain Trust, particularly Moley, argued that domestic policy was the key to recovery.[4] Complex issues were involved. One need not adopt the internationalist theory of the depression to believe that cooperation between nations could alleviate it. But Brandeis and

Frankfurter focused on domestic policy. Roosevelt's own attitude changed in the weeks preceding the conference. Since the New Deal's recovery program was focused on domestic policy, the president wanted coordinated governmental action while the French and British believed "that the removal of commercial barriers would automatically provoke a revival."[5] Preconference negotiations indicated that agreement would be difficult and, to make matters worse, the American delegation was itself badly split on policy issues which put the negotiators "in a fog much denser than ... [they] might encounter in the North Atlantic."[6]

Brandeis and Frankfurter did not expect much from the conference because Herbert Feis kept them informed about the difficulties and uncertainities connected with preconference planning. He reported in early April that "there could hardly be worse difficulty and confusion than exists,"[7] and in June Frankfurter reported to Brandeis that the "London sky looks dark."[8] Frankfurter's foreboding proved accurate. While the American delegation in London floundered, Roosevelt concluded that the time was not right for currency stabilization.[9] In a "bombshell" message to the conference on 3 July, he reminded the delegates that the conference had been called to produce "greater prosperity to the masses of all Nations" and that it should not "allow itself to be diverted by the proposal of a purely artificial and temporary experiment affecting the monetary exchange of a few Nations only."[10]

Although the reaction was "violent"—the *Manchester Guardian* referred to the message as a "Manifesto of Anarchy"—Roosevelt did have some distinguished European support. Keynes congratulated Roosevelt for "throwing the gauntlet of a nationally managed currency in the face of the gold standard." A group of Oxford economists, including Keynes's biographer Roy Harrod, greeted the president's message with enthusiasm.[11] Frankfurter observed:

Whatever else they may say, it's now clear F.D.R. is his own "brain trust." Keynes' support of F.D. is significant but the whole London Conference sheds glory on no one.[12]

Frankfurter told Brandeis that the message was Roosevelt's own work, written aboard the *Indianapolis* "when only Louis Howe was with him."[13] Yet, putting the best face possible on things, he congratulated Roosevelt on his "forthright rejection of that London Formula, with all its mischievous ambiguities—a literary shell-game if there ever was one."[14]

Brandeis replied that

> Keynes notwithstanding, the tone and circumstance of F.D.'s July 3 proclamation to the World Conference are to all very disquieting as a symptom. This may be a manifestation of the disintegrating effect of absolute power on mind and character.... Remember—we have no Congress until Jan. '34.[15]

Brandeis ignored the economic policy and focused on the arrogance of Roosevelt's edict. Both Brandeis and Frankfurter disapproved of the way Roosevelt handled the conference because, "Keynes notwithstanding," it was the "tone and circumstance" of the message that was bad. Brandeis and Frankfurter were content with a mild form of internationalism which preserved diplomatic amenities while avoiding serious commitments. The president's message, however, was needlessly blunt and, for Brandeis at least, a sign that power was adversely affecting Roosevelt's judgment.

Roosevelt's "bombshell" message presaged a turn to domestic remedies, and fiscal policy, for a time, became the panacea. Rather than seek stabilization abroad, Roosevelt sought higher prices at home. The basis of the policy was George Warren's theory that a reduction in the gold value of the dollar would raise prices and restore a balance between the prices of raw materials and consumer goods.[16] Warren's theory had remained in the background until a drastic fall in prices in July gave it new

relevance. A continuing drop persuaded Roosevelt that action
was necessary. On 16 August he told Morgenthau to buy gold "in
the open market at more than the prevailing price."[17]

Brandeis and Frankfurter regarded this fiscal policy with
growing disapproval. The first objectionable action was the
abrogation in June of the gold clause in public and private
contracts. Brandeis asserted that this action was "terrifying in its
implications" because the government had repudiated a "solemn
obligation" which it had entered into freely. Brandeis concluded
that "taxation would have afforded an honorable way out" of a
genuine emergency.[18] "Yes," Frankfurter replied, "what you say
of Govts own default on obligations is only too true & so
needless."[19] Though Brandeis was "calm about going off gold,"
he was disturbed about the government's breach of contract.[20]

Roosevelt's decision to buy gold set off a vigorous debate
within administration circles which Brandeis and Frankfurter
followed with interest. Acheson recalled that Morgenthau and
Herman Oliphant headed a group supporting the policy, while the
opposition was led by Oliver Sprague, Lewis Douglas, and James
P. Warburg.[21] Corcoran told Frankfurter that Acheson himself
was one of the leaders of the opposition.[22] In late August Brandeis
showed Acheson a memorandum written by Harold Stephens
which argued that the gold buying was illegal. Within a week,
however, Stephens received from Homer Cummings a memorandum by Oliphant supporting the policy. Acheson asked
Brandeis for advice, and he recalled that Brandeis's reply

> was Delphic, but clear enough to me. I can hear him now
> saying, "Dean, if I wanted a legal opinion, I would prefer to
> get it from you than from Homer Cummings."[23]

By mid-July Sprague was unhappy over Roosevelt's policy, but
had decided to remain in the Treasury Department counting on
the support of Douglas and Acheson.[24] The conflict intensified.
The climactic White House conference to discuss legality was
held 19 October.[25] Acheson protested gold buying vigorously,
while Cummings fumed at him "in impotent fury."[26] Brandeis

wrote to Frankfurter that "things have not bettered since I wrote
you last week—the gold purchasing project ... has augmented
the uncertainties. To me the whole scheme is unintelligible."[27]
Frankfurter replied that Roosevelt had left him with the
conviction that his gold purchase policy "was a complete leap in
the dark."[28] He later observed that "FDR seems bent on a policy
of monetary stunts which not one economist here ... believes in
& very few even pretend to understand."[29] But while Frankfurter
was openly critical in his correspondence with Brandeis, his
comments to the president were guarded.

In transmitting to Roosevelt a letter from some British
economists, Frankfurter remarked that they "have refused to be
worshippers of the golden calf theory of currency."[30] In his most
extensive written comment to Roosevelt about gold buying,
Frankfurter observed:

> Through the fog of the currency debate is the clear trend of
> business improvement.... As a result of our discussion
> about gold buying with Will Woodin ... I have felt quite
> clearly that you were giving that policy a tentative trial to
> see what it could do without committing yourself to that
> theory any more than to any other theory as a solvent. I
> don't understand why more people who are sympathetic to
> your efforts don't understand that.

He asserted that after the deflationist and inflationist wings in
Congress neutralized each other, Roosevelt could "mobilize
general consent."[31] This letter has been cited as evidence that
Frankfurter agreed with Roosevelt's monetary experiments.[32]
But this assertion ignores both Frankfurter's way of handling
people (particularly Roosevelt) and the letter itself. Frankfurter
was trying to influence Roosevelt away from gold buying by
stressing the "tentative" nature of the policy, and by depicting
the president as standing in statesmanlike superiority to the
monetary tinkerers.

Far from approving of the policy, Frankfurter criticized it more
than Brandeis did. He approved of Sprague's resignation and

public statement "not the least for F. D.'s good."[33] He regarded
Acheson's resignation with equanimity, but he was disturbed
over indications that he had been forced out.[34] In December
Frankfurter reported to Brandeis that Keynes believed gold
buying to be "puerile," and he later observed that "F.D. is
retreating on Warren's theory & so Sprague's outbursts were all
to the good."[35] As late as January 1934, Frankfurter was
complaining about Roosevelt's "dollar gyrations."[36] Roosevelt
finally gave up on gold buying later in January. He proposed a
stabilization of the dollar, and Congress passed the Gold Reserve
Act which ended the day-by-day fluctuations.[37] It is unlikely that
Brandeis and Frankfurter had anything to do with Roosevelt's
decision. He abandoned the policy because it did not work.

The episode sheds light on Frankfurter's strategy in handling
Roosevelt. He did not strongly oppose a settled presidential
policy, but was circumspect in discussing gold buying. When he
did not agree with Roosevelt's ideas, he did not discuss them any
more than necessary. As long as Roosevelt was undecided,
however, Frankfurter expressed his opinions forcefully.

The year 1934 was a low ebb for Brandeis and Frankfurter. The
president was uncertain, and his advisers were offering a variety
of solutions. Conservative business leaders, suddenly haunted by
the specter of Leviathan, trumpeted concern about threatened
liberties.[38] Frankfurter's presence in England from September
1933 until August 1934 was a disadvantage because, although he
was in constant touch with Roosevelt, Brandeis, and others, he
was nonetheless more a spectator than a participant. Throughout
this period, Brandeis and Frankfurter continued to lobby for
their recovery program. As early as August 1933, Brandeis
prepared a preliminary balance sheet on the New Deal. He
approved of the TVA, labor reform, the CCC, and the PWA, but
he saw danger in the NRA, AAA, repudiation of gold contracts,
aid to business by the RFC, and inflation.[39]

Brandeis also feared Roosevelt's power, and agreed with Al
Smith about the necessity of editorial criticism and the need for
political opposition. He suggested that Ellery Sedgewick, editor
of the *Atlantic Monthly*, get Harold Laski to write an article on the

theme.[40] Brandeis was worried about Roosevelt's friendship with Vincent Astor and speculated that this was "responsible in large part for F.D.'s disinclination to tackle heavy estate taxes."[41] Brandeis talked comprehensively with Sam Rosenman

> on regularity of employment—the small unit, smaller executive corporation salaries, and heavy estate taxes. He asked what you thought of these views and said that he was to see F.D. this weekend and would talk fully with him on these matters.[42]

Frankfurter hoped that Rosenman was "a full and accurate reporter of your views to F.D."[43] In September Brandeis again saw Rosenman, who reported that he had taken Brandeis's opinions to Roosevelt. The president "was much interested & took some notes."[44] Brandeis outlined his program, including specific legislative proposals, to Moley in September.[45] Moley had written to Brandeis several days earlier that he had enjoyed "a long talk" with Frankfurter "on a variety of subjects, principally public works," and that Frankfurter had suggested he might see him before the Court convened.[46]

Frankfurter, however, apparently failed to set up an appointment for Brandeis with Roosevelt before he left for England because Brandeis wrote to Frankfurter later: "As F.D. has gone to Hyde Park— no request for conference came; for which I am glad, as I have outlined fully to Moley and others what I should have said to F.D."[47] This comment shows that Brandeis preferred not to speak with Roosevelt directly. While this reluctance was at least partly due to Brandeis's sense of judicial propriety, it may also have stemmed from his disillusionment with Roosevelt.

Frankfurter's disillusionment, while never so great as Brandeis's, was also strong. In late October he observed that Farley's "pretty bad" performance had occurred "with F.D.'s approval."[48] A little later he commented that news from America "too thoroughly illustrates the doubts & difficulties you have felt."[49] By November Brandeis had almost completely lost faith in Roosevelt. He referred to him sarcastically as "the great

Experimentalist," and took comfort in the thought that "each day brings Congress' convening nearer."[50] Indeed Brandeis was glad that Frankfurter was in England:

> You could not have averted F.D.'s aberrations and plunges. They were the inescapable penalties paid for conferring absolute power. Next year you may—because you were not in this mess—be effective in helping us out of the mire.[51]

He predicted that "Liberalism and Experimentation will have received a severe set-back & the reactionaries will be strengthened in their error."[52] Frankfurter sadly agreed.[53]

Despite this disillusionment, however, Brandeis and Frankfurter did not give up hope. They continued to press their views on Roosevelt. A constant factor in the thought of both men was hostility to businessmen. They continually reminded Roosevelt of the invidious intentions of big business. Frankfurter wrote to him shortly before he left for England and stressed that "the forces of opposition—business, financial and political forces are stirring beneath the surface, ready to become overt."[54] In late October he wrote to Roosevelt that the news in England was "tinctured . . . with the Wall Street bias."[55]

In November while Frankfurter and Brandeis were exchanging gloomy comments about the direction of the New Deal, Frankfurter was adroitly urging Roosevelt to launch a massive public works program. He congratulated him on the Civil Works Administration, stating that it should encourage industry and concluding that he had long "believed that nothing is as important for the recovery program as that you should give your personal impetus to a vigorous public works program."[56] There was little in the CWA to indicate the advent of such a program, but Frankfurter was using an occasion of congratulation to urge Roosevelt tactfully to move in a new direction.[57] Brandeis was alarmed by the very success of the temporary CWA program. He asked how the government could permit men to fall back into unemployment when neither business nor the PWA could take up the slack.[58] Frankfurter agreed that Harry Hopkins "has been too successful."[59]

While in England, Frankfurter served as a conduit for suggestions he thought Roosevelt needed to hear. So his view on public works was fortified by a memorandum from some British economists.[60] Roosevelt assured Frankfurter that

> The memorandum from your economist colleagues was read by me to one of my little confidential gatherings— Morgenthau, Cummings, Governor Black, George Harrison, Warren, Rogers, and Oliphant—and the comment was that the Oxonians are thinking much in our terms and that since their memorandum was written we had already put several suggestions into practical effect. ... You can tell the professors that in regard to public works we shall spend in the next fiscal year nearly twice the amount we are spending in this fiscal year but there is a practical limit to what the Government can borrow.[61]

Frankfurter must have winced at the participants in the "little confidential gathering," for not one of his friends was present. He might also have smiled ruefully at Roosevelt's comment that "the Oxonians are thinking much in our terms." Brandeis, who observed that Roosevelt's budget messages indicated that he has "consented to follow Roper," said that the president's letter was "just like him."[62]

At times Brandeis nearly gave up hope that anything could be done until Frankfurter returned. In December he wrote: "I continue glad you are not here. You could not help matters & might have impaired your chances of helping F. D. et al. hereafter."[63] Still, Brandeis occasionally had some good things to report. He approved of Roosevelt's tariff proposal and observed that his message on stock exchange legislation was well done.[64] But Brandeis's compliments were few, and about matters of marginal importance.

One of the minor reforms which Brandeis and Frankfurter

advocated was the abolition of contingent fees for lawyers, particularly in tax cases. Brandeis had called for abolition as early as 1928[65] and discussed it with Frankfurter several times. In the spring of 1933 Frankfurter gave Roosevelt the draft of a bill abolishing contingent fees.[66] The draft had been forgotten in the rush of the first hundred days. In January 1934, Frankfurter reopened the subject by describing the huge savings that the bill could produce: "Between ourselves, L.D.B. passed on that bill before I submitted it to you." He also recommended a great expansion of the postal savings program which Brandeis had long urged as a way of limiting the power of bankers.[67] In reporting to Brandeis about his correspondence with Roosevelt, Frankfurter commented: "I put it to him hard."[68]

These proposals, however, dealt with minor matters and reflected the powerlessness of Brandeis and Frankfurter during this period. They won no major battles. But by maintaining contact with Roosevelt, Frankfurter was able to make some gains in personnel placement. With the passage of the Securities Exchange Act in the summer of 1934, two young proteges of Brandeis and Frankfurter attained positions of greater importance.

Thomas Corcoran and Benjamin Cohen did not begin their New Deal careers while Frankfurter was in England. Indeed both had been known by Brandeis and Frankfurter before the New Deal, and both had been involved in drafting the Securities Act. Corcoran had been one of Frankfurter's most promising students. In 1926 he served as secretary to Justice Holmes and then worked for a prosperous New York law firm. In 1932 he became a counsel for the Reconstruction Finance Corporation and, after a brief interlude in the Treasury Department, he retained the RFC post until 1941 when he left government service. Eugene Meyer, the first chairman of the RFC, had asked Frankfurter to recommend some capable young lawyers for him. Frankfurter promptly mentioned Corcoran, and Meyer took him solely on that recommendation.[69] So Corcoran, the liberal gadfly, entered government service during the Hoover administration to work for a conservative businessman.

In addition to helping with securities legislation, Corcoran worked as a recruiter. In early May Brandeis saw Acheson and suggested that he discuss personnel matters with Corcoran. This was Brandeis's first mention of Corcoran.[70] Until late 1933, Brandeis made only scattered references to him, occasionally misspelling his name; he did not meet him until the fall.[71] Frankfurter was closer to Corcoran. In June 1933, he tried to arrange for him to act in Moley's stead when Moley went to London. Frankfurter wrote to Moley:

> I hope you can pull off the Corcoran arrangement, or rather that FDR will. I think the way to do it is for him to do it. It really is, if I say may so, an excellent adjustment during your absence.[72]

The phrase "if I may say so" implies that the proposed arrangement was Frankfurter's idea, but there is no evidence that Moley responded to the suggestion.

Nevertheless by the summer of 1933 Corcoran was already serving as a one-man intelligence unit.[73] In July Frankfurter wrote to Brandeis that Corcoran called him nightly.[74] Once Corcoran had proved his usefulness, Frankfurter was eager to place him in a more significant position. He introduced him to Missy LeHand, the president's secretary:

> I venture to give this note to a very dear friend of mine, Thomas G. Corcoran, and at present an assistant to the Secretary of the Treasury. He is a most valuable public servant and one of the most indefatigable workers for the success of this administration. From time to time he may come to you about matters, and I commend him to you warmly. He is a person of entire dependability.[75]

Corcoran was important in Frankfurter's plans before he left for England, and Frankfurter's absence enhanced his importance for he served as Frankfurter's eyes and ears. Brandeis became involved also. In October Corcoran wrote to Frankfurter: "I've been seeing L.D.B. regularly and of course will so long as le bon Dieu gives me the chance."[76] Later he reported that there was talk of a Frankfurter-Brandeis bloc, and that he was "under suspicion in the Treasury" and planned to return to the RFC.[77] Moley was aware of a connection for he wrote to Frankfurter that he had been in contact with his "various children"—including Corcoran.[78]

Frankfurter steered both Corcoran and Cohen to Brandeis for advice.[79] In late December 1933 Corcoran assured Frankfurter:

> But even if you haven't had anything but cables you can always be comfortable that ... I always take advice—and that I haven't moved and won't move an inch in a general course of direction without going to L.D.B.[80]

Brandeis supported this statement, for he expected Corcoran to relay information to Frankfurter. He wrote to him that he had seen Corcoran several times and "doubtless he is keeping you fully informed." He was "a great joy" and was "handling himself admirably."[81]

Throughout the first half of 1934 Corcoran figured prominently in the Brandeis-Frankfurter correspondence.[82] He helped Acheson fight against the gold-buying policy, and soothed the temperamental Cohen.[83] He testified on the Securities Exchange bill.[84] In addition to these tasks, Corcoran was also helping develop Brandeis's ideas on social security.[85] So by the summer of 1934, Frankfurter was giving more thought to placing Corcoran properly. He told Brandeis that Solicitor General Biggs offered to make Corcoran his assistant. Frankfurter, however, again tried to persuade Moley to take Corcoran on as his "resident Washington representative." Brandeis agreed that Corcoran

> should remain on the RFC payroll with the free hand hitherto enjoyed: and it would be fine to have his status such that he would be in fact F. D.'s advisor and carry out F. D.'s policies through "Tom's boys." Doubtless that could

be effected by his being Moley's resident representative. . . .
But it must be borne in mind that Moley is mercurial.[86]

Frankfurter agreed that Moley was "mercurial" but said it was "a
case of working with the tools we have."[87]

This plan did not work out, but Frankfurter did not give up.[88]
In March 1935 he wrote Roosevelt a long letter about his need for
a special assistant. The person must be anonymous, aloof from
politics, discreet, highly intelligent, and committed to the New
Deal:

> You will say that I am giving the specifications for a
> paragon. Well, I am, but there is one such, strangely
> enough, ready to hand. I mean Tom Corcoran . . . very, very
> rarely do you get in one man such technical equipment,
> resourcefulness, powerful and persuasive style, unstinted
> devotion, wide contacts and rich experience in legal,
> financial, and governmental affairs.[89]

Frankfurter suggested that Corcoran be in charge of all the
"preliminary sifting" of material submitted to Roosevelt. He was
"shocked" at the way reports were submitted to the president
"without any intellectual traffic directions."[90] After years of
effort, Frankfurter finally succeeded, for he wrote to Missy
LeHand in late March expressing his gratification at "the
arrangements made by the President for annexing for his
immediate help the resourceful talents of Tom."[91] Frankfurter
and Brandeis finally had their own representative at the
president's side.[92]

Benjamin Cohen was closely linked with Corcoran in New Deal
circles. Cohen received his law degree in 1916 from Harvard,
where he met Frankfurter. During World War I he was an
attorney for the United States Shipping Board and from 1919 to
1921 was counsel for the American Zionists. Then he became
secretary to Judge Julian W. Mack of New York. Cohen was
brought into government by Frankfurter in connection with the

Securities Act in 1933.[93] A brilliant legislative craftsman, Cohen was associate general counsel for PWA in 1933, and from 1934 to 1937 he served as general counsel for the National Power Policy Committee. In both positions he worked closely with Harold Ickes.[94]

Cohen's role was similar to Corcoran's for, like Corcoran, he was a keen observer of the Washington scene and kept Frankfurter and Brandeis informed of developments.[95] He used his personal influence to help shape policy, and he was in demand as a speechwriter.[96] He worked best at drafting legislation.[97]

The two men had different personalities. Corcoran was the extroverted front man, while Cohen preferred to work out of the limelight.[98] In many ways the two complemented one another and, for all their differences in temperament, made a formidable team.[99] Cohen played a key role in the passage of the Securities Exchange Act on 6 June 1934, shortly before Frankfurter returned from England. The main burden of drafting and lobbying was carried by Landis, Corcoran, and Cohen.

Roosevelt had appointed a committee in 1933 to consider stock exchange regulation. Chaired by Daniel Roper and John Dickinson, the committee also included A. A. Berle and Landis. Roper, in the best Commerce Department tradition, advocated self-regulation. Landis began to work independently, but he quickly involved Cohen and Corcoran. They received encouragement from Ferdinand Pecora and Max Lowenthal.[100] Over the Christmas holidays Corcoran, Cohen, and Landis produced a draft.[101]

The outlook for an effective bill was not favorable. As early as October 1933, Corcoran had expressed dissatisfaction with the president's committee, and he noted later that Roosevelt had showed signs of yielding to conservative pressure.[102] But despite these difficulties, an effective bill was introduced on 10 February 1934.[103] Frankfurter, still in England, wrote to Landis:

Having been given a good opening, I sent the Skipper my views regarding the Securities Act. Not knowing what is going on behind the scenes, I wrote in the dark, but I

expressed myself very stiffly. This is for your exclusive
information.[104]

Frankfurter did not know the details and so he urged the
desirability of reform on the president in general terms.

Brandeis, however, was closely involved with the bill in an
advisory capacity. He saw Lowenthal in late October, and they
carefully analyzed the proposed legislation.[105] Corcoran mentioned Brandeis frequently in his correspondence with Frankfurter. In November he cabled Frankfurter: "Had a long talk with
Isaiah . . . don't worry."[106] He wrote later to reassure Frankfurter
again about his frequent consultations with Brandeis.[107] This was
during the period when Corcoran, Cohen, and Landis were
putting the bill into final form.[108] Another indication of
Brandeis's influence is the stringency of the bill, which alienated
some members of Congress.[109] Corcoran told Frankfurter that
while the bill was well received by the press, there were
"indications of a terrific fight in which Skipper's position
doubtful." He urged Frankfurter to support the bill in his
correspondence with Roosevelt, and Frankfurter complied.[110]

Frankfurter mentioned to Roosevelt an article by Bernard
Flexner in the *Atlantic* which argued that bankers would "operate
under the act once they are denied hope of amendments which
would weaken permanent gains of the act."[111] Several days later,
he wrote that stock exchange regulation was "long overdue."[112]
Toward the end of the month Frankfurter commented:

> The New York papers also bring the full text of the Stock
> Exchange Bill. That is an astonishingly careful and acute
> piece of draftsmanship. The Bill reveals real mastery of the
> intricacies of the Exchange and addresses itself with
> knowledge to them.[113]

Roosevelt resisted appeals from Wall Street for concessions, and
the Senate and House bills were reconciled in late May. The final
form confided to the discretion of the new commission some of
the authority explicitly written into the earlier draft.[114] But all

the drafters were satisfied with the result. Frankfurter told Roosevelt that he was "getting a stock exchange control act with a good set of teeth."[115] When Roosevelt signed the measure into law, Frankfurter sent his congratulations.[116] And yet this act, like the Securities Act, was not central to the Brandeis-Frankfurter recovery plan.

Frankfurter and Brandeis became increasingly disillusioned with Roosevelt and the course of his administration from the summer of 1933 to the summer of 1934. Despite such gains as the Securities Exchange Act and the placement of Corcoran, little progress had been made in combating the depression. The possibilities for future error seemed greater than the prospects for substantive reform. Frankfurter and Brandeis both urgently felt the need for a fresh start.

CHAPTER VII

A New Beginning

The second New Deal is often regarded as the triumph of the Brandeisian philosophy. Turning from the shambles of the first New Deal, Roosevelt, after a period of vacillation, took a fresh approach. Having failed to control bigness at the beginning of his administration, the president tried to limit it by a "revitalization of the competitive sector." The result was the triumph of the "neo-Brandeisians."[1] This has become a standard interpretation of the second New Deal.[2] This discussion involves a reassessment of this view. Did the second New Deal fulfill the Brandeis-Frankfurter recovery program? Their program involved heavy taxation (particularly of corporations and estates), massive public works expenditures, and regularity of employment. They also wished to limit bigness and to introduce greater competition and flexibility into the economy.

Historians have largely overlooked the recovery program and focused entirely on the war on bigness. The result has been a distortion of how Brandeis and Frankfurter reacted to the second New Deal. Its failure to achieve their long term ends was more significant to Brandeis and Frankfurter than the limited gains which were made. The second New Deal was not a triumph for the Brandeisian philosophy. Yet, paradoxically, the influence of Brandeis and Frankfurter was never higher than during 1935, even as the second New Deal was becoming a disappointment.[3]

101

That they were able to exert such influence was due both to circumstances and to their skill in personal relations.

Brandeis and Frankfurter had a long way to come from the dark days of 1934. Their position was not promising. They had been almost completely out of sympathy with the early New Deal. The men they had placed in the administration were good reporters, but were seldom in a position to shape policy.[4] Their contacts in Congress were few.[5] In addition Frankfurter had been away a year, and his influence and contacts had weakened. Frankfurter's relationship with Roosevelt was the best advantage they possessed, and Brandeis valued this connection highly. He attached great importance to Frankfurter's return from England, eagerly anticipating his quick reentry into the Washington arena. In May Frankfurter told Brandeis that he planned to leave England about the first of July, adding that he saw "no purpose in getting involved in Washington matters during the summer," and asking Brandeis if he thought it worthwhile to approach Roosevelt with suggestions before the fall.[6]

The reaction was immediate. Brandeis, Corcoran, and Cohen all wrote to Frankfurter urging him to return immediately.[7] Brandeis told Frankfurter that he should quickly begin making plans for the next session of Congress.[8] Corcoran alluded to difficulties with Moley.[9] Cohen testified to Frankfurter's leadership:

> It is difficult to urge you too strongly knowing your desire to grasp the opportunity of your European contacts ... particularly when one cannot underwrite what can be accomplished by your return but there is no question of the need of real personal force over here. The men attached to you are working hard, but their spirits are a little low and their consciousness of any coherent program is somewhat dulled.[10]

Brandeis was implacable. In early June he wrote to Frankfurter that he hoped to see him "very soon after July 10—which day he [Corcoran] tells me you are due."[11] When Frankfurter arrived,

Brandeis greeted him with a request to arrange a meeting with Corcoran, Cohen, Lowenthal, and Brandeis's daughter Elizabeth Raushenbush.[12] Frankfurter quickly plunged into activity. He followed Brandeis's advice and had Moley "spend hours" taking him "into all the high-ways & by-ways of F. D.'s movements ... & the personal relations."[13] By the end of August Frankfurter felt sufficiently reoriented to have a conference with Roosevelt.[14]

In early August Brandeis reemphasized the need for a huge public works program and tax reform. He went over old ground, arguing that all of the projects would be socially useful and thus "would stimulate prosperity and broaden the tax base in the future," clearly intending for Frankfurter to relay these views to Roosevelt.[15] Frankfurter was also to cover "much ground" during his meeting with the president in late August. He observed that Roosevelt seemed to be his old self. Frankfurter presented Brandeis's views on the "irrepressible conflict" between government and business interests. Roosevelt agreed that Brandeis had "put his finger on the crux of the situation." When the president wondered whether to "baby them along," wait for a fight, or declare war himself, Frankfurter told him that Brandeis "wouldn't have him declare verbal war, but recognize that here is war & act on that assumption."[16] Frankfurter urged Roosevelt to launch a large public works program with emphasis on housing.[17] When Roosevelt argued that he could not borrow three billion dollars a year, Frankfurter asserted that high unemployment "is intolerable & destructive of American institutions." He went on to stress the necessity of programs to produce regularity of employment.[18]

This was a long-standing concern for Brandeis. In the Frankfurter Papers there is a memorandum dealing with the subject dated June 1911, which sets out his position in detail. Brandeis asserted that "irregularity of employment is ... the greatest of industrial wastes, and one of the main causes of social demoralization." He believed that the only good way of encouraging regularity was to make it benefit the employer, and his plan was designed to do this. After determining the average employment in a particular industry for a year, the employer would place a "certain part" of the wages in a trust fund. The amount deposited would depend on the annual employment rate. If the rate was less than average, the employee would receive the principle plus interest. If the rate was greater than average, the employer received part of the money. If there was full employment, the employer would receive the principle plus interest. Furthermore, the fund could provide unemployment compensation when needed. This plan was essentially the one which Brandeis advocated in the 1930s.[19]

Brandeis never lost interest in the employment issue. In 1928 he urged Paul Kellogg of the *Survey Graphic* to take up regularity of employment, which he characterized as "the fundamental remedy."[20] But during the 1920s nothing was done even in Wisconsin.[21] The depression stimulated new interest in the subject, however, and Brandeis was pleased to learn that Paul Douglas had been appointed acting director of the Swarthmore Unemployment Institute in 1930, even though he did not always agree with Douglas on methods.[22] Douglas was willing to work with trade associations. Although it is not difficult to imagine what Brandeis thought of this tactic, he contented himself with the tactful understatement: "I think his the less hopeful method of attack."[23]

In 1931 Raushenbush drafted a bill which Harold Groves introduced to a special session of the Wisconsin legislature. The mutual insurance plan of the Commons version was dropped and a system of individual accounts substituted, but emphasis remained on prevention of unemployment. The bill was passed on 28 January 1932.[24] Brandeis wrote to Harold Laski:

The Unemployment Reserve Act recently adopted in Wisconsin is our first step in grappling with irregularity of employment. Possibly you saw Elizabeth's recent articles in the Survey Graphic. She and Paul have had the largest part both in drafting the bill and in securing its passage.[25]

This success, however, aggravated a division between the

supporters of the Wisconsin plan and the supporters of the Ohio plan advocated by Abraham Epstein.[26]

Epstein argued that unemployment reserve bills had failed to pass in every state but Wisconsin because they were "essentially utopian and meaningless," and did not reflect an understanding of "the practical processes of legislation." Epstein said that the benefits (the maximum in Wisconsin was ten dollars a week) were insufficient and that the depression made the provisions inadequate. He argued that the provision that the employer bear the complete cost was unwise "because it had the effect of spurring selfish forces to greater opposition." Security for the unemployed "can only be achieved by a pooled fund operating on true insurance principles."[27]

Elizabeth Brandeis Raushenbush replied that the benefits could be increased in the future and that emphasis should be on preventing unemployment.[28] She defended the company reserve clause by saying that even if unemployment were largely unpreventable, "there would still be a definite advantage in allocating its cost in so far as possible to the industries and concerns that are its proximate cause."[29] This difference of opinion was never resolved and became a major source of conflict once the question of social security legislation reached the national level.

In the summer of 1933, Paul and Elizabeth began to consider federal legislation designed to stimulate state action on unemployment compensation laws. Wagner's tax credit proposal had not won much support.[30] When they discussed the matter with Brandeis, he asked them, "Have you considered the case of Florida vs. Mellon?" After some thought, they grasped the analogy, for if

the Federal estate tax law could constitutionally permit . . . the crediting of State inheritance taxes against the Federal estate tax, maybe a new Federal payroll (unemployment) tax on employers might permit and encourage the crediting of similar State payroll taxes on employers, levied by the States for jobless benefit purposes.[31]

Brandeis was firmly convinced that administration should be left wholly to the states, and suggested that the federal government should levy an excise tax on every employer refusing to comply "under some adequate state law." The tax revenue should, he argued, go into the general fund and not some special fund "lest by so doing we start national provision."[32] Elizabeth replied that she and Paul "were intensely interested" in his suggestion and that Paul would be "delighted to draft you a bill."[33] She also criticized Isador Lubin's proposal to stimulate state legislation by permitting deductions from federal income tax.[34] Brandeis reassured her that he had seen Lubin, who accepted his proposal and agreed to talk to Frances Perkins about legislative possibilities.[35]

During the Christmas vacation of 1933 a meeting was held at the Washington home of Lincoln Filene, a friend of Brandeis's. The Raushenbushs presided, and the idea began to gain support. Paul Raushenbush spent several weeks in Washington with Thomas Eliot, the associate solicitor of the Labor Department, working on a draft of a federal payroll tax bill. Raushenbush urged Roosevelt in January 1934 to support the Wisconsin plan.[36] Elizabeth observed hopefully: "If Felix gets into action too, why something may happen!"[37]

The Raushenbush-Eliot draft was cleared first with Frances Perkins and then with Senator Wagner and Congressman Lewis, who agreed to accept the payroll tax idea.[38] After the draft was reworked, Wagner and Lewis introduced it in March 1934. The bill, though it had passed through several hands, was essentially Brandeis's. He wrote Frankfurter that Corcoran was doing "grand work" and it looked "as if he would get through my federal excise tax to effect regularity of employment."[39] Frankfurter replied that he was "delighted over the introduction of your excise tax on payrolls to effect regularity," though he expected a struggle before final success was obtained.[40] His premonitions were justified for Roosevelt appeared to have doubts about the Wagner-Lewis bill. Writing to Tugwell, the president said:

I have told Miss Perkins and Bob Wagner that I have no

objection to its being reported by the Committees, but I do
not think the adjournment of the Session should be held up
by it. As you say—it will require a good deal of overhauling
and would necessarily cause much debate.[41]

Elizabeth noted that Roosevelt was not committing himself one
way or the other while he waited to observe the response.[42]

During this period Elizabeth continued to ask her father for
help in influencing others. She suggested that Corcoran arrange
for him to see Harry Hopkins who was "ace high with the
President and hence very important." She concluded one of her
letters by exclaiming: "Well, if you can fix Tugwell and get Harry
Hopkins interested!"[43] There is no evidence that Brandeis was
able to do either. Despite the best efforts of Brandeis and the
Wisconsin group, Roosevelt remained aloof. In a letter to
Congressman Robert L. Doughton, chairman of the Committee
on Ways and Means, Roosevelt approved of the Wagner-Lewis
bill, saying that "the general principles . . . seem to me sound . . .
and I hope that the bill will be passed by Congress at this
session."[44] After this endorsement, however, Roosevelt hesi-
tated.[45] On 3 June 1934 he finally sent a message to Congress,
approving the idea of social security and establishing a
Committee on Economic Security to formulate a program.[46] The
best efforts of the Wisconsin group could not obtain a quick,
decisive victory.

The committee was headed by Frances Perkins and included
Morgenthau, Cummings, Wallace, and Hopkins.[47] Edwin Witte,
a professor at the University of Wisconsin, was named executive
director and Arthur J. Altmeyer was made chairman of the
Technical Board. Although both supported the Wisconsin
approach, division quickly surfaced among committee members.[48]
While Brandeis and Frankfurter rarely alluded to unemployment
compensation during early 1934, the subject became prominent
in the summer. Corcoran and Moley arranged for Brandeis to see
Roosevelt in June. Corcoran reported that

Isaiah did not like the scheme in the Skipper's mind because
it left administration completely in the Federal Government

as opposed to the States. The Skipper gave the impression that there was nothing as yet cut and dried about the scheme and that it was all in the making.[49]

Brandeis himself reported to Elizabeth that he had told Roosevelt that he was "all wrong," and discussed the issue with him for about forty-five minutes "& I think convinced him of the error."[50]

The first time Brandeis saw Frankfurter after his return from England, he and Elizabeth talked with him about "unemployment reserve."[51] The nationalist subsidy plan had considerable support. The plan would "impose the tax and then provide subsidies equal to a stated percentage of the specified federal standards."[52] Frankfurter observed that supporters of the Wisconsin plan will "have a long slow, hard job of deflating the grandiose proposals of insurance scheme."[53] In mid-July Frankfurter argued with Moley against the nationalistic scheme, and suggested that Cohen be drawn into the legislative planning. He was hopeful that Perkins would be on the right side.[54] A week later Brandeis urged Frankfurter at his upcoming meeting with Roosevelt "to reinforce what I said to him on employers' bearing the whole cost;—which seemed to impress him very favorably."[55]

There were, however, continuing anxieties. Brandeis was uneasy about the personnel of the Committee on Economic Security. He worried about Witte who was "never a fighter," and who favored the Wisconsin plan only "because he thought the act most likely to get enacted . . . and not because of a conviction to its fundamentals."[56] He expressed similar misgivings about Altmeyer who was "probably convinced that we should have state action—knowing the inherent difficulty of administering an act."[57] This kind of pragmatism disturbed Brandeis, who preferred deeper commitments. Brandeis saw Witte sometime in August and although the details of the visit are not recalled, it seems to have been productive. Frankfurter reported that Witte "was well invigorated by his visit to you. He will, I think, be solid on national insurance act, but has to be kept at on many aspects of ballyhoo & nonsense about President's 'commitments' on this & that."[58] Brandeis and Frankfurter believed that the committee was being guided by sympathetic leaders, and this may account for the way Frankfurter handled the subject of social security when he saw Roosevelt in late August. He did not go into detail on the issue but let Witte's committee "impress him with facts."[59]

Indeed, Frankfurter did not press Roosevelt on this issue. His correspondence with him contained few references to social security, and this was unusual when Frankfurter felt deeply about a particular issue. He did write Roosevelt a lengthy letter on the subject adopting an apparently neutral tone:

> The relative advantages and disadvantages of a single, national scheme as against a scheme through the States but sponsored by the nation, or fostered by it, calls for long careful exploration and thereafter a matured process of formulation.

He warned against "the constitutional obstacles in the way of an all-embracing national scheme," and urged Roosevelt not to commit himself to either a national or a state plan "which may gravely embarrass the attainment of your aims."[60] He advised the president, who was planning to give a speech in Wisconsin on 9 August, to mention "the characteristic pioneer legislation of Wisconsin in dealing with unemployment legislation." He concluded by urging Roosevelt to support state initiative:

> You will remember Mr. Justice Holmes' observation . . . that our Federal system gives us the great advantage of making social experiments in the "insulated chambers of the individual states." That aspect, not of state rights but of state opportunities, might be emphasized with particular advantage in the state of Wisconsin.[61]

Frankfurter's neutral facade was thin; he was clearly urging the Wisconsin plan on Roosevelt.[62]

The two men conferred in September at Hyde Park,[63] and saw each other again in October. Commenting on the latter meeting, Brandeis wrote: "We shall watch eagerly for the fruits of your session."[64] It seems likely that social security was discussed at these meetings, although the Frankfurter-Roosevelt correspondence of this period focuses on public works and tax reform. In the late fall and winter of 1934, the committee strenuously debated the issue, and an advisory council voted for the nationalist subsidy plan.[65] In early November, however, the Technical Board came out for the Wagner-Lewis plan. On 14 November a national conference on economic security was held in Washington. When Roosevelt addressed it, he came out in favor of a federal-state approach.[66]

But even Roosevelt's pragmatic solution did not settle matters entirely, as Henry Wallace and Tugwell kept up the fight for a nationalist program. Perkins recalled that Roosevelt's speech "had been prepared by and approved in substance by the Committee."[67] Irritated at the interminable debate, she took matters into her own hands. During Christmas week of 1934 Perkins issued an ultimatum: the committee would meet one evening at her house with the telephone disconnected until it decided "the thorny question once and for all." And she later reported:

> We sat until two in the morning, and at the end we agreed reluctantly and with mental reservations, that for the present the wisest thing we could do was to recommend a federal-state system.[68]

Roosevelt decided to include the committee's recommendations in his 1935 legislative program.[69] Frankfurter got this information from Moley and wrote to Brandeis: "I know not how accurate this is—I do know that the President was furious against subsidy."[70] Tugwell felt that his viewpoint had suffered a major defeat, but he did his best to minimize the loss. He pressured the president to see the light,

but the Frankfurter and Brandeis influence has just been

too strong . . . the most I could do in conjunction with Harry Hopkins . . . was to get the Economic Security Report to the President rewritten so that it minimized the part of unemployment reserves in a national security scheme and threw the emphasis upon a works program as the real effort towards security.[71]

Brandeis was not completely satisfied with the committee's work, either. In late December he wrote to Frankfurter complaining that what was needed was a return "to the Wagner-Lewis bill with only real perfecting amendments." He was against any compromise on the question of pooling, saying that they should "strive for the simon pure article."[72] In January he wrote to Frankfurter that Paul Raushenbush was in Washington working on a model bill for the states. He deeply regretted Roosevelt's decision to deviate from the Wagner-Lewis provisions, attributing it to "political considerations."[73]

The fate of the bill in Congress gave further cause for concern. Robert and Philip LaFollette wired Roosevelt in support of the Wisconsin approach.[74] Wyzanski reported to Frankfurter in January 1935 that "the things in which you are most interested, the federal-state character of the scheme . . . can hardly be easily altered."[75] Roosevelt's intentions, however, were discouraging to Frankfurter who now looked to Robert LaFollette for help.[76] Congressional conservatism also struck at some of the bill's provisions.[77] By March, Brandeis's pessimism had deepened, and he wrote gloomily to Frankfurter:

Unemployment insurance has been so much bedeviled by refusal to pass the Wagner-Lewis bill at the last session— that I shall not be sorry if it should go over to 1936. Anything passed this year will be unutterably bad—and we can't get state action in any event in most states until 1937.[78]

After this discouraged observation, neither Frankfurter nor Brandeis had much to say on the subject.

When Congress finally passed the Social Security Act in August 1935, neither man made any comment in their correspondence. Frankfurter did not write his usual congratulatory letter to the president.[79] Unfortunately neither Frankfurter nor Brandeis rendered a written critique of the act so it is difficult to know exactly how they felt about it. The act did have the tax offset feature as well as merit rating which strengthened its decentralist character. In fact it was in some ways even weaker (from a nationalist perspective) than the earlier Wagner-Lewis bill. This was not entirely due to Brandeisian scruples, but to Congressional conservatism which gave the states power out of a suspicion of federal power. Congress also deleted the original requirement that the states select personnel on merit.[80]

Still, the silence of Brandeis and Frankfurter probably did not indicate total disapproval. The act was not as good as the earlier Wagner-Lewis bill, but at least it followed the Wisconsin plan in broad outline. Brandeis continued to believe in the efficacy of that plan, citing evidence to Frankfurter two years later of the fine record compiled by the Wisconsin program in helping to achieve regularity of employment.[81] By 1939, however, the administration of the national plan had disillusioned him and he was informing his visitors of "the heresy of the prevailing unemployment compensation system."[82] The passage of the Social Security Act was at best only a partial victory.

Throughout this long period of struggle, it was only unemployment compensation that engaged the attention of Brandeis and Frankfurter. They ignored the question of old age insurance. When the Committee on Economic Security "adopted a national system of contributory old-age and survivors insurance without anxiety or fuss," Brandeis and Frankfurter showed no concern.[83]

This indifference, however, reflected the attitude of Frankfurter and Brandeis to relief. There are few references to the subject in their correspondence. Brandeis made one revealing comment about Hopkins and the Civil Works Administration when he noted in early 1934 that Hopkins did "an extraordinary job" in getting four million men on the CWA rolls. But he complained about the temporary nature of the employment:

> the success is alarming. How can the government let go?
> And it seems most improbable that private business or PWA
> can produce the jobs within the next 3 months.[84]

Frankfurter agreed: "Yes, it looks as though Hopkins has been too successful."[85] It was not that Brandeis and Frankfurter were indifferent to suffering, or that they begrudged help to the needy. They accepted relief spending as a necessity, but felt it was at best a palliative. They were concerned with ending the depression and not merely with easing its symptoms.

Tax reform and public works were the pillars of their recovery program. Because the early New Deal had proved inadequate, Brandeis and Frankfurter pushed their ideas with renewed vigor after Frankfurter returned from England. Frankfurter had one conference with Roosevelt in late August and another in October.[86] He had requested the latter meeting because he wanted to discuss "two or three matters of major importance ... following up the discussion at Hyde Park."[87] One of the subjects was undoubtedly public works. In late November Frankfurter urged the president to push a public works program amounting to five billion dollars a year. He denied that it would involve "a public borrowing of five billion dollars" because

> The stimulating of business through such a program will, of
> course, increase the national income, and thereby greatly
> augment the yield of our present taxes, and make possible
> the payment of higher rates of taxation with less real
> hardship than the existing rates impose.[88]

Several days later Frankfurter argued the benefits of a large public housing program.[89]

Others in the administration shared this concern about public works. Ickes recalled in September 1934 that Hopkins had urged Roosevelt to adopt a program of five billion dollars a year for five years. He noted later that Roosevelt committed himself to spend about five billion dollars in 1935.[90] Frankfurter and Brandeis did not mention the subject in their correspondence between November 1934 and the passage of the Emergency Relief Appropriation Act in April 1935.

Frankfurter briefly congratulated the president on the passage of the act, but his remarks did not indicate much enthusiasm.[91] In mid-April Brandeis wrote to Frankfurter that Roosevelt seemed to be gaining strength, but he did not mention the appropriation.[92] Brandeis and Frankfurter believed that the president did not go far enough even though the act "authorized the greatest single appropriation in the history of the United States or any nation."[93] Although five billion dollars was spent during the first year, appropriations tapered off to six billion for the next six years.[94] The act had other defects. Projects were selected in which the cost of materials was low, and this ruled out vital housing projects. The new agency was not permitted to compete with private industry, and many projects were "make-work assignments of scant value."[95] As was so often the case, this New Deal measure was only half a step in the right direction.[96]

Taxation was closely related to public works in the minds of Frankfurter and Brandeis, and perhaps no subject was discussed so thoroughly in their correspondence. In 1932 Brandeis urged a "super income tax" on trusts.[97] Such taxes were directed at the "super-rich" and his formula for this was not "distributing wealth" (which Huey Long favored) but "distributing power."[98] He cited figures showing the low inheritance tax rate and commented that "you can never get the 'New Deal' under any such scale."[99] Frankfurter became convinced that Roosevelt "meant business as to tax matters." He told Brandeis that, as a result of his (Frankfurter's) conversations with the president, Morgenthau asked for his cooperation on tax matters. Frankfurter could not resist a little gloating:

> Poor H. M. Jr. evidently inferred from F.D.'s talk that the President cares for what I say—for this is practically the first time H. M. Jr. and I ever talked.[100]

On 11 December 1934, the Treasury Department presented a "sweeping tax program" to Roosevelt. The program included not only gift and inheritance tax increases, but also an intercorporate dividend tax, a graduated tax on corporate income, and a tax on undistributed corporate profits.[101] Despite Frankfurter's belief that Roosevelt "meant business as to tax matters," there was little evidence to support such a view. The president only reluctantly came to see the necessity for major tax reform. Brandeis and Frankfurter had long urged such reform but as late as January 1935 Roosevelt, in his budget message, expressed no need for new tax legislation in the fiscal year 1936.[102]

Moley recalled that when he dined at the White House in February 1935, Roosevelt handed him a brief outline of a tax program written by Herman Oliphant. The president seemed only "mildly interested" at the time.[103] His interest did not revive until June, and then may have been a result of the pressures of the "Share Our Wealth" program and the need for new political initiatives.[104] But it is difficult to know how Roosevelt thought about the matter. In the fall of 1934 Frankfurter was convinced that he had sold him on tax reform, yet he waited until June to push actively for reform. The delay might have been a matter of tactics, but this seems unlikely. When Roosevelt did act, it was from political considerations rather than from conviction.

Such behavior caused widespread liberal apprehension about the president's intentions. In early 1935 Brandeis, far from satisfied with the course of events, observed that "it is the business of a leader to lead."[105] In mid-March he wrote: "From what I heard yesterday it seems that the relations of F.D. to the progressive Senators will need much revising."[106] Other people were concerned about Roosevelt's relations with the liberals.

In late April David K. Niles wrote to Frankfurter saying that Roosevelt and the liberals needed to get together, observing that "a frank talking-things-over between the President and . . . liberal and progressive leaders from all over the country should be of real help."[107] Frankfurter passed this letter on to the president and then discussed the possibility of a meeting. Roosevelt agreed.[108] It seems likely that Brandeis and Frankfurter engineered this. Brandeis had implied that such a meeting was needed; Frankfurter had known Niles "for a good many years" and thought highly of him.[109] Frankfurter, acting on Brandeis's suggestion, may have solicited the letter from Niles, passed it on to Roosevelt, urged that a conference be called, and then helped to arrange it. This would have been Byzantine maneuvering, but well within his capacity.

Frankfurter and Niles were instrumental in planning for the conference. Niles sounded out Sen. George Norris, who urged that the group be kept small. They decided that six senators and cabinet members (Ickes and Wallace) be included along with Frankfurter and Niles. The six senators were Norris, Edward Costigan, Bronson Cutting, Hiram Johnson, Robert LaFollette, and Burton K. Wheeler, all of whom had been members of the National Progressive League.[110] Brandeis and Frankfurter hoped that the conference would steel Roosevelt to continue the fight against the old order with renewed determination. They also hoped that the progressives would support him in a new reform effort. The conference was held on 14 May, and Frankfurter seemed pleased with the results. He wrote to Roosevelt two days later that the senators were "very happy" with the meeting. Wheeler was satisfied, and LaFollette would continue as a "dependable friend and helper."[111]

Ickes recalled that Roosevelt asked for "a very frank discussion of the legislative and political situation" and that this request was "taken at its face value." LaFollette and Wheeler did most of the talking, urging the president "to assert the leadership that the country is demanding." Frankfurter reported that Brandeis asserted it was "the eleventh hour." Ickes left the conference believing that Roosevelt intended "to take a firm stand on his progressive policies and force the fighting along that line."[112] According to Frankfurter it was not only the senators and cabinet members who were happy, but Brandeis as well. Frankfurter wrote to Roosevelt:

I wish you had seen Brandeis's face light up when I gave him

your message about your tax policy and the forthcoming
message about it. His eyes became glowing coals of fire,
and shone with warm satisfaction. He asked me to tell you
how deeply he rejoiced to have had the message from you,
and with what eagerness he is looking forward to the
enunciation of your policy.[113]

Frankfurter was pleased with the conference, but he believed
that he should maintain close contact with Roosevelt.[114] In July
he wrote to Brandeis that the president wanted him "around on
odds & ends & there are diverse matters of policy . . . on which I
do what I can."[115] Ickes observed in August that Frankfurter
"has been spending the better part of every week at the White
House recently and he sees the President on occasions when the
President can talk freely."[116]

One important result of the conference was a renewal of
Roosevelt's interest in tax reform. Frankfurter had told Brandeis
that the president was behind a stringent tax program; events in
the spring and summer seemed to prove this. Roosevelt was
committed to the "must" legislation (which included a tax bill)
and intended to keep Congress in session if necessary.[117] In
mid-June Frankfurter wrote to Brandeis that "tax matters are
really moving & here is ideal determination on the part of F.D. I
must say Treasury is also good."[118] Moley recalled that in June
Roosevelt

read a message employing the Oliphant scheme to Frankfurter and me and invited our views. Frankfurter, reflecting
Brandeis's ideas of paying for public works with heavier
inheritance taxes and increased levies on higher incomes,
was enthusiastic.[119]

Moley did not know that Frankfurter's enthusiasm was also due
to his involvement in drafting the legislation.

Roosevelt's tax message went to Congress on 19 June. The
message assailed bigness and called for inheritance and gift taxes
to control excessive concentrations of wealth. The president

requested higher income taxes for the wealthy, and taxes on
corporate profits scaled to the size of the firm. An intercorporate
dividend tax was designed to prevent evasion of the graduated
profits tax.[120] The thrust of the message "was the neo-
Brandeisian conviction that cutting down towering fortunes and
breaking up massive corporate empires would help the small man
and stimulate 'creative enterprise.' "[121] Brandeis wrote to Frankfurter that "the tax message confirmed your encouraging
prognosis of last week."[122]

However, the tax bill quickly ran into trouble in Congress, and
Roosevelt mishandled the situation. Without warning, he
demanded prompt action from congressional leaders in late June
and succeeded only in plunging "the legislative situation into an
unseemly mess."[123] During July there was a bitter struggle
merely to preserve the bill in a recognizable form. Frankfurter
described business hostility to Brandeis, who replied by saying
that Roosevelt must realize that the conflict is "irrepressible."[124]
At the end of the month Frankfurter reported that though the
progressive senators were encouraged by Roosevelt's actions,
"conservatives are correspondingly more & more bitter."[125]

While the struggle continued, Frankfurter remained in
Washington to steel the president in the fight. Robert H. Jackson,
general counsel of the Bureau of Internal Revenue, emerged as a
powerful proponent of tax reform. In testimony before the
Senate Committee on Finance, he said:

> We do not wish to discourage the growth of small concerns.
> It is the existence of healthy and profitable small concerns
> that gives our economy the elasticity and flexibility in
> production and prices that are so valuable.[126]

Brandeis observed that Jackson was doing a good job, and
Frankfurter replied that it was "grand" that Roosevelt's
"fighting qualities are being ever more aroused."[127] The bill,
however, did not escape Congress unscathed. When it finally
emerged, there was no provision for an inheritance tax, and only
a token version of the corporate income tax. The surtax on

excessive corporate profits was not increased. The rates of the
gift tax were increased, but a number of loopholes made evasion
possible.[128] Despite such dilution, Roosevelt signed the bill on 31
August.[129]

Yet Brandeis was gratified, if not completely satisfied, with the
bill. The day before the president signed it, Brandeis wrote to
Frankfurter that he had "rendered a great service—F.D. comes
out on top."[130] Roosevelt had been persuaded of the effectiveness
of taxation as an instrument of social policy, and he had fought
for a strong law despite strenuous business opposition.[131]
Although the bill was much less than they wanted, Brandeis and
Frankfurter could hope for greater gains in the future. The tide
seemed to be running in their direction.

Roosevelt also showed a heartening determination with regard
to the attack on holding companies. The desire to limit the size of
these companies was an important part of the fight against
bigness. In 1931 Brandeis wrote Gifford Pinchot a revealing
memorandum in which he stated:

> To present the case against the Holding Company in a few
> words is necessarily to state it dogmatically and ... leaves
> out the emotional considerations—which, perhaps in the
> last consideration—are the more important reasons for
> opposition.[132]

In August 1932 Frankfurter discussed the power of holding
companies with Roosevelt.[133] In February 1933 he wrote to
Moley telling him that the president was concerned about the
companies, and suggesting the creation of an informal drafting
committee to discuss the problem.[134]

But nothing was done until the July 1934 creation of the
National Power Policy Committee, which gave the holding
company issue top priority.[135] At the suggestion of Morris Cooke,
Ickes transferred Cohen from PWA to the committee, and Cohen
became a principal figure in the drafting process.[136]

Differences quickly surfaced among the reformers themselves.
Cohen's draft did not provide for the abolition of holding

companies because he believed instead that the companies should be regulated and restricted "to a sphere where their economic advantages may be demonstrable."[137] Roosevelt, however, had called for the elimination of holding companies in the fall of 1934.[138] This policy, strange to say, was too rigorous for Brandeis and Frankfurter. Frankfurter opposed a revision produced by a committee headed by Cummings which deleted Cohen's tax provisions and added a "death sentence."[139] He spoke against the revision at a White House conference and, as he reported to Stimson, "really got rapped for it."[140] It is no wonder that Frankfurter could report to Brandeis that Roosevelt "is wholly untouched by all the ballyhoo of the utility crowd," and that he "was really hot on holding cos (companies) & for drastic action."[141]

A conference held in January 1935 hammered out some of the differences and produced new emphasis on the gradual extinction of the holding companies.[142] Corcoran, who remembered how the stock exchange bill was weakened, was "glad to build up the draft in order to leave room for the 'sweat-down' in the legislative process." Title One of the draft gave the Securities Exchange Commission the power to propose simplifications of the holding company system. Corporate cooperation would be voluntary until the beginning of 1940, and then the commission could compel dissolution of those companies which could not produce a sound economic reason for existence.[143]

It seems strange that on this issue Frankfurter appeared to be more conservative than Roosevelt. Although Brandeis never expressed a direct opinion in his correspondence with Frankfurter, he undoubtedly agreed with him. But the reason becomes clear when one recalls their opinion of the Sherman Act. They believed that that act was worse than useless because its inflexibility caused it to be undermined by judicial subversion. Regulation by means of taxation was not subject to the same constitutional objections as outright elimination. Frankfurter's misgivings about the holding company bill were based on tactical considerations rather than disagreement about the ultimate purpose.

On 6 February 1935, Burton K. Wheeler introduced the
holding company bill in the Senate, and Rayburn did so in the
House.[144] The measure aroused the predictable wrath of the
business community. John W. Davis told the American Bar
Association that it constituted "the gravest threat to the liberties
of the American citizen that has emanated from the hall of
Congress in my time."[145] On 12 March, Roosevelt sent a strong
message to Congress urging passage of the bill.[146] Brandeis,
watching the pressure mount, wrote to Frankfurter uneasily in
late March: "It will be a very serious matter for F.D. . . . if he
weakens on the Holding co. bill."[147] Frankfurter was more
sanguine and, after the message was sent, he told Brandeis that
Roosevelt "certainly moved into action on Holding Cos."[148]

During the period from the introduction of the bill in February
to its passage in August, Frankfurter encouraged the president to
stand firm. Moley recalled that at times, "notably in the hot fight
over the Holding Company bill, Frankfurter lived for a
considerable period at the White House almost completely
unnoticed by the Press."[149] Even Frankfurter grew concerned
over the pressure Roosevelt faced. In mid-April he acknowledged
that "the pressure on F.D. re holding cos. is terrific. It will be a
test of him."[150] Frankfurter also worked with progressives in
Congress on the bill. He wrote to Burton Wheeler:

> Senator Norris was here yesterday and we both rejoiced
> over the help that the President's remarks ought to bring to
> your bill. I know there is a hard row still to be hoed, but
> under your persistent, courageous and informed leadership
> I should think you could overcome even the obstacles
> which Norris tells me are stronger in the House than in the
> Senate.[151]

When the bill passed the Senate on 11 June, after a narrow vote
on the death sentence provision, Frankfurter congratulated
Wheeler for his skillful conduct of the floor fight.[152]

Frankfurter predicted a tough battle in the House, but he said
that Roosevelt was showing admirable determination.[153] Bran-

deis, expressing satisfaction with the president's tax message, concluded: "It needs only a complete victory on the Holding Company bill to set the required foundation."[154] Frankfurter's prediction of a difficult fight proved all too accurate. The legislative struggle was complex,[155] but by 1 August the bill was in conference. At Rayburn's insistence the matter was reopened on the House floor, and the death sentence was voted down again. By 17 August it seemed that the bill would die before adjournment.[156]

Frankfurter, alarmed at the prospect of an impasse, labored behind the scenes to produce a workable compromise. In August, when Frankfurter was "living in the White House," he pushed for a settlement by drafting "an opaque compromise on Section II" which gave the holding companies greater leeway under certain conditions.[157] Roosevelt, somewhat disgruntled, told Moley in Frankfurter's presence that "Felix sounds just like John W. Davis."[158] Congress accepted the compromise version of the bill, and the president signed it on 26 August. Frankfurter's willingness to compromise on this issue is a measure of how important it was to him. What he and Brandeis thought in detail about the final version is difficult to say.[159] Undoubtedly it was less than they wanted. It did not possess the taxing provisions which they supported, and it lacked the rigor they had wanted. Yet the challenge to the utility companies was a source of satisfaction.[160]

Public works, taxation, social security, and holding company legislation were the subjects on which Frankfurter and Brandeis concentrated in 1935. The other reforms of the period were less important to them. They had never been close to Senator Wagner despite his prominence as a progressive.[161] Tugwell characterized Wagner as a new nationalist, and his support of the NRA demonstrates this.[162] In September 1933 Wagner wrote: "When I framed the National Industrial Recovery Act and steered it through Congress, I felt that the greatest victory in my war against human misery had been achieved."[163] Wagner's National Labor Relations Act of 1935 was one of the most significant pieces of New Deal legislation which did not originate in the executive branch. Yet Frankfurter and Brandeis rarely mentioned

it. In mid-March Frankfurter observed in a detached fashion that
Roosevelt "will support Wagner bill. Bob LaFollette & Bob
Wagner seem to have done a good job with him."[164] Several
months later Frankfurter noted that Norris "supported strongly
Prest's support of Wagner labor bill."[165] Brandeis did not
respond to these remarks and when the act passed neither
Frankfurter nor Brandeis commented. Indeed, Brandeis never
abandoned his commitment to the preferential shop rather than
a closed shop. He believed that unions should be protected
against the power of corporations, but he also feared that the
closed shop principle would create the same bigness in unions
that he had been fighting in business.[166] So the Wagner bill
passed without the support or indeed the sympathy of
Brandeis.[167]

The legislation of 1935 has been called a triumph for the
Although other laws were enacted in 1935, Brandeis and
Frankfurter were not significantly involved with them. Though
they undoubtedly supported the establishment of the Rural
Electrification Administration in May 1935, there is no reference
to it in their correspondence.[168] The Guffey Act was likewise
ignored, but it must have been an unwelcome indication that New
Nationalist ideas were still alive.[169] They did not believe that the
Banking Act of 1935 was very important.[170]

The legislation of 1935 has been called a triumph for the
"neo-Brandeisians," and it does represent the high-water mark of
New Deal reform. The influence of Frankfurter and Brandeis was
never stronger than during this period. But this conjunction, far
from proving a triumph, shows how limited their influence really
was. What had been accomplished? Some progress had been
made in the areas of taxation, public works, social security, and
the regulation of holding companies. And yet in each case the
results fell far short of what Frankfurter and Brandeis had
wanted. In retrospect it seems evident that the satisfaction they
took in the events of 1935 derived more from what these tentative
advances promised than for what they actually accomplished.

CHAPTER VIII

The Supreme Court

Brandeis's advocacy of a recovery program is separable from his judicial role. While his position prevented him from openly supporting certain policies, Brandeis had been accustomed to operating with such restraint. From the beginning of the New Deal until the spring of 1935, his place on the Court was not important in his relationship with Frankfurter and Roosevelt. After this point, however, that was no longer true. It was inevitable that New Deal legislation would be challenged in the courts. All would have been well had Brandeis upheld the New Deal laws, but he did not always do so; his position on the Court strained his relationship to Roosevelt and placed Frankfurter in the awkward role of mediator.

For a time in 1934, it seemed as though the conservative Court was changing direction. In January the Court sustained a Minnesota mortgage moratorium, and in March it upheld a New York statute regulating milk production. In both cases Brandeis voted with the majority.[1] Neither of these cases involved New Deal legislation, but they did embody state economic experimentation which the Court had rejected earlier.

An ominous hint of the Court's attitude toward the NRA was given in the "hot oil" cases. Section 9 (c) of the NRA Act had given the president the authority to prohibit the transportation in interstate commerce of oil produced or stored in excess of state limitations.[2] The object was to conserve oil and raise its price.[3] The Court invalidated this part of the act. Chief Justice Hughes wrote the majority decision which asserted that section 9 (c) contained improperly vague delegation of authority.[4] Paul Freund reported to Frankfurter that Brandeis questioned

> at length on the availability of orders and regulations, and on steps taken thus far in that direction. L.D.B. was chiefly concerned, on the constitutional side with delegation under 9 (a), which permits the President to declare acts a crime without making findings.[5]

But Frankfurter was unhappy with the decision. He wrote to Wyzanski: "What really troubled me about the majority decision was the unabashed way in which they have now made finding 'in the case of delegated power' to the President a constitutional requirement."[6] He did not, however, express any misgivings to Brandeis.

The *Gold Cases* challenged the right of Congress to nullify the gold clause in private and public contracts.[7] Hughes again wrote the majority decision upholding the government by a vote of five to four. The "Four Horsemen" dissented. Hughes argued that there is nothing in the Constitution which prevents Congress from invalidating contracts in the pursuit of government policy.[8] Brandeis concurred in a decision clearly based on economic expediency:

> It is a relief to have the gold clause case out of the way; but I feel little satisfaction with the administration's performance. McReynolds' talk was very different from his opinion—was really impressive; better than anything I have ever heard from him.[9]

The case of *Stewart Dry Goods* v. *Lewis* in early 1935 involved a graduated state tax on retail sales based on volume. The tax was held in violation of the equal protection clause of the Fourteenth Amendment. Roberts wrote the majority decision, and Cardozo wrote a dissenting opinion in which Brandeis and Stone concurred. Cardozo argued that graduated taxes better served social justice by producing "a more genuine equality."[10] Brandeis also dissented in the Railroad Retirement case. Roberts wrote the majority opinion overturning benefits for railroad workers by arguing that the law was arbitrary and in violation of the Fifth Amendment. Hughes wrote a dissenting opinion in which Cardozo, Stone, and Brandeis concurred. Hughes took a broad view of the commerce clause, arguing that the power delegated to Congress over interstate commerce "does not require that its government should be wise, much less that it be perfect. The power implies a broad discretion even of mistakes."[11]

Still, down to 27 May 1935 (the so-called "Black Monday"), Brandeis's performance on the Court had not caused any difficulties. But on that day the Court handed down three unanimous decisions which embarrassed the administration. Brandeis wrote the decision in the case of *Louisville Bank* v. *Radford*, which invalidated the Frazier-Lemke Act of 1934. The act, designed to relieve the plight of farm mortgagors, had been sustained by two unanimous circuit courts and five district court judges. Nevertheless, Brandeis concluded that the act had the effect not merely of impairing the obligation of contracts, but also of taking property without compensation, and he held the act in violation of the Fifth Amendment.[12]

The Frazier-Lemke Act was not an administrative measure, and Roosevelt never indicated any displeasure at the decision. However, he did have reason to resent the Court's decision in the case of *Humphrey's Executor*. In October 1933, Roosevelt dismissed William E. Humphrey, a conservative member of the Federal Trade Commission who had served since Coolidge's day. Humphrey fought dismissal tenaciously, filing suit in the United States Court of Claims. The legal struggle continued after his death in February 1934.[13] When the case reached the Supreme Court, the administration was confident of victory. *The Meyers* case in 1926 had apparently settled the question of the presidential removal power. Chief Justice Taft had argued for the Supreme Court that "the President's removal power was an inherent part of executive prerogative, apart from any authority specifically delegated to him by the Constitution."[14]

When Roosevelt named Stanley Reed solicitor general in early 1935, Attorney General Cummings suggested that he pick an easy case for his first argument before the Court. Reed selected the case of *Humphrey's Executor*,[15] but his optimism was not justified. Speaking for a unanimous Court, George Sutherland voided the President's action by asserting that the authority of Congress "in creating quasi-legislative or quasi-judicial agencies" required it to act in discharge of its duties independently of executive control.[16] This decision angered Roosevelt because it seemed to have the "sting of personal animus."[17] But there was certainly no personal animosity in Brandeis's stance. In the *Myers* case Brandeis had decided against the presidential removal power.[18] James Landis, Brandeis's law clerk at the time, recalled:

> Brandeis' dissent in that case, I believe, exhibits more research than any other opinion in the law books. For weeks, at his suggestion, I literally combed the Journals of the Senate from the Civil War to the present to establish the consistent practice of the President and the Senate over some fifty years which contradicted the allegation to the contrary in the Chief Justice's opinion.[19]

Landis said that Brandeis's dissent was "as thorough a piece of historical research as you would find in the Supreme Court reports anywhere."[20]

The effect of this decision, however, was to put Brandeis at odds with Roosevelt and strain his relationship with Frankfurter, who had approved of the dismissal of Humphrey.[21] Frankfurter said nothing which indicated that he had changed his mind, but Brandeis was firmly convinced that this limitation of presidential power was essential to the preservation of liberty. He asked reporters, "What would happen if Huey Long were President and such a doctrine prevailed?"[22] Thus Brandeis's distrust of bigness, whether in business or government, brought him into disagreement with Frankfurter.

In the *Schechter* case a unanimous Court declared title one of the National Industrial Recovery Act unconstitutional. Hughes wrote the opinion for the Court, and Cardozo and Stone wrote concurring opinions. Hughes asserted that "extraordinary conditions do not create or enlarge constitutional power," and concluded that "the code-making authority thus conferred is an unconstitutional delegation of legislative power."[23] Cardozo, the lone dissenter in the "hot oil" cases, denounced the delegation of power in the NRA Act in terms more vivid than those used by Hughes, asserting that the delegated power in the NRA "is not canalized within banks that keep it from overflowing. It is unconfined and vagrant."[24]

Thus Roosevelt suffered two major defeats from a unanimous Court on the same day. He commented caustically that the Court was relegating the country "to a horse-and-buggy definition of interstate commerce."[25] Although Roosevelt seemed calm, he took the decisions badly.[26] He had apparently not completely given up on the NRA since he wrote William C. Bullitt that "the principles of NRA must be carried on in some way."[27] Brandeis's response put him at odds with the president. He told reporters that 27 May was "the most important day in the history of the Court and the most beneficent" because the decisions "compelled a return to human limitations." The NRA embodied the characteristic American error of trying to get things done the easy way.[28] Corcoran chatted with Brandeis in the robing room immediately after the decisions, and he reported to Harry Hopkins that Brandeis said:

> This is the end of this business of centralization, and I want you to go back and tell the President that we're not going to let this government centralize everything. It's come to an end. As for your young men . . . tell them to go home, back to the States. That is where they must do their work.[29]

Cohen noted that Brandeis seemed "visibly excited and deeply agitated." He told Corcoran and Cohen to

phone Felix and have him down in the morning to talk to the

President. You must see that Felix understands the
situation and explains it to the President. You must also
explain it to the men Felix brought into the Government.
They must understand that these three decisions change
everything. The President has been living in a fool's
paradise. . . . Make sure that Felix is here in the morning to
advise the President. The matter is of highest importance.
Everything must be considered most carefully in the light of
these decisions by a unanimous Court.[30]

This stance placed Frankfurter in an awkward position.[31] He had
recognized the danger earlier, and had tried to avoid it by
suggesting some changes in the NRA designed to prevent a court
test.[32]

The government initially sought to make its case for the NRA
in defense of the lumber code, but the case *U.S.* v. *Belcher*, was
dismissed due in large part to Frankfurter's behind-the-scenes
activity.[33] He consulted with Solicitor General Reed and reported
to Roosevelt that he had

made clear to him what seemed to me the decisive reasons
for dismissing this appeal. . . . He indicated that the NRA
people are anxious for a ruling from the Supreme Court
even if adverse in order to guide the new legislation. I told
him I thought that was a suicidal policy from any point of
view. He, himself, believes the case should be dismissed but
wondered whether the views of the NRA people . . . were not
a reflection of yours. I assured him that if he were
convinced as he is, of the wisdom of dismissing the appeal,
he would have your support.[34]

In early April Frankfurter told Brandeis that Reed's action in
moving for the dismissal "showed real wisdom and courage."[35]

This did not end the matter, however. On 4 April Corcoran
reported to Roosevelt that Frankfurter had learned that
Cummings "intends announcing to the press this afternoon that

government will immediately expedite to Supreme Court a new NRA case from second Circuit in New York involving poultry code." Frankfurter urged the president to "hold whole situation on NRA appeals in abeyence."[36] It was too late. Frankfurter believed that Richberg, who had urged Cummings to take the action in the first place, delayed Roosevelt's vetoing cable to Cummings.[37] Frankfurter wrote to Brandeis that Richberg "has been incredibly short-sighted & I am sorry to say, worse in maneuvering an appeal on N.R.A. during F.D.'s absence."[38]

Frankfurter tried to prevent the *Schechter* case from coming before the Court. Corcoran had told Roosevelt that yielding on the case would be "most impolitic and dangerous ... because fundamental situation on court not changed."[39] Given the mood of the Court, Frankfurter knew that the NRA would be overturned, and he also knew that Brandeis would decide against it. Frankfurter also disapproved of the NRA, but preferred it to die a natural death which would avoid strained relationships and embarrassment for the administration.

David Riesman, Brandeis's law clerk for the 1935 term, reported to Frankfurter in November:

> As for the Justice, work on opinions gives me an opportunity to see how he works and how he thinks. We have had several good scraps about policy, but remembering your warning, I don't push him when I see his mind is made up—as it generally is.[40]

Frankfurter knew that Brandeis could be inflexible and that argument was sometimes futile. He realized that Brandeis firmly supported the "Black Monday" decisions, and he also feared what Roosevelt might do. Tugwell recalled that Frankfurter admitted to him and Roosevelt that "we needed a constitutional amendment but thought that we had to have some more adverse Supreme Court decisions before we got to it."[41]

Frankfurter submitted two memos to the president, outlining possible responses to the "Black Monday" decisions. In the first,

he suggested that Roosevelt play a waiting game with the Court
while pushing ahead with his reform program:

> Let the Court strike down any or all of them [reform bills]
> next winter or spring, especially by a divided Court. *Then*
> propose a Constitutional amendment giving the national
> Government adequate power to cope with national eco-
> nomic and industrial problems.[42]

He warned Roosevelt against a "general attack on the Court"
since it would give opponents "a chance to play on vague fears of
a leap in the dark and upon the traditionalist loyalties the Court is
still able to inspire."[43] In the second memo, he advised Roosevelt
to support a bill which would enable the president "to attach fair
labor clauses to contracts for Government purchases and to
contracts made with the proceeds of Government loans and
grants."[44] Such an act would affect industry directly and
indirectly and "would draw a much wider support to the
standards promulgated by the Government."[45]

Frankfurter suggested that "the administrative mechanism"
or an appropriate part of the NRA be continued at least until
March 1937. This would encourage the establishment of fair
labor standards and stimulate appropriate action by the states.[46]
Frankfurter also urged that Roosevelt "vigorously proceed with
legislation now pending, like the Social Security Bill, the Holding
Company Bill and the Wagner Bill."[47] He recommended
legislation which would enable a state to prohibit the importation
of goods "produced under conditions not conforming to the labor
policy of that state." Frankfurter suggested that Roosevelt call a
conference of governors which

> could be used as the occasion for a rounded presentation of
> the New Deal aims and the diverse methods by which they
> are being pursued. This is, I believe, essential, to take out of
> the public mind the false equation that N.R.A. = New Deal
> instead of being simply one means of realizing some of its
> purposes.[48]

These memos outline Frankfurter's strategy of avoiding a direct clash with the Court and continuing the reform program he and Brandeis desired. Although Frankfurter had spoken to Tugwell and Roosevelt of a constitutional amendment, it is doubtful if he approved such a step except possibly as a last resort.[49] In June he wrote to Brandeis:

> The Progressives—particularly Bob LaF. [LaFollette]—are pushing hard for a constitutional amendment. I gather this from what Moley phoned me yesterday—and he was with the Prest. friday night. Moley asked me to get after Bob and make him hold his horses. But it's as hard for me to try to do anything with Bob on this, as with Norris on TVA.[50]

Frankfurter opportunistically used the *Schechter* decision as justification for turning from NRA centralization to a reform of labor standards.

Frankfurter also wished to prevent the president from doing anything impulsively. Roosevelt's immediate reaction was the "horse-and-buggy" press conference of 29 May where he launched into a lengthy critique of the Court's narrow interpretation of the commerce clause.[51] Frankfurter was quick to assure Brandeis that he had nothing to do with Roosevelt's remarks:

> F.D. gave me no indication whatever that he was going to do the press conference. I knew nothing of it until Marion told me just as we were coming to lunch with you. I assume that F.D. purposely did not consult me or tell me—why I know not, except perhaps that he had political purposes & so naturally would not consult me.[52]

Twenty years later Frankfurter told Samuel Rosenman that he "had not the slightest inkling that he was going to make a speech about the Supreme Court or that he was going to say what he said." Roosevelt, Frankfurter concluded, received "awful ignorant advice ... from those who were in on the secret."[53]

Fortunately the press conference was not the beginning of a presidential offensive against the Court, but only an expression of pique. Frankfurter was relieved that there was no follow-up, and he was delighted when Roosevelt turned with renewed interest to his 1935 legislative program.[54] Yet the relationship of Brandeis, Frankfurter, and Roosevelt remained strained for a time.

In July 1935 Roosevelt wrote to Norman Hapgood:

> Our Cape Cod friend is a grand person and I hope he will help us to find ways of answering the people who can only say either "don't do it" or "you can't do it" whenever constructive action of any kind is proposed.[55]

This statement reveals an impatience which Roosevelt must have known Hapgood would communicate to Brandeis. In November Ickes asked the president whether any vacancies would soon occur on the Court. Roosevelt said not, and then

> went on to say that Justice Brandeis, as he got older, was losing sight of the fundamentals. I asked him what Felix Frankfurter thought of Brandeis's changed attitude, and he said that he was heartbroken over it and did not like to discuss it.[56]

Philip Kurland, however, recalled that he had never heard Frankfurter express "any feeling of disappointment in Brandeis's position on New Deal legislation before the Court."[57] Frankfurter probably did think Brandeis too rigid at times, and he may well have told Roosevelt this. However, there is no evidence that Frankfurter was "heartbroken" about Brandeis's judicial stance. This exaggeration may have come from Roosevelt. Frankfurter probably regretted the zeal with which Brandeis helped strike down the NRA in part because he was himself more flexible on the issue, and in part because he was put in the middle. But while the "Black Monday" episode may have strained friendships, no serious rupture occurred.

Matters soon returned to normal. In September Frankfurter
and Brandeis were discussing Justice Cardozo's health and
means of lessening his work load.[58] Brandeis's later decisions did
not cause difficulty. In *Colgate* v. *Harvey* the Court invalidated a
Vermont tax law. Brandeis, along with Cardozo and Stone,
dissented with Frankfurter's approval.[59] Brandeis also dissented
in the *Butler* case, in which the Court invalidated the AAA.
Stone's notable dissent referred to the majority decision as "a
tortured construction of the Constitution," and asserted that
"courts are not the only agency of government that must be
assumed to have the capacity to govern."[60] Frankfurter wrote to
Stone: "A Court that can do that . . . deprives us of all intellectual
criteria for plotting the future orbit of adjudication."[61] Fortunately, Brandeis was not implicated.

In February 1936 Hughes wrote a decision for the Court which
upheld the TVA. Brandeis concurred, but argued that the
judgment of the circuit court should have been affirmed without
the Supreme Court passing on it. Brandeis argued that the suing
stockholders never showed "fraud, oppression, or gross negligence," and insisted that judicial review is limited to "actual
cases and controversies."[62] Frankfurter, enthusiastic about
Brandeis's opinion, wrote Charles E. Clark that it was "one of the
high water marks of Supreme Court jurisdiction in constitutional
controversy."[63]

In May, however, the Court dealt the New Deal another severe
blow when it invalidated the Bituminous Coal Act.[64] In ruling the
act unconstitutional, Justice Sutherland ignored the stream of
commerce doctrine. His precedents included the notorious
Knight case of 1895 and the *Schechter* case.[65] The coal case split
the Court three ways. Butler, McReynolds, Van Devanter, and
Roberts joined Sutherland. Hughes wrote a concurring opinion
in which he agreed that the act's labor provisions were invalid,
but argued that the Court erred in "voiding the price-fixing
provisions in defiance of the will of Congress."[66]

Cardozo challenged the majority in a stinging dissent. Noting
that wrongs attributed to the act did not exist, Cardozo observed
that "the complainants have been crying before they are actually

hurt."[67] Brandeis and Stone concurred.[68] So Brandeis, who
viewed with disapproval a blanket attempt to regulate the
national economy with the NRA, showed himself willing to
countenance the regulation of specific industries. Roosevelt took
this decision badly. High, who saw him the evening the decision
was announced, reported:

> The President was obviously tired and apparently dis-
> couraged. Mac who came in with me . . . tried to get in a few
> wise cracks but they just didn't catch on. I'd never seen the
> boss so low.[69]

Roosevelt talked indignantly of the Court's unwillingness to
approve humanitarian legislation.[70]

He soon had even greater cause for discouragement. On 1 June
1936, the Court reached the judicial nadir in the *Morehead* case.
Butler, writing for a divided Court, struck down a New York
minimum wage law as an impairment of the constitutionally
dubious "freedom of contract."[71] This antediluvian decision was
too much even for the conservative Hughes, who wrote a
vigorous dissent in which Brandeis, Stone, and Cardozo
concurred. He concluded:

> It is difficult to imagine any grounds, other than our own
> personal economic predilections, for saying that the
> contract of employment is any the less an appropriate object
> of legislation than are scores of others, in dealing with
> which this Court has held that legislatures may curtail
> individual freedom in the public interest.[72]

The decision was so scandalous that even Herbert Hoover
protested that action would have to be taken to "give back to the
States the powers they thought they already had."[73]

Roosevelt, though involved in his reelection campaign, was
considering judicial reform. Sometimes this calculation had its
lighter side. High reported that the president

frequently returns to a discussion of the Supreme Court—
wonders how long some of its ancient judges will hold
out—Tom [Corcoran] said the other evening: "I just saw
Van Devanter. He looks very bad." We all laughed.[74]

This banter was the prelude to serious action. New Deal
legislation did not come under judicial scrutiny until January
1935. Between this time and the end of the fall term of 1936, the
Court proved to be a consistent opponent of the New Deal.
Hostility between the judicial and executive branches grew,
culminating in Roosevelt's court plan of 1937 which adversely
affected Brandeis's relationship with Frankfurter and with the
president.

CHAPTER IX

The Court Fight

On 15 January 1937, Roosevelt concluded a letter to Frankfurter with the words: "Very confidentially, I may give you an awful shock in about two weeks. Even if you do not agree, suspend final judgment and I will tell you the story."[1] Frankfurter promised to be patient and observed: "You certainly tease my curiosity when you threaten me with something with which I may not agree. That, certainly, would be a great surprise."[2] The "awful shock" was the plan to reform the federal judiciary. Roosevelt proposed that whenever any federal judge reached seventy years of age and failed to retire within six months, the president be permitted to "appoint one additional judge to the court to which the former is commissioned." The maximum number of Supreme Court justices permissible under the plan would be fifteen.[3] Although these provisions applied to all federal courts, the Supreme Court was the real target.

The plan was presented to Congress on 5 February. Two days later Frankfurter wrote to Roosevelt:

Yes, you "shocked" me by the deftness of the general scheme for dealing with the mandate for national action which you received three times . . . the momentum of a long series of decisions not defensible in the realm of reason nor justified by settled principles of Constitutional interpreta-

139

tion had convinced me, as they had convinced you, that means had to be found to save the Constitution from the Court and the Court from itself.

Frankfurter concluded that "some major operation was necessary," and expressed deep faith in Roosevelt's ability to make the wise choice.[4] Frankfurter was not among the very few advisers who participated in the planning which lasted from 4 November to 31 December 1936.[5] In mid-December Roosevelt gave Cummings responsibility for developing an acceptable solution. Cummings recalled that when Justice McReynolds was attorney general in 1913, he had recommended that additional judges be appointed to lower federal courts if the judges did not retire at the proper time. Cummings presented this idea to Roosevelt, who adopted it without telling many of his close associates.[6]

Rosenman recalled that he received the president's permission to tell Corcoran about the proposal after a conference on 30 January .[7] This was the first Corcoran had heard of it. Hopkins said that

Neither Tommy Corcoran nor Ben Cohen had anything to do with the court fight.... Once the President moved, Tommy and Ben did what they could, but Cummings and Richberg were jealous of all other legal advice and kept Tommy at arm's length.[8]

Corcoran worried about Brandeis's reaction, saying: "I've got the Boss's O.K. to go down and tell him [Brandeis] in confidence what's coming. He sure won't like it."[9] Corcoran, having gotten permission,

crashed the sacred robing room—he walked with me in the hall while the balance of the Court filed by ... Brandeis asked me to thank the President for letting him know, but said he was unalterably opposed to the President's action and that he was making a great mistake.[10]

The day after the plan was made public Brandeis asked
Frankfurter who had advised Roosevelt on the idea, inquiring
pointedly: "Has he consulted you on any of his matters of
late?"[11]

While Brandeis was expressing disapproval of the plan,
Frankfurter was being drawn by Roosevelt into a closer
involvement with it. In a letter of 9 February marked
"privatissimo," Roosevelt explained the reasoning behind the
plan and asked for Frankfurter's help in preparing a fireside
chat.[12] Frankfurter said he would be glad "to go over the situation
with Tom and then have him convey to you the way the matter
lies in my mind."[13] In mid-February Frankfurter dispatched a
memorandum to Roosevelt, saying that in his opinion the
problem was "basically an educational one."[14] The heart of the
memorandum was a critical analysis of the Court's recent
behavior, buttressed by quotations from those who protested the
arbitrary way "some of the Justices have identified the
Constitution with their private social philosophy." Frankfurter
concluded:

> It is necessary not only to protect the Constitution, but to
> protect the judiciary itself from losing its essential
> safeguards. For its security depends ultimately upon the
> confidence of the people. Only thus will the necessary
> independence of the judiciary be assured. But the first
> requirement of an independent judiciary is that judges
> should be intellectually free to make impartial judgments.
> Judges who cannot rise above their private views are not
> free judges.[15]

Throughout this extended passage, Frankfurter focused his
attention exclusively on the abuses of the Court. Nowhere did he
mention the details of the court plan.

Frankfurter's position has been variously interpreted. The
consensus is that he opposed the plan, but kept silent out of a
sense of loyalty to the president.[16] He did not discuss it even in

situations where there seemed a professional obligation to do so. One of his students recalled that when asked about the plan in one of his classes, Frankfurter replied that more information was needed. Discussion was deferred until the end of the course, and the question never came up again.[17] Frankfurter's writing prior to 1937 contains opposition to plans such as the one Roosevelt proposed. In 1930 Frankfurter argued that

It is idle to abuse abuses, and equally futile to fall back upon mechanical contrivances when dealing with a process where mechanics can play but a very small part. . . . The ultimate determinant is the quality of the Justices.[18]

In his article on the Supreme Court written for the *Encyclopedia of the Social Sciences*, Frankfurter dealt specifically with the optimum number of justices, asserting that experience "is conclusive that to enlarge the size of the Supreme Court would be self-defeating."[19]

Frankfurter's position was clear. Therefore it seemed reasonable to assume that he would oppose the president's plan. Yet he acted as Roosevelt's adviser throughout the entire episode. Max Freedman, speaking with what he claims to be Frankfurter's authorization, asserts that after the plan was announced, Roosevelt asked Frankfurter to "help him out of this mess even though he strenuously disliked many parts of the court-packing plan." Frankfurter agreed out of friendship for the president, out of a belief that the Court had "provoked reprisals by its abuse of judicial power," and "out of the justified belief that his legal scholarship would save the President from more flagrant blunders."[20] This stance cost Frankfurter a good deal. His health suffered, and his friendship with Brandeis was strained.[21] The essential agony, however, was that he was caught in an inescapable dilemma.[22] While he did not approve of the plan, his indignant realization of the Court's failure and his close relationship to Roosevelt led him to defend it as best he could in private.

Perhaps Frankfurter's most candid statement about the plan

came in a letter he wrote to Brandeis in March 1937. The letter, written in reference to Hughes's statement to the Senate Judiciary Committee, was never sent, probably because Frankfurter thought it was too harsh. He commented:

> Tampering with the Court is a very serious business. Like any major operation it is justified only by the most compelling considerations. But no student of the Court can be blind to its long course of misbehavior. I do not relish some of the implications of the President's proposal, but neither do I relish victory for the subtler but ultimately deeper evils inevitable in a victory for the Hughes and the Butlers and their successors.... It is a complicated situation and an unhappy one that F.D.R. has precipitated, but the need, it seems to me, more important than any is that in a handful of men ... the fear of God should be instilled so that they may walk humbly before their Lord.

Frankfurter asked Brandeis to look at the proposal not as a thing in itself, but in relation to its deterrent effect on future justices.[23] Frankfurter's position was made more painful because some of his old friends opposed the plan. Norman Hapgood predicted that it would split Congress and damage the New Deal program.[24] Justice Stone found the situation "very distressing," and told Frankfurter that it might have been avoided "with a little forbearance on all sides."[25] Frankfurter's friend Charles C. Burlingham, a venerable giant of the bar, challenged him:

> You who know the business of the Court—that it needs no relief, that a court of 15 is absurd ... that constitutional questions can be taken up by the S. C. speedily ... that every member of the Court is in full *mental* vigor ... you are the one to speak out loud and clear against the proposal.[26]

Burlingham put Frankfurter on the defensive at the outset, and Frankfurter never gained the initiative. He professed to be a "bit puzzled" by Burlingham's insistence on projecting him into "the political cauldron," saying that if he had wanted to get into politics, he would have yielded to the "terrific temptation" to become solicitor general.[27] Included with this letter was one Frankfurter wrote to another friend in which he argued that he remained silent on the plan because he was "the symbol of the Jew, the 'red,' the 'alien,'" and that to speak out "would only fan the flames of ignorance, of misrepresentation, and of passion."[28] Neither of these arguments was persuasive. Frankfurter's statements revealed he was unsure of himself and his position, in contrast to his usual posture as a skilled debater with incisive wit.

Brandeis and Frankfurter continued to correspond during March as the debate grew in intensity.[29] Until the end of the month, however, they did not discuss the controversy. Hughes's letter to the Senate Judiciary Committee emerged as a matter of particular sensitivity. Hughes recalled that three senators, including Burton K. Wheeler, called on him on 18 March to request him to appear before the committee. Hughes was "entirely willing" to do so, but he believed that at least one other member of the Court should accompany him, "preferably Justice Brandeis—because of his standing as a Democrat and his reputation as a liberal judge." When Hughes consulted Brandeis, however, he discovered that Brandeis was opposed to any member of the Court appearing before the committee. Hughes then suggested that he might write a letter to the committee, and Brandeis agreed to this.[30]

After having also secured Van Devanter's approval, Hughes phoned Wheeler on the morning of 19 March to tell him

> that there was a very strong feeling that the Court should not come into the controversy in any way, and that it was better that I should not appear; but that if the Committee desired particular information on any matters relating to the actual work of the Court, I should be glad to answer in writing giving the facts.

Hughes recalled that Wheeler, having seen Brandeis "in the

interval," called the following day for a letter. Hughes wrote the
letter and had it approved on Sunday, 21 March, by Brandeis and
Van Devanter. He maintained that he had no time to consult the
other justices.[31]

Hughes's account indicates that he had taken the initiative and
was willing to testify personally before the committee. Wheeler
recalled that during the height of the battle, Mrs. Brandeis paid a
social call on one of his daughters. As she was leaving she asked
her hostess to "tell your obstinate father we think he is making a
courageous fight." This overture encouraged Wheeler to make
an appointment with Brandeis.[32] Wheeler approached the justice
with misgiving, knowing his views on judicial propriety.
Nevertheless he asked Brandeis about the state of the Court, and
Brandeis suggested that he talk to Hughes. Wheeler replied:

> "Yes, but I don't know the Chief Justice." "But the Chief
> Justice knows you, and what you're doing," commented the
> wiry veteran of many political battles, leading Wheeler to
> the telephone.[33]

According to Wheeler, Brandeis took the lead in bringing Hughes
and himself together.

A contemporary account has a similar emphasis: Hughes
refused to testify at Wheeler's request; Wheeler saw Brandeis
and asked him to speak to Hughes; Brandeis refused but "after
some urging" gave Wheeler permission to telephone Hughes
from his apartment. "No doubt the fact that Wheeler had the
tacit consent of Brandeis behind him gave an extra persuasiveness
to his demands."[34] Brandeis was deeply involved in the effort to
lay the Court's case before Congress, and this, coupled with his
views on judicial propriety, is a vivid indication of his opposition
to the Roosevelt proposal.[35]

Frankfurter, however, resented Hughes's letter. In his
unmailed letter to Brandeis, Frankfurter argued that while all
Hughes's facts were true, the total impression was nonetheless
false because "while he professes not to deal with policy, it

powerfully affects the issues of policy which alone really matters in this case."[36] He continued:

> I resent the C.J.'s putting you on the front line even with your approval. The majority of the Court who have abused their powers and gravely jeopardized our constitutional system by a long course of departure from their constitutional duty should go into the arena and defend the Court, if defense is to be made.[37]

Though Frankfurter did not say he resented Brandeis's actions, the implication was clear. Five days after the unmailed letter was composed, Frankfurter wrote a more tactful one which still communicated deep feeling. The case of the *West Coast Hotel Co.* v. *Parrish* provided the impetus.

This decision, handed down on 29 March 1937, upheld a Washington State minimum wage law. Hughes wrote the opinion for the Court, but it was a narrow five to four margin with the "Four Horsemen" in predictable dissent. While one might have expected Frankfurter to be cheered by this positive turn, he reacted angrily, writing bitterly to both Brandeis and Roosevelt. He told Brandeis that the day of the decision was "one of the few real black days in my life."[38] A point of irritation for Frankfurter was the famous shift by Justice Roberts. In *Morehead* v. *New York ex rel. Tipaldo,* Roberts had voted against a minimum wage law.[39] In the Washington case, however, he voted with Hughes.[40] Frankfurter asserted that this reversal had "not a discoverable, legally relevant factor," and was "a shameless, political response to the present row."[41]

Having disposed of the case and Justice Roberts, Frankfurter turned to Hughes's letter to the committee:

> As for the Chief—I have long written him down as a Jesuit—I deplored his letter and certainly its form. Of course the President was given unreliable and untrue figures (I know not by whom), but that hardly excuses the Chief Justice for intervening in a political fight by

pretending not to, and doing so in the form in which he did—his disingenuous claim that there wasn't time to consult the whole Court . . . I am very sorry to write thus, but I am very, very sad.[42]

Frankfurter also complained about the Hughes letter to Roosevelt, observing that Brandeis's willingness "to allow the Chief to use his name is a source of sadness to me that I need hardly dwell on to you."[43] Brandeis's reply was brief: "I reserve comment on what you say until there is chance for a talk, saying only that you are laboring under some misapprehensions."[44] Sometime between 5 and 25 April they talked, but unfortunately there is no record of their conversation.[45] This was undoubtedly the closest they ever came to an outright split, "and once tempers had cooled, they agreed not to discuss the Supreme Court crisis for a time to avoid placing such a strain on their friendship again."[46]

This agreement was apparently kept, for Brandeis did not allude to the Court fight again in his correspondence with Frankfurter.[47] Other judicial matters, however, were mentioned, and these discussions revealed differing perspectives on judicial matters. On 18 May Van Devanter announced his retirement. Frankfurter's comment must have been critical of his work, for Brandeis replied that while his estimate was qualitatively correct "quantitatively no one could fully appreciate his value who has not observed his work in conference . . . and who has not watched his performance in Court."[48] Another indication of Brandeis's high regard for a conservative colleague came when George Sutherland resigned. Brandeis observed that his resignation was "like all his other acts—motivated solely by a sense of patriotic duty." Brandeis explained that Sutherland felt he would soon be unable to do his share of the work, and wished to give Roosevelt time to name a successor and "get him worked in before the end of the term."[49]

While not alluding again to the Court plan, Brandeis took two opportunities to praise his conservative colleagues in surprisingly generous terms. There may be a clue here to explain, at least in

part, Brandeis's opposition to the Court plan. Brandeis and
Frankfurter had different perspectives because, unlike Frankfurter, Brandeis was a member of the Court. For him it could
never be simply an aberrant institution needing reform; it was a
group of acquaintances.

Brandeis never ignored substantive differences in the interest
of harmony. It was simply that he had seen men like Sutherland
and Van Devanter from a different perspective. He saw virtues
not readily apparent to any outside observer, however sensitive.
There is another factor to be considered also. The justices
frequently agreed on many of the routine cases handled by the
Court. Looking only at the major cases involving New Deal
legislation introduces a distorted focus which not even so close a
student of the Court as Frankfurter could entirely overcome.
These large areas of agreement stimulated a communal feeling
among the justices. Frankfurter and Brandeis were in agreement
on the major New Deal issues, where both were on the outside
functioning as lobbyists for a recovery program and as personnel
officers for various agencies. On Court matters, however, their
positions were different. It is not surprising that judicial matters
caused the most serious difficulty in their relationship.

The president's plan was in trouble from the beginning.
Despite all the tarnish its response to the New Deal had produced,
the Court still enjoyed enormous prestige as a force for stability
in a changing world. Although Roosevelt waged a vigorous
campaign—"Corcoran and the other administration agents put it
up to Senators in stiff terms to back the President"—it was not
enough.[50] By late March and early April, "popular support for the
plan steadily ebbed away."[51]

Although Frankfurter and Brandeis stopped discussing the
Court plan, Frankfurter continued to correspond with Roosevelt.
Indeed Frankfurter's letters to the president became even more
appreciative than usual in the spring and summer of 1937. On 12
April 1937, the Court upheld the National Labor Relations Act in
another five to four decision.[52] Frankfurter agreed with the
decision, but he believed it was politically motivated. He wired
Roosevelt: "After today I feel like finding some honest

profession to enter."[53] He saw the president on 20 April, having
been asked by him to "slip into town" for "a good long talk."[54]
Later he wrote to Roosevelt that after

> long happy exhilarating hours with you I was, as it were, on
> wings and you put more spirit into me than possibly could
> any Bacardi rum—or any that you will have put in wood,
> even for forty years in the Virgin Islands!... The Good Lord
> keep you strong and fit—and may the principle of luck
> continue to mark you as its own.[55]

Frankfurter came to oppose any compromise on the Court
plan. Burlingham wrote to Roosevelt arguing that, since the
Court had changed direction and Van Devanter had retired, he
should withdraw "those portions of the bill which affect the
Supreme Court."[56] When Frankfurter saw this letter, he advised
Roosevelt "to accept no compromise."[57] But compromise was
being forced on the president. His party was badly divided on the
issue. Van Devanter's retirement created problems because, by
offering Roosevelt the chance to make a liberal appointment, it
seemed to lessen the urgency of the situation. In addition, the
president's commitment to nominate Senate Majority Leader
Joseph Robinson to the Court had become embarrassing.

Finally Roosevelt turned the floor fight over to Robinson, and
offered a compromise permitting the president to appoint one
justice a year for any justice who failed to retire at age seventy-
five. But Robinson, worn out by the long struggle, died on 14
July. With Robinson went the bonds of personal loyalty in the
Senate on which Roosevelt had depended. Vice-president Garner,
having counted votes on Robinson's funeral train, reported to
Roosevelt on 20 July:

> "How did you find the court situation, Jack?" Roosevelt
> asked. "Do you want it with the bark on or off, Cap'n?"
> "The rough way," Roosevelt said with a laugh. "All right.
> You are beat. You haven't got the votes."[58]

Frankfurter wrote to Brandeis on the occasion of Robinson's
death, saying that he had "gained real respect for his power and
integrity." He asserted that Robinson

> showed more character and candor and restraint than, I am
> sorry to say, Bert Wheeler ... Wheeler's canonization of
> Hughes is positively indecent, considering the views I heard
> him express about the Court two years ago, and I deeply
> resent his persistent effort to identify you with the Court,
> and to use you as a screen for hiding its grave abuses in the
> past.[59]

Frankfurter wrote a marginal note on his copy of the letter
admitting that it was "perhaps unwise," but that he sent it

> for the same old reason, to try to have as much content of
> candor in our relationship as possible, partly to ease talk ...
> by letting him know as tactfully as I can, as much as possible
> of my views.[60]

Brandeis did not respond to Frankfurter's comments directly, but
contented himself with hoping that Roosevelt would appoint
someone to the Court quickly.[61]

As the fight was being lost, Frankfurter identified himself more
closely with Roosevelt, at least in private. When Gov. Herbert
Lehman of New York came out against the plan in July,
Frankfurter told Roosevelt that he was "hot all over." He
regarded Lehman's action as something which violated "the
decencies of human relations and offends the good taste and the
decorum of friendship."[62] Despite Frankfurter's exertions, the
death of Robinson made the defeat of the Roosevelt proposal
inevitable. A meaningless bill which left the Court untouched
was finally passed. Nothing could conceal Roosevelt's surprising
defeat.[63]

Frankfurter continued to stand by the president. He sent him
some notes for his state of the union address in which he asserted
that the Court had given "tortured constructions of the

Constitution," and was "acting as a super-legislature." He also noted that the Court had reversed itself, and credited the Court plan for the change. The Court altered its course

> only after it had become the duty of the President to protest the want of cooperation between the judicial and legislative branches of Government and to insist that what was needed was not a change in the Constitution but a proper interpretation of our fundamental law.[64]

Frankfurter suggested that Roosevelt review the obstructions created by the Court before his plan was presented. While there existed a bare majority on the Court who understood their proper function, Frankfurter asserted that "unceasing vigilance is required to preserve the constitutional rights of a free and democratic people." Linking the president's position with a respectable tradition, Frankfurter suggested that he quote Theodore Roosevelt's statement that "judges, like executives and legislators should hold sound views on the questions of public policy which are of vital importance to the nation."[65] Frankfurter was trying to help a defeated president make the best of a bad situation by taking the offensive.[66]

Yet nothing could conceal the magnitude of Roosevelt's defeat. Frankfurter's loyalty to him during the struggle only deepened their relationship.[67] The friendship between Brandeis and Frankfurter was too strong to be permanently damaged, but Brandeis's ties with Corcoran were broken as a consequence of the Court fight. Cohen saw Brandeis on 10 October and reported to Frankfurter that he looked well, but he observed that Brandeis had expressed disappointment

> that Tom was not with me. He mentioned Tom several times. I told him that Tom was working with the Skipper ... he hoped that he would come soon. When I told Tom, he closed his jaws and said, "I am not going to see him. He did not shoot straight with us last year, and it is best not to renew the relationship. The Skipper is very bitter, and I think it is best

that he should not think we are in touch with him. I went to say goodbye at the close of the year as a matter of courtesy, but I don't want to go back as we can't restore the old relationship."

Cohen suggested that Frankfurter talk to Corcoran. Tact would be needed, however, because Corcoran believed Brandeis had "stayed" Frankfurter's hand during the Court fight. Moreover, Cohen said that Corcoran was bitter because Brandeis would "not even consider resigning under circumstances which might mean your appointment." Cohen concluded by stating that Corcoran believed Frankfurter was "tied too much emotionally with Brandeis."[68] Corcoran was deeply embittered. He visited Brandeis in November but not, apparently, thereafter.[69]

Corcoran, however, probably exaggerated Roosevelt's anger to justify his own refusal to attempt a reconcilation. While there undoubtedly was tension, it did not endure. Brandeis saw Roosevelt on 25 January 1938 and reported that he and his wife had "a pleasant social call with only Missy LeHand present."[70] The initiative for the visit came from Roosevelt through the mediation of Brandeis's kinsman, Louis B. Wehle. When Roosevelt saw Wehle in December, he hinted that he would like to see Brandeis. Wehle thought that Brandeis would agree and that a time during the Court recess in January would be convenient.[71] The visit was not significant in itself, but it eased the tension. The Court fight was over and there was no reason to hold grudges.

Even Owen Roberts ceased to be a villain. Frankfurter saw him in July 1938, and reported to Brandeis that he was "most friendly & he looks fit and handsome again."[72] Years later Frankfurter wrote:

It is one of the most ludicrous illustrations of the power of lazy repetition of uncritical talk that a judge with the character of Roberts should have attributed to him a change of judicial views out of deference to political consideration.[73]

This was a far cry from Frankfurter's angry assertion in 1937 that "with the shift by Roberts, even a blind man ought to see that the Court is in politics, and understand how the Constitution is 'judicially' construed."[74] The Court fight strained the Roosevelt-Frankfurter-Brandeis alliance. But if it was not completely restored, it was put in working order again. The problem was that the Court fight had both revealed and created divisions within the Democratic party. The Roosevelt coalition and the New Deal suffered a setback from which they never fully recovered. By early 1938 Brandeis and Frankfurter were once more ready to renew the struggle, but the chance for victory had vanished.

CHAPTER X

The Later New Deal

The spring and summer of 1935 marked the high point of the New Deal. Not until Lyndon Johnson's first year as president was reform achieved on such a scale. In the summer of 1935 Brandeis and Frankfurter could anticipate a continuation of progress. But this was not to be, and the rest of the story can be told quickly. Was there a waning of the New Deal, a decline of the reform impulse? Certainly the administration ran into difficulties. William E. Leuchtenburg's masterful treatment of the era chronicles the years 1936-40 with such chapter titles as "A Sea of Troubles" and "Stalemate." It was not so much that liberalism weakened, as that conservatism gained strength.[1] Roosevelt tried, with occasional vacillation and uncertainty, to move forward, but he was stymied by the conservative coalition in Congress.

The Brandeis-Frankfurter collaboration encountered formidable external obstacles to success. Yet a study of the collaboration in these years also shows a loss of vitality, difficult to pinpoint but impossible to ignore. There was a decline in intensity. Several reasons may be suggested for this. Brandeis and Frankfurter realized their limitations in the light of the conservative resurgence. Foreign affairs, particularly the rise of fascism and the plight of European Jews, attracted more of their attention. Lastly, Brandeis's age (he was to retire in 1939 at the age of

eighty-three) may have begun to limit his capacity for close
day-by-day involvement in Washington developments. The later
period of the Brandeis-Frankfurter collaboration began in 1936, a
difficult year to characterize because there were no major
legislative goals to crystalize their efforts to specific ends. Apart
from the election, which dominated planning in the second half
of the year, 1936 resembled 1934 as a year of administrative drift.
In both years Roosevelt appeared baffled by success and unsure
of how to proceed.

Brandeis and Frankfurter continued to discuss some of their
long-standing concerns with the president. In December 1935
Brandeis again argued for limitations on contingent fees, noting
that "there is no escape otherwise from the continuing
degradation of the legal profession."[2] Frankfurter urged Roosevelt to take action in January 1936, saying that few things "are
more needed in the interests of the Treasury, and not less to
improve the morality of the bar."[3] And on 19 February
Frankfurter, pleased that Roosevelt had approved the suggestion,
wrote to him that a proposal to limit contingent fees had been
drafted. He asserted that if such legislation had not been blocked
earlier many things might have turned out differently, since the
real "general staff of the opposition, the lawyers, would not have
been pork-fed by unconscionable fees."[4]

Taxation, particularly of corporate profits, continued to
demand attention. In December 1935 Brandeis noted that it
would soon be possible to "determine the great increase in
[corporate] profits during '35," and that the figures "should
afford great ammunition in many ways."[5] In early March 1936,
Frankfurter congratulated Roosevelt on his message which called
for the taxation of surplus corporate profits.[6] Brandeis expressed
concern about the fate of the bill because he thought the gains
made in "taxing bigness" were in danger of being lost.[7] Despite
some opposition, however, the Revenue Act passed in June.
Substantive issues, however, were lacking in 1936. One
indication of this is the extensive treatment Frankfurter and
Roosevelt devoted to a disagreement with A. Lawrence Lowell,
president of Harvard, over the nature of Roosevelt's participation

in the celebration of Harvard's tercentenary.[8] While Lowell's behavior was boorish, Frankfurter and Roosevelt would not have given the matter such attention if they had had more important issues to think about.

Later in 1936 political concerns again came to the center of the stage. As in 1932, Brandeis and Frankfurter did not act as political strategists. But they did attempt to shape the policies of Roosevelt closer to their own outlook. Brandeis, for example, discussed the value of adopting a strong antibusiness stance.[9] Frankfurter's involvement in the campaign was deeper than Brandeis's, but even he was detached. In fact Frankfurter went to England in the summer and his letters to Brandeis dealt mostly with Palestinian matters.[10] Shortly before he left, he wrote to Roosevelt expressing his disapproval of the Democratic party's preliminary platform; it was "wishy-washy, uninspiring, much worse than tame cat." Frankfurter wanted the platform to be a statement of Roosevelt's own philosophy, a "call to arms." He sent a draft for Roosevelt's "improvement and stiffening."[11]

Frankfurter's draft contained no new ideas, but was an eloquent restatement of his basic convictions. The plight of the nation during the depression was due to "virtual surrender by Government to the blind control of a dominant few." By timely reforms the New Deal had saved the "traditional system of individual enterprise and free competition." Frankfurter listed New Deal reforms, and stated that they "have not only brought immediate relief; they have started the recuperative process of recovery."[12] Frankfurter also mentioned broad principles which would produce lasting recovery. Permanent employment could be achieved and maintained by means of a vigorous program of public works. He included a statement about governmental fiscal policy:

> Balancing the budget through increased tax revenues or decreased expenditures, as the national income is restored, is an indispensable element in the eventual and complete success of a program of permanent recovery requiring Government intervention entailing deficit-financing when

an economic recession is imminent and entailing debt-curtailment when inflation or excessive speculation threaten the stability of the national economy.[13]

Private enterprise was "at the basis of our American system." Frankfurter warned that competition "is the life of trade in a system of individual enterprise." When competition is destroyed, capitalism is also destroyed. The trend toward concentration must be reversed if "a private socialism in this country as alien to traditional Americanism as state socialism" is to be avoided. Warming to his task, Frankfurter argued that the trend toward concentration is motivated by

> The creed of greed ... there is no practical way to regulate the economic oligarchy of autocratic, self-constituted and self-perpetuating groups.... It is necessary to destroy the roots of economic fascism, which engulfed freedom in other lands.[14]

This draft was "marked and annotated" by Roosevelt, and "strengthened his own concept of the general philosophy he should advocate in the 1936 campaign."[15]

During the campaign, correspondence between Frankfurter and Roosevelt diminished. Frankfurter contented himself, for the most part, with sending the president encouraging notes and congratulatory telegrams about particularly effective speeches. Brandeis, likewise, watched from the sidelines, writing Frankfurter anxiously in late September that "Voters are so far from the homo sapiens of which men tell that one cannot help having anxiety."[16] After the election Brandeis commented that the job was "thoroughly done" and said: "Our task must be to make sure that F.D. does not forget."[17] This cryptic comment is an apparent allusion to the necessity of keeping Roosevelt on a progressive course.

The early part of 1937 was dominated by the Court fight. In May, Roosevelt took the offensive with a message to Congress which combined a request for wage and hour regulation with a

plea for action to prevent income tax evasion.[18] He separated the
tax evasion issue from the question of new tax rates, and stated
that no new taxes would be recommended. He then expressed the
strictures of Brandeis and Frankfurter against their own
profession:

> It is a matter of deep regret to know that lawyers of high
> standing of the bar not only have advised and are advising
> their clients to utilize tax avoidance devices, but are actively
> using these devices in their own personal affairs. We hear
> too often from lawyers as well as from their clients, the
> sentiment, "It is all right to do it if you can get away with
> it."[19]

Frankfurter wired Roosevelt his approval as well he might, for he
"had been advising the President to adopt such measures almost
from the day he first entered the White House."[20]

In June Frankfurter sent Roosevelt "a detailed technical
memorandum" on the labor situation, which outlined the "law of
peaceful picketing and . . . the scope of collective bargaining, with
the obligations imposed on the employer no less than the
worker."[21] Despite the disruptive sit-down strikes of 1937, the
labor situation drew little comment from Brandeis.[22] Nor did it
figure significantly in the Frankfurter-Roosevelt correspondence,
although the president admitted that the strikes were "a real
headache."[23]

In the fall, Frankfurter returned to the vital subject of
taxation.[24] He submitted a memorandum on tax policy which
dealt with the three phases of tax legislation he had previously
discussed: an undistributed profits tax, tax exemptions, and a
capital gains tax.[25] He began with the undistributed profits tax,
giving the rationale behind the tax and considering the Supreme
Court's decision in *Eisner* v. *Macomber* (252 U.S. 189), which
prohibited corporations from distributing their profits in the
form of taxable stock dividends. Frankfurter noted that the case
had been decided in 1920, with Brandeis and Holmes dissenting.[26]
Frankfurter then turned to the question of tax exemptions. He

observed that for over twenty years "an unbroken line of
Secretaries of the Treasury has reported to Congress the growing
evils of tax exempt securities." Beyond this, however, Frankfurter asserted that "neither law nor economics nor morality"
can justify ignoring "the existence of income free from tax
exempt securities in fixing the rate of the surtax on all additional
income." The problem was that the law assumed not only that
"income from tax exempt securities is not taxable, but that such
income does not exist."[27]

While Frankfurter wanted to correct this situation, he was
after even bigger game. He suggested an end to "the unwarrant-
able shelter, which tax exempts now afford a large proportion of
the wealth of the country." Tax exemptions of governmental
securities, he claimed, were never constitutional requirements
"but are merely the creations of Supreme Court decisions."
Since the Court's doctrine is an expression of policy, Congress
should define the scope and limits of the policy. Frankfurter
concluded:

> I, therefore, suggest that the Congress should authorize the
> States to tax income from future federal obligations, so long
> as there is no discrimination against the federal borrowing
> power, and that, by the same token, the federal government
> should assume authority to tax without discrimination
> income from state and municipal obligations.[28]

Frankfurter also analyzed the capital gains tax. He argued that
there is no tax which "can so readily and equitably be borne." He
conceded, however, that since the nation faced a possible housing
shortage, "we might well consider the exemption from the capital
gains tax of any investment actually made to construct new
dwelling houses and apartments." Frankfurter rejected the
argument that the tax had deterred investment in new business.[29]

Along with this memorandum, Frankfurter also submitted a
message, prepared at Roosevelt's request, which contained three
recommendations. Frankfurter called for "a definite increase in
the taxes now levied upon very great individual net incomes." He

then suggested that the principle of graduated taxation should be applied to corporations as well as to personal income. The tax rate should have a sliding scale, with heavier taxes being levied on the larger corporations. Frankfurter's final recommendation was that taxation be used to encourage the simplification of corporate structures "through the elimination of unnecessary holding companies in all lines of business."[30]

This extended treatment of tax policy indicates its importance for Brandeis and Frankfurter. Frankfurter did not break any new ground in this discussion, but emphasized ideas which he and Brandeis had always stressed. In a sense, they had run out of ideas. Yet since their ideas had never been consistently tried, they could be excused for insisting on their implementation before casting about for newer remedies.

Certainly Roosevelt and an increasingly rebellious Congress seemed powerless as the nation was suddenly hit with a serious recession beginning in August 1937. The relative prosperity of early 1937 was due to deficit spending. In June Roosevelt, worried about the danger of inflation, cut back on expenditures for the WPA and the PWA. The government had not only stopped priming the pump but was even "taking some water out of the spout."[31] This new crisis touched off vigorous debate within the administration, but it did not lead to any extension of the influence of Frankfurter and Brandeis. Most of the people who took up the fight for deficit spending were not close to them.[32] One such person was Leon Henderson, who allegedly predicted the recession six months in advance. Henderson never became friendly with Corcoran or Cohen and "was not considered one of the inner New Deal circle."[33]

Moreover, Congress did not fill the gap created by the lack of presidential leadership. Brandeis and Frankfurter could find little in the legislative achievement to cheer them.[34] In fact the Revenue Act of 1938 was a bitter blow because it drastically reduced the undistributed profits tax.[35] Opposition to the tax had grown to the point where even men like Eccles and Hopkins urged concessions. Rosewell Magill, a Treasury official, complained to Roosevelt that he no longer knew whether he was being shot at by

his friends or his enemies.[36] The president resignedly permitted
the bill to become law without his signature.[37]

Perhaps the most significant victory in this period was the
passage of the Fair Labor Standards Act in June 1938. The basic
idea of the bill—that the government had power under the
Constitution to determine the labor conditions under which
goods moving in interstate commerce were manufactured—had
been given to Frances Perkins by Frankfurter in 1932. It had
been embodied in the Walsh-Healy Public Contracts Act of
1935.[38] Perkins had never been satisfied with the act's
limitations, and in the spring of 1937 Roosevelt called for a
comprehensive measure, securely codifying some of the reforming features of the NRA.[39]

A clear measure of the detachment of Brandeis and Frankfurter
from Washington events is provided by their reaction to the
antimonopoly drive of 1937-38. Much of the rhetoric of the
campaign was cast in the Brandeis tradition; many of the
speeches used by the leading spokesmen, Harold Ickes and
Robert Jackson, were written by Corcoran and Cohen.[40]
Nevertheless, Brandeis was not enthusiastic. He regarded the
campaign as superficial trust-busting which failed to cope with
the basic issue of bigness. In November 1937, he wrote to
Frankfurter that

> 47 years of the Sherman law futility ought to be as
> convincing as the 39 years of Smyth v. Ames rule failure. I
> hope F. D. will not forget that not monopoly but bigness is
> the curse and that through taxation the evil may be
> averted.[41]

Not even an antimonopoly campaign, theoretically congenial to
"Brandeisians," could animate Brandeis and Frankfurter.

In 1934 when Roosevelt seemed to be groping indecisively,
Frankfurter and Brandeis criticized him severely. There was not
much criticism in this later period. This was due to genuine
bafflement. In June 1938, Frankfurter noted that there was

evidence of an economic upswing, but he observed:

> It's all strangely obscure—why things go down so disas-
> trously & why they gradually seem to be climbing up. Of
> course there is still deep darkness—railroads, steel,
> unemployment generally, but there is a new feel in the air.[42]

Despite the "new feel" this observation betrays bewilderment,
not optimism. Brandeis concurred: "The improvement in
business must be a great relief to the country, but I see in it
nothing which suggests a solution of our problems."[43]

Another factor of growing importance was the European scene
(particularly after Munich in 1938), which attracted the
attention of Brandeis and Frankfurter. Reporting on a conversation he had with Roosevelt in October, Brandeis noted that "F. D.
went very far in our talk, in his appreciation of the significance of
Palestine—the need of keeping it whole and of making it
Jewish."[44] Brandeis argued further that increased immigration
would stimulate the demand for capital goods and help end
unemployment. Undoubtedly most of the immigrants would be
Jewish refugees. Brandeis combined a desire for economic
recovery with concern for European Jews.[45] In 1938 much of
Frankfurter's correspondence with Roosevelt focused on the
European situation. Both Frankfurter and Brandeis were
consistent opponents of isolationism. They encouraged the
president to take a strong stand against fascism, but they did not
confine their efforts entirely to him. Alben Barkley recalled the
he

> often used to visit the Justice and Mrs. Brandeis at their
> modest apartment in Washington. It was Justice Brandeis
> who largely fired my zeal for Zionism and my interest . . . in
> seeing that the homeland of the Jewish people was
> restored.[46]

Though aroused over foreign developments, Brandeis and

Frankfurter did not ignore such judicial matters as the appointment of Hugo Black to the Court. Brandeis had hoped that Roosevelt would quickly replace Van Devanter, who had retired in May.[47] In September Roosevelt appointed Black after controversy following the disclosure of his brief membership in the Ku Klux Klan. Brandeis and Frankfurter did not comment on the controversy prior to the appointment, but Frankfurter expressed concern about how Black would be welcomed. He believed that Stone was hostile to him. Brandeis, however, denied that there was any trouble on Stone's side:

> You do Harlan grave injustice. Every member of the Court has been uniformly friendly & some surprisingly fraternal. No one has been so considerate & helpful as Harlan & he has gone out of his way to give much of his time—when there was occasion.[48]

Aside from Court matters and foreign affairs, the Brandeis-Frankfurter correspondence reflected the absence of issues. Both men commented briefly on the final resolution of the TVA struggle. Frankfurter asserted that Arthur Morgan was "pathological," and Brandeis agreed that his career was a tragedy "of one public spirited and with high purposes who is not wholly sane."[49] Frankfurter commented briefly on the Barkley-Chandler senatorial primary in Kentucky by observing that great sums of money were being pumped into Chandler's campaign from outside the state to secure a defeat for Roosevelt.[50] When Chandler was defeated, Frankfurter noted with relief that the country had been saved "from a demagogue with the mind of Huey Long."[51]

In the latter half of 1938, Court matters again demanded attention. Cardozo, whose health had been failing for some time, died in July. The question of a successor was one which, by this time, involved Frankfurter personally. He seemed to many to be the logical choice. Before Cardozo's death there had been speculation that Frankfurter would be appointed if Brandeis resigned. In October 1937, Cohen reported to Frankfurter that

Corcoran was "particularly bitter that Brandeis should not even consider resigning under circumstances which might mean your appointment."[52] Ickes, reporting this sentiment in July 1938, wrote that Harold Laski told Brandeis he should resign in favor of Frankfurter. According to Ickes, Brandeis observed "he was not sure that Frankfurter could not do more by teaching the younger generation."[53]

In May 1938 Roosevelt speculated with Henry Morgenthau about possible appointments in the event of Brandeis's resignation. Landis and Frankfurter were mentioned, with Morgenthau favoring Landis. Roosevelt said that while Frankfurter would be the more popular appointment, he would have "a terrible time" getting him confirmed by the Senate.[54] Frankfurter did not expect to be nominated because Roosevelt had told him it would be politically impossible.[55] In the late summer after Cardozo's death, however, public support for Frankfurter's appointment grew. While national polls made him the favorite candidate, some Jews were alarmed at the prospect because they thought his appointment would stimulate anti-Semitism.[56] Corcoran believed that by September Roosevelt had decided to appoint Frankfurter, but had encountered Jewish opposition. Ickes reported that there was still hope that Brandeis would resign and that this would enable Roosevelt to appoint Frankfurter with less opposition.[57]

If Roosevelt had already decided on Frankfurter, he kept it to himself. Farley recalled that the president had told him in December that

> Felix Frankfurter wants to get on [the Court] in the worst way. Some months ago I had to tell him at Hyde Park that I just couldn't appoint him for many reasons. In the first place the appointment has to go west. In the second place, I told Felix that I could not appoint another Jew.... [58]

Nevertheless the pressure on Roosevelt to appoint Frankfurter increased. Robert Jackson recalled that he urged the appointment in December 1938 by arguing that only Frankfurter could stand up to Hughes, and that the appointment "would bequeath to

posterity another Brandeis who will be a bridge to the next liberal
administration if that is deferred." Jackson also reported that
Hopkins supported Frankfurter.[59]

Hopkins appears to have taken the lead in applying pressure on
Roosevelt. On 2 January 1939, Ickes reported that Hopkins had
spoken to Jackson about the matter and was thinking about
asking Senator Norris to contact the president.[60] All these
pressures at last produced the desired result. Frankfurter was
informed of his nomination on 4 January 1939.[61] Ickes wrote on
15 January, "my own guess is that until it was all over the
President did not realize that we had ganged up on him for
Frankfurter."[62]

Brandeis retired shortly after Frankfurter went on the Court.
In April 1938 Acheson reported to Frankfurter that Mrs.
Brandeis was concerned over her husband's condition.[63] In the
middle of January 1939, Ickes reported rumors of Brandeis's
impending retirement.[64] Brandeis was not present when Frankfurter was sworn in early in February. Finally, bowing to the
inevitable, he resigned on 13 March 1939.[65] Frankfurter wrote to
Brandeis that his retirement revealed "the poignancy of human
finitude," but that its essential theme was

> that of triumphant accomplishment: the uttermost exertion
> of extraordinary powers to great ends, and unflagging
> serenity in fair weather and foul. The work is done, in so far
> as one man can do it, and others must carry on where you
> leave off, inspired by your example and energized by the
> driving force of your best achievement.[66]

Brandeis's two years in retirement were peaceful, although at
times he grew despondent. In May 1940 he told his niece Fanny
Brandeis that "all I can do now is let people talk to me and
imagine I help them, I don't. . . . "[67] But these moods passed.
Brandeis remained a close observer of the political and diplomatic
scene. He watched Roosevelt's performance during 1940 and
1941 with growing approval, terming the president's address to
the Democratic convention "noble."[68] He supported the

destroyer deal.[69] In August 1941 he wrote: "The good reports on F.D.'s health are indeed a comfort. To have carried the burden throughout these months is an amazing exhibition of strength."[70] During these retirement years, Brandeis continued to consult with Roosevelt. The central concern was the Jewish victims of fascism. In one of his last letters, Brandeis requested Roosevelt to ask Churchill for assurances that the Jews in Palestine would be afforded the means of self-defense.[71]

In these latter communications there was a note of affection which had been lacking earlier. Roosevelt gained stature in Brandeis's estimation during the years of international travail. Shortly after Brandeis's death on 5 October 1941, Frankfurter wrote to Roosevelt that at his last meeting with Brandeis, "a day before the blow came," Brandeis had praised the president as "greater than Jefferson and almost as great as Lincoln."[72] Frankfurter had long had a great affection for Roosevelt which continued to grow during the years of global conflict. He was shattered by Roosevelt's death, and his esteem grew in retrospect during the rest of his own life. Max Freedman reported that two days before he died

> Mr. Justice Frankfurter had me summoned urgently. He asked me to stand beside his bed so that I could hold his hand all the time we were together.... "Tell the whole story," he said slowly and gravely. "Let people see how much I loved Roosevelt, how much I loved my country, and let them see how great a man Roosevelt really was."

His last dream was of being in heaven and seeing Churchill coming forward to welcome him, "promising a good long talk with Roosevelt."[73]

CONCLUSION

It has been said that every life is a failure as seen from within. Certainly Brandeis and Frankfurter were no strangers to deep frustration. Although they were influential figures, their successes were limited and their failures were disappointing. As Roosevelt supporters in 1932, they optimistically awaited the launching of the new administration. Their hopes quickly faded; they suffered through the first hundred days, enduring grimly the implementation of policies they opposed. With growing impatience they watched Roosevelt flounder in 1934, and their gloom did not disappear until the spring of 1935.

But for the most part, even then their hopes were thwarted. The second burst of reform legislation failed to produce an effective recovery program, while the magnitude of Roosevelt's triumph in 1936 helped pave the way for the disastrous Court fight of 1937. Though the reform impulse never disappeared, growing political opposition and the diplomatic anxieties of the late thirties prevented substantive progress. With the outbreak of conflict in Europe, "Dr. New Deal" gave way to "Dr. Win the War."

The New Deal simply did not do what Brandeis and Frankfurter wanted it to do. It never grappled successfully with bigness. Taxation was not used effectively as an instrument of reform and recovery. Roosevelt never committed himself to a spending program large enough to pull the nation out of the depression. It is difficult to see any significant impact by Brandeis and Frankfurter on these fundamental issues. They tried diligently, but it was a Sisyphean labor.

This is not to say, however, that they had no influence during the New Deal period. While they failed to control the course of policy—and who (including Roosevelt) could really claim to do so?—they did enjoy some success. They helped shape legislation to their own ends, particularly the Securities Act, the Securities Exchange Act, the Social Security Act, the Revenue Act of 1935, and the Public Utility Holding Company Act. The impact of Brandeis and Frankfurter on the New Deal, moreover, cannot be limited to their influence on legislation. They seem to have affected presidential policy even when the results were not reflected in specific legislation. Roosevelt appears to have absorbed something of the Brandeis-Frankfurter distrust of large corporations, of businessmen and their legal advisers, while acquiring a sense of the importance of the right people for the right jobs.

And so a complete analysis of their impact on the New Deal must include a study of the many people they placed in government service. Such men as Corcoran, Cohen, Margold, Frank, Lilienthal, and Wyzanski had influential public careers. This list is far from complete; scores of men were scattered throughout the government by the Brandeis-Frankfurter placement service. This not only extended their influence in government circles, but also provided them with many sources of information which they skillfully exploited. Their wide circle of friends and proteges made them among the best informed men in Washington.

The role played by Brandeis and Frankfurter was inspired by their underlying philosophy, which was essentially Brandeis's advocated by Frankfurter. Brandeis's outlook represented a significant intellectual reaction to the industrialization and business consolidation prominent since the late nineteenth century along with the growing power of the federal government. This philosophy, with its unyielding emphasis on the curse of bigness, has been called outdated, but it seems more energetic than passive acquiescence to "inevitable" growth. It seems ironic that while Brandeis's opposition to bigness has been called reactionary, his Keynesian recovery program has been denounced as radicalism.

Also basic to Brandeis's philosophy was an emphasis on personnel. All structural reform of institutions is meaningless in the absence of competent and responsible leaders. Thus the interest of Brandeis and Frankfurter in recruiting public servants was not an egocentric attempt to extend their power, but a practical expression of their approach to government and reform. To them, virtue and intelligence were essential for public service. In the last analysis, the estimate of the significance of Brandeis and Frankfurter must be based on more than a bookkeeping notion of profit and loss, or a pragmatic emphasis on results. Brandeis and Frankfurter were dedicated public servants for whom a well-fought battle was itself a kind of victory. Their enemies were greed, dishonesty, and injustice. To lose to such perennial and formidable foes is painful but not disgraceful. The careers of Brandeis and Frankfurter illustrate the truth of one of their deepest convictions—that the richest resource of democracy is dedicated people in the public service.

APPENDIX:

Brandeis's Recovery Program and the Historians

Historians have analyzed the role of Brandeis as a policy advocate during the New Deal from a limited perspective. According to this outlook, Brandeis, Frankfurter, and their followers, variously called "Brandeisians" and "neo-Brandeisians," offered only the outworn remedies of atomization and competition for the curse of bigness. Brandeis's recovery program, however, has been virtually ignored, and the result has been a consistent misunderstanding of what he advocated as a way out of the economic crisis.

This historiographical distortion seems to have originated with Brandeis's contemporary opponents, particularly the members of the Brain Trust. As we have already seen, Tugwell and Berle showed no awareness of Brandeis's recovery plan, and Moley acknowledged its existence (while dismissing it contemptuously) only in a later work.[1] It is not surprising to find that the historians of the period have, for the most part, passively followed this lead in their treatments of the New Deal era. An exhaustive survey of the historians' discussions of this issue would be a work of supererogation. A brief sampling of some representative works, however, will help bring the issue into sharper focus.

Although it is now over thirty years old, Alpheus Mason's biography of Brandeis is still the nearest thing we have to a definitive treatment; a fresh synthesis is long overdue. The book is particularly weak on the New Deal period. The chapter on

Brandeis's reaction to the New Deal, entitled "The New Deal: Yes and No," presents a critique based entirely on Brandeis's reaction to the curse of bigness and does not discuss his recovery program.[2] In his political biography of Roosevelt, James M. Burns deals with Brandeis only in passing, chiefly in connection with judicial matters. Only once does he allude to Brandeis as a presidential adviser, and then mentions merely his "passion for hard facts and statistics."[3]

By contrast, Arthur M. Schlesinger's exhaustive study of Roosevelt's first term contains many references to Brandeis's philosophy. Schlesinger asserts that he enjoyed more influence on public policy in 1935 than at any other time in his long career.[4] Yet Brandeis's influence was expressed in his proposed remedies for the curse of bigness as he looked toward "a diversified economy and a decentralized society."[5] Schlesinger interprets the second New Deal as a neo-Brandeisian triumph while asserting that, although the "first New Dealers" had a recovery program, the Brandeisian philosophy "in its antibusiness essentials, was a program only for reform."[6] Schlesinger is also aware, however, that Brandeis supported a comprehensive public works program and discusses Frankfurter's relationship with Keynes.[7] But he does not present a complete picture of Brandeis's recovery program; his discussion limits Brandeis's proposals to the traditional antitrust, curse-of-bigness categories.

William Leuchtenburg's highly regarded one-volume survey of the New Deal also interprets Brandeis's philosophy essentially in antibusiness terms. The planners, Leuchtenburg observes, had advocated "fundamental structural reforms" but by 1935 they had been overcome by the "atomistic" Brandeisians.[8] Leuchtenburg mentions Brandeis's draconian tax policy, but he interprets it only in connection with his distrust of business without relating it to a recovery program.[9] Indeed for Leuchtenburg, Brandeis did not have a program for recovery.

Ellis W. Hawley's work on monopoly and the New Deal is justifiably one of the most respected monographs on the period. Hawley's work provides an excellent sustained analysis of the "economic ambivalence" of governmental policy toward monopoly in the 1930s. And yet his characterization of the Brandeisian program relies on what had already become the traditional categories. He observes that "if the philosophy of the Brandeis-Frankfurter adherents and their allies could be summed up in one word, that word would probably be 'decentralization.' "[10] At one point Hawley hints at a broader perspective when he points out that some antitrusters were "accepting elements of the Keynesian analysis and trying to weave the spending and antitrust approaches together. Brandeis, Frankfurter, Corcoran, Cohen, and Coyle, were all advocates of a spending program.... "[11] Hawley never follows up this lead, however. In his discussion of tax policy, he asserts that the "neo-Brandeisians were interested in taxation as a weapon against bigness."[12] And so they were. But he never mentions Brandeis's advocacy of the use of increased tax revenue to finance a comprehensive public works program massive enough to lift the country out of the depression.

In his study of the "old" progressives' attitude to the New Deal, Otis Graham lumps Brandeis in with the Wilsonians of an earlier era who opposed planning as a matter of principle. While Brandeis was not in the anti-New Deal camp, he "staunchly and for the most part successfully opposed the planning features of the New Deal, and most of its centralizing tendencies."[13] Graham describes the Wilsonians in unflattering terms, saying that their "quaint" ideas reflected the intellectual climate of an earlier era.[14] He concludes this negative portrait by asserting that the advice of the Brandeisian progressives to Roosevelt "could only be destructive: dismantle, decentralize, localize."[15]

Frank Freidel sees Brandeis's philosophy in similar terms. For him the emphasis of Brandeis's "ideology" (a questionable word to use in this context) was on "policing the 'money trust.' "[16] Freidel seems to give credence to the view that Brandeis's ideas were becoming obsolete. In the spring of 1933 he was "proposing specific solutions that seemed limited and naive. Like Holmes, he was becoming an ancient monument, more revered than followed."[17] Elliot A. Rosen also interprets Brandeis's philosophy in such restricted categories. He mentions the "Brandeis-Frankfurter group's dependence on free markets and its stress on a regression to small-scale production."[18] He quotes with apparent approval comments by Berle and Tugwell on the outmoded "neo-Brandeisian anti-trust" views.[19]

This brief survey of representative works has revealed a lack of understanding on the part of the historians of the New Deal as to the existence and nature of Brandeis's recovery program. They have correctly seen that Brandeis had deep reservations about the New Deal. However, they have not realized that the reservations came not simply from a failure of antitrust policy, but from a failure to adopt a truly radical Keynesian program to end the depression. Historians have written confidently about "Brandeisianism" and even "neo-Brandeisianism." One may be pardoned for wondering, however, if Brandeis himself was a "Brandeisian" in the limited sense in which the term has been defined. One thing seems clear: if Brandeis really was a "Brandeisian," he was a good deal more also.

ABBREVIATIONS

AAA	Agricultural Adjustment Administration
BP	Brandeis Papers, University of Louisville
CCC	Civilian Conservation Corps
COHC	Columbia Oral History Collection, University of Columbia
CWA	Civil Works Administration
DELP	David E. Lilienthal Papers, Princeton University
DRP	Donald Richberg Papers, Library of Congress
EBRP	Elizabeth Brandeis Raushenbush Papers, University of Wisconsin
EGP	Emmanuel A. Goldenweiser Papers, Library of Congress
FDRL	Franklin D. Roosevelt Library, Hyde Park, New York
FP	Frankfurter Papers, Library of Congress
FPHLS	Frankfurter Papers, Harvard Law School
G	Government Files, BP
GOF	Governor's Office File, FDRL
HP	Charles E. Hughes Papers, Library of Congress
HMP	Herbert S. Marks Papers, FDRL
I	Insurance Files, BP
JMLP	James M. Landis Papers, Library of Congress
M	Miscellaneous Files, BP

MLCP	Morris L. Cooke Papers, FDRL
NIRA	National Industrial Recovery Act
NMF	Nutter, McClennon, Fish Files, BP
NRA	National Recovery Administration
P	Palestine Files, BP
PPA	Samuel I. Rosenman, ed., *The Public Papers and Addresses of Franklin D. Roosevelt*, 13 vols. (New York: Random House, 1938-50)
PPF	President's Personal File, FDRL
PSF	President's Secretary's File, FDRL
PWA	Public Works Administration
RFC	Reconstruction Finance Corporation
RTP	Rexford Tugwell Papers, FDRL
SC	Supreme Court Files, BP
TVA	Tennessee Valley Authority
WPA	Works Progress Administration

NOTES

INTRODUCTION

[1] Raymond Moley, *The First New Deal* (New York: Harcourt, Brace & World, 1966), p. 228. Moley lists five philosophies. Such schematizations are sometimes suggestive but never definitive. For a discussion of the concept of two New Deals, see William H. Wilson, "The Two New Deals: A Valid Historical Concept?" *Historian* 28 (1966): 268–88.

[2] Daniel R. Fusfeld, *The Economic Thought of Franklin D. Roosevelt* (New York: Columbia University Press, 1956). Fusfeld argues that Roosevelt entered the White House with a definite economic philosophy. This view has not won wide acceptance.

[3] Rexford G. Tugwell, "New Deal Diary," 22 December 1932, RTP.

[4] Representative contemporary views are: Joseph Alsop and Robert Kinter, *Men Around the President* (New York: Doubleday, Doran & Company, 1938); and John F. Carter and Ernest K. Lindley, *The New Dealers* (New York: Simon and Schuster, 1934).

[5] The phrase "Brandeis-Frankfurter philosophy" indicates great similarity in outlook but not complete agreement, for the two men had their differences.

179

CHAPTER I
Brandeis, Frankfurter, and Roosevelt:
The Background of Their New Deal Relationship

[1]Liva Baker, *Felix Frankfurter* (New York: Coward-McCann, 1969), p. 17; Alden Todd, *Justice on Trial: The Case of Louis D. Brandeis* (New York: McGraw-Hill, 1964), p. 256.

[2]Elting E. Morison, *Turmoil and Tradition: A Study of the Life and Times of Henry L. Stimson* (Boston: Houghton Mifflin Company, 1960), p. 97.

[3]Ibid. See also "Felix Frankfurter," *Fortune Magazine*, January 1936, pp. 87–88.

[4]Frankfurter to William O. Douglas, 16 January 1934, FP, box 10.

[5]Frankfurter to Hans Zinsser, 1 November 1932, FP, box 114.

[6]Frankfurter to Brandeis, 18 March 1932. The letter is cited by Alpheus T. Mason in his *Brandeis: A Free Man's Life* (New York: The Viking Press, 1946), pp. 373–74.

[7]Melvin I. Urofsky, "Wilson, Brandeis and the Trust Issue," *Mid-America* 49 (1967): 3–28. See also Norman Hapgood, "Justice Brandeis: Apostle of Freedom," *The Nation*, 5 October 1937, pp. 330–31. Hapgood said that Brandeis was "the most powerful intellect assisting Mr. Wilson to expound the principles of democracy applied to the problems of a machine age." Moley, reflecting an animus against Brandeis in the New Deal period, characterized him as Wilson's "dark angel." Rexford Tugwell, *The Brains Trust* (New York: The Viking Press, 1968), pp. 60–61.

[8]These men differed among themselves, but their approach to socio-economic problems was similar.

[9]Frankfurter to Elihu Root, 15 March 1916, NMF, box 77, folder 2.

[10]Brandeis to Frankfurter, 14 June 1910, NMF, box 29, folder 4, printed in Melvin I. Urofsky and David W. Levy, *The Letters of Louis D. Brandeis*, 5 vols. (Albany: State University of New York Press, 1972), I: 350–51. The Illinois case was *Ritchie* v. *Wayman*, 244 Ill. 508 (1910). The Ballinger-Pinchot case was a conservation dispute in 1909 between Richard A. Ballinger, President Taft's secretary of the interior, and Gifford Pinchot, the chief forester. Brandeis acted as Pinchot's attorney before a joint congressional committee. For a good brief account, see George E. Mowry, *The Era of Theodore Roosevelt and the Birth of Modern America, 1900–1912* (New York; Harper & Row, 1962), pp. 250–59.

[11]Brandeis to Frankfurter, 12 June 1912, FPHLS, printed in Urofsky and Levy, *Letters*, 2:648.

[12]Max Lowenthal, "Felix Long Ago," in *Felix Frankfurter: A Tribute*, ed. Wallace Mendelson (New York: Reynal and Company, 1964), p. 127. This "House of Truth" was an omen of things to come. Much later there was the "little red house" where Thomas Corcoran, a Frankfurter protégé, held court during the early days of the New Deal. See Max Stern, "The Little Red House," *Today*, 19 May 1934, p. 5.

[13]Lowenthal, "Felix Long Ago," pp. 127–29.

[14]Herbert B. Ehrmann, "Felix," in *Felix Frankfurter: A Tribute*, p. 95.

[15]Baker, *Felix Frankfurter*, p. 41.

[16]Brandeis to Winfred T. Denison, 12 July 1913, NMF, box 1, folder N-1, printed in Urofsky and Levy, *Letters*, 3:134–35.

[17]Brandeis to Roscoe Pound, 12 July 1913, printed in Urofsky and Levy, *Letters*, 3:135–36.

[18]Alfred Lief, *The Social and Economic Views of Mr. Justice Brandeis* (New York: The Vanguard Press, 1930), p. 298.

[19]Frankfurter to the committee on admissions, Cosmos Club, Washington, D.C., 19 January 1915, FP, box 24.

[20]Frankfurter to Elihu Root, 15 March 1916, NMF, box 77, folder 2. Frankfurter's letters indicate that he was deeply involved in the fight for Brandeis's confirmation. For a good account of the struggle, see Todd, *Justice on Trial*. There is a seeming incongruity in Frankfurter's linking Brandeis and Stimson in this way but, though poles apart in political philosophy, they were both older men of great integrity who functioned as Frankfurter's mentors. Gardner Jackson, Boston journalist and somewhat erratic New Dealer, recalled that Stimson was "a completely moral man" and said that this profoundly influenced Frankfurter. See Gardner Jackson, "Reminiscences," COHC, p. 229.

[21]Archibald McLeish, "Law and Politics," in *Felix Frankfurter: A Tribute*, p. 224.

[22]Baker, *Felix Frankfurter*, pp. 55–57.

[23]Ibid., p. 63.

[24]Ibid., pp. 76–79.

[25]Holmes to Laski, 5 October 1919, printed in *The Holmes-Laski Letters*, ed. Mark deWolfe Howe (New York: Atheneum, 1963). All subsequent references to this correspondence will be to this edition.

[26]Baker, *Felix Frankfurter*, pp. 99–100.

[27]Ibid. Yonathon Shapiro has suggested that Brandeis joined the Zionist movement after many Jews had opposed his suggested entry into Wilson's cabinet in 1913 in order to secure Jewish support for his appointment to the Supreme Court. See Yonathon Shapiro, *Leadership of the American Zionist Organization, 1897-1930* (Urbana, Illinois: University of Illinois Press, 1971), pp. 67-70. This view has not won wide acceptance. See Melvin Urofsky's review in the *Journal of American History* 59 (1972): 17-18. See also Ezekiel Rabinowitz, *Justice Louis D. Brandeis: The Zionist Chapter of His Life* (New York: Philosophical Library, 1968), pp. 15-16.

[28]Brandeis to Emma Frankfurter, 14 November 1916, FPHLS, printed in Urofsky and Levy, *Letters*, 4:265.

[29]Brandeis to Harold Laski, 3 August 1925, M, box 18, folder 3.

[30]Brandeis to Harold Laski, 29 November 1929, M, box 18, folder 3.

[31]Frankfurter to Alpheus T. Mason, 18 December 1945, FP, box 83.

[32]Brandeis to Julian Mack, 11 March 1934, P, box 59, folder 1.

[33]Brandeis to Frankfurter, 19 November 1916, FPHLS, printed in Urofsky and Levy, *Letters*, 4:266-67.

[34]Brandeis to Frankfurter, undated, P, box 57, folder 1. The year can be deduced from dated references to the project, e.g., Brandeis to Frankfurter, 11 April 1929, FP, box 27.

[35]Frankfurter to Brandeis, undated, FP, box 29. Brandeis had considerable wealth at his disposal to use in this way. This wealth resulted from his early lucrative law practice, conservative investments, and a Spartan style of life. His estate before taxes amounted to over three million dollars. A generous man, during his life he gave away one and a half million dollars, a half million of which went to relatives and friends. See Mason, *A Free Man's Life*, pp. 638, 692.

[36]Frankfurter to Brandeis, undated, FP, box 29. The date is difficult to pinpoint; Marion Frankfurter had repeated medical problems. This letter begins with the formal "Dear Mr. Brandeis" salutation.

[37]Frankfurter was an ardent supporter of Al Smith, but Smith had his own set of advisers and the relationship between the two was not close.

[38]Brandeis to Frankfurter, 14 November 1928, FP, box 27.

[39]Frankfurter to Roosevelt, 21 November 1928, FP, box 97. Frankfurter's letter to Roosevelt, which contained Brandeis's views, was marked "confidential." He consistently stressed confidentiality when passing Brandeis's views to Roosevelt. This reflected concern for judicial propriety—of

importance to Brandeis, who regularly rejected requests for extrajudicial activities with the terse notation "precluded." According to Frankfurter, this was one of Brandeis's favorite words. Frankfurter to Alexander Bickel, 4 February 1958, FP, box 127.

[40]Brandeis to Frankfurter, 14 November 1928, FP, box 27.

[41]Brandeis to Frankfurter, 19 December 1929 and 24 March 1930, FP, box 27.

[42]There is not, however, the same wealth of detail and intense interest which characterized their correspondence during the New Deal years.

[43]Harlan B. Philips, ed., *Felix Frankfurter Reminisces* (New York: Reynal & Company, 1960), p. 265.

[44]Laski to Holmes, 30 November and 27 December 1930. Laski is one of the relatively few people to give an unfavorable portrait of Brandeis, and he does it with a vengeance. He characterized Brandeis as suspicious, domineering, dogmatic, and, as a sort of blanket condemnation, "not quite human in his contacts." It may be that Laski, who was himself not a Zionist, was incapable of seeing Zionism other than as fanaticism. Judge Mack once noted that Laski "was pretty rough shod in some of his statements about the Zionists." Mack to Brandeis, 29 December 1934, P, box 59, folder 1. Frankfurter, however, did not receive equal censure.

[45]Their later differences, for example during the Court fight, did not lead to recriminations.

[46]Philips, *Frankfurter Reminisces*, pp. 235–36; Baker, *Felix Frankfurter*, p. 24. Grenville Clark, a 1906 graduate of the Harvard Law School, was a lawyer in New York.

[47]Philips, *Frankfurter Reminisces*, p. 236.

[48]Ibid.

[49]Fusfeld, *Economic Thought*, p. 68. Brandeis was an ardent advocate of the Taylor system.

[50]Philips, *Frankfurter Reminisces*, p. 236.

[51]Baker, *Felix Frankfurter*, p. 87.

[52]Frankfurter to Roosevelt, 28 December 1928, FP, box 97.

[53]Baker, *Felix Frankfurter*, p. 131. Bernard Bellush, *Franklin D. Roosevelt as Governor of New York* (New York: Columbia University Press, 1955), has scattered references to Frankfurter's role as adviser during these years.

[54]Roosevelt to Frankfurter, 10 January 1931, FP, box 97; Frankfurter to Roosevelt, 27 June 1931, FDRL.

[55]Fusfeld, *Economic Thought*, p. 148.

[56]Frankfurter to Roosevelt, 27 June 1929, FP, box 97.

[57]Frankfurter to Missy LeHand, 9 March 1935, FP, box 98. Frankfurter commented: "As you know, I have consistently refrained from pestering the President about appointments, except on inquiries from him." Frankfurter wrote John J. Burns of the Securities and Exchange Commission, "You will have noticed that I have been very careful not to initiate suggestions of personnel. But I should be less than fair if I did not add my word about former students that I know intimately when I know that they are otherwise under consideration." Since Frankfurter was seldom interested in recommending anyone who had not been his student or whom he did not know well, his limitation was academic. In any case, the Frankfurter method overcame all obstacles. Frankfurter to Burns, 24 May 1935, FP, box 135. In a cable to Tom Corcoran from Oxford, Frankfurter wired: "Send bill and supporting statement. Is it possible to have Costigan suggest Ben Skipper and invite my opinion?" Frankfurter to Corcoran, 13 February 1934, FP, box 116. With good reason Calvert Magruder referred to Frankfurter's "Oriental guile" in personnel matters. Magruder to Frankfurter, 10 October 1933, FP, box 80. Brandeis recognized Frankfurter's skill in personnel matters as early as 1914 when he wrote an acquaintance that Frankfurter had "a faculty, rarely equalled, of hearing about 'possible opportunities' for men capable of doing good work." Brandeis to Roger Barton Hull, 31 January 1914, NMF, box 48, folder 2, printed in Urofsky and Levy, *Letters*, 3:242.

[58]Frank Freidel, *Franklin D. Roosevelt: The Triumph* (Boston: Little, Brown, and Company, 1956), p. 102.

[59]Brandeis to Charles Warren, 8 October 1913, NMF, box 58, folder 1, printed in Urofsky and Levy *Letters*, 3:190.

[60]Brandeis to Alice Brandeis, 23 January 1914, EBRP, printed in Urofsky and Levy, *Letters*, 3:237.

[61]Frankfurter to Roosevelt, 5 January 1929, GOF.

[62]Frankfurter to Roosevelt, 24 January 1929, GOF.

[63]Frankfurter to Roosevelt, 28 February 1930, GOF.

[64]Brandeis to Frankfurter, 16 April 1930, FP, box 27.

[65]Frankfurter to Roosevelt, 18 April 1930, FP, box 97.

[66]Roosevelt to Frankfurter, 5 July 1929, FP, box 97; Roosevelt to Frankfurter, 24 November 1928, FP, box 97; Roosevelt to Frankfurter, 6 February 1930, FP, box 97; Roosevelt to Frankfurter, 1 December 1930, FDRL.

[67]Roosevelt to Frankfurter, 7 August 1932, FP, box 97.

[68]Philips, *Frankfurter Reminisces*, p. 239.

[69]Frankfurter to Walter Notestein, 17 December 1931, FP, box 86.

[70]Frankfurter to Samuel E. Morison, 9 June 1932, FP, box 85.

[71]Frankfurter to Al Smith, 24 October 1932, FP, box 164. About a month earlier, Brandeis had written Frankfurter: "Al Smith's outlook declines . . . he is 'lost totally.'" Brandeis to Frankfurter, 4 October 1932, FP, box 28.

[72]Frankfurter to Roosevelt, 10 November 1932, FP, box 97.

[73]Frankfurter to Hans Zinsser, 1 November 1932, FP, box 114.

[74]Baker, *Felix Frankfurter*, p. 36.

[75]Frankfurter's perceptive wife observed that Roosevelt seemed too accessible and too agreeable. Frankfurter to Brandeis, 7 August 1932, G, box 9, folder 2.

[76]Rexford Tugwell tried to deal with the more puzzling aspects of Roosevelt's personality. See his *The Democratic Roosevelt* (New York: Doubleday and Company, 1957).

[77]Frankfurter to Brandeis, 7 August 1932, G, box 9, folder 2.

CHAPTER II
The Social Philosophies of Brandeis and Frankfurter

[1]Charles E. Wyzanski, "Brandeis," *Atlantic Monthly*, November 1956, pp. 70-71.

[2]Frankfurter to Alexander Bickel, 13 November 1936, FP, box 24.

[3]David Riesman to Frankfurter, 22 May 1936, FP, box 127. Melvin Urofsky observed that Brandeis "had a curious gap in his knowledge of things religious" (*A Mind of One Piece: Brandeis and American Reform* [New York: Charles Scribner's Sons, 1971], p. 98). It is possible, however, to overstate the case.

Brandeis's letters, particularly in the early years, show familiarity with the Old Testament. Indeed, his moral system, with its strong emphasis on social justice, has a strong affinity with the prophetic tradition.

[4]Fanny Brandeis, "Conversation with Louis D. Brandeis," 19 May 1940, BP, Addendum File, box 1, folder 7.

[5]Dean Acheson, *Morning and Noon* (Boston: Houghton Mifflin, 1965), p. 96.

[6]Arthur M. Schlesinger, Jr., *The Politics of Upheaval* (Boston: Houghton Mifflin, 1960), p. 222.

[7]Brandeis to Alfred Brandeis, 2 June 1920, M, box 4, folder 4.

[8]Brandeis to Alfred Brandeis, 21 March 1929, M, box 4, folder 4.

[9]Brandeis to Alfred Brandeis, 27 April 1927, M, box 4, file 4, folder 4. He knew, however, that the prosperity of the 1920s was spotty. His letters to Alfred show an awareness of the farmers' plight during the decade.

[10]Ruth Bryan to Brandeis, 10 August 1933, SC, box 13, folder 1. Miss Bryan, youngest daughter of William J. Bryan, asked for permission to quote Daniels's letter to her father which was dated 31 March 1924. She included a copy of the letter, doubless to refresh the justice's memory.

[11]Felix Frankfurter, ed., *Mr. Justice Brandeis* (New Haven: Yale University Press, 1932), p. 117.

[12]Acheson, *Morning and Noon*, pp. 52–53. In 1908 Brandeis defended before the Supreme Court the constitutionality of an Oregon law limiting the hours of female employees in certain establishments to ten a day. In the case of *Muller* v. *Oregon* (208 U.S. 412 [1908]), Brandeis presented a brief which devoted two pages to constitutional precedents and over a hundred to sociological data. See Alfred H. Kelly and Winfred A. Harbison, *The American Constitution: Its Origins and Development*, 4th ed. (New York: W. W. Norton, 1970), pp. 529–30.

[13]Louis D. Brandeis, *The Curse of Bigness and Miscellaneous Papers* (New York: Viking Press, 1934), p.76.

[14]Holmes to Laski, 16 January 1923.

[15]Holmes to Laski, 1 March 1923.

[16]Holmes to Laski, 18 May 1919. Lawrence, in the northeastern part of Massachusetts on the Merrimack River, was an important textile center.

[17]Edwin George to Brandeis, 14 March 1934, G, box 8, folder 2.

Notes   187

18Herbert Aptheker to Brandeis, 14 March 1934, G, box 7, folder 2.

19Ibid.

20Milo Perkins to Tugwell, 5 June 1935, quoted by Tugwell in "New Deal Diary," RTP.

21Brandeis to Frankfurter, 9 November 1933, FP, box 115.

22Brandeis to Frankfurter, 14 May 1928, FP, box 27.

23*Liggett Company* v. *Lee*, 288 U.S. 517 (1933).

24Ibid.

25Ibid.

26Ibid. Brandeis's library included a critical study of the chain store issue by Charles G. Daughters entitled *Wells of Discontent: A Study of the Economic, Social, and Political Aspects of the Chain Store* (New York: Newson and Company, 1934). The author's inscription acknowledged that Brandeis's "warnings of thirty years ago have an important place in this book." See Carl G. Ryant, "The South and the Movement Against Chain Stores," *Journal of Southern History* 39 (1973): 210.

27*New State Ice Company* v. *Liebmann*, 285 U.S. 262 (1932).

28Ibid.

29One young man, upon hearing this advice, recoiled in horror exclaiming, "But Mr. Justice—Fargo, North Dakota?" Schlesinger, *Politics of Upheaval*, p. 222.

30Brandeis to Alfred Brandeis, 18 February 1925, M, box 4, folder 4.

31Holmes observed to Laski: "I am pleased to know that Brandeis who used to uphold it [the Sherman Act], doesn't think it does any good." Holmes to Laski, 5 March 1925. Emmanuel Goldenweiser, "Confidential Memoranda, 1934–1942," EGP, box 7.

32Brandeis to Frederic Howe, 22 March 1938, SC, box 22, folder 1. As early as 1922 Brandeis outlined a draconian tax policy designed to restrict "capitalistic power," which included graduated state and national income taxes, graduated state and national inheritance taxes, super corporation taxes, and national "super inheritance taxes." Brandeis to Frankfurter, 30 September 1922, FPHLS, printed in Melvin I. Urofsky and David W. Levy, *The Letters of Louis D. Brandeis*, 5 vols. (Albany: State University of New York Press, 1972), 5:67–68.

[33]Louis D. Brandeis, *Other People's Money—and How the Bankers Use It* (New York: Frederick A. Stokes Company, 1914).

[34]Goldenweiser, "Confidential Memoranda."

[35]Ibid.

[36]See "Savings Bank Insurance" in Louis D. Brandeis, *Business: A Profession* (Boston: Small, Maynard & Company, 1914), pp. 154-81. Brandeis was deeply involved in savings bank insurance over a number of years, and his correspondence reflects this concern. See Beulah Amidon, "Other People's Insurance: The Social Invention of Louis D. Brandeis," *Survey Graphic*, November 1936, pp. 598-602, 638-40.

[37]Goldenweiser, "Confidential Memoranda."

[38]Louis D. Brandeis, "The Incorporation of Trade Unions," reprinted in *Business: A Profession*, pp. 86-89. See also Louis D. Brandeis, "How Far Have We Come on the Road to Industrial Democracy?—An Interview," reprinted in *The Curse of Bigness*, pp. 43-47.

[39]Brandeis to Lincoln Steffens, 26 February 1912. Quoted in A. T. Mason, *Brandeis: A Free Man's Life* (New York: The Viking Press, 1946), p. 303.

[40]Ibid.

[41]*New York Times*, 29 July 1910. Quoted in Mason, *Brandeis*, pp. 296-97.

[42]Ibid.

[43]Ibid., p. 314.

[44]In 1890 Brandeis wrote his fiancee Alice Goldmark that Thayer "was my best friend among the instructors at the Law School and we have been quite intimate ever since." Brandeis to Alice Goldmark, 13 October 1890, EBRP, printed in Urofsky and Levy, *Letters*, 1:92-93.

[45]James B. Thayer, "The Origin and Scope of the American Doctrine of Constitutional Law," *Harvard Law Review* (1893): 144.

[46]Ibid.

[47]Frankfurter, *Mr. Justice Brandeis*, p. 96.

[48]Brandeis to Frankfurter, 26 May 1937, FP, box 28.

[49]297 U.S. 288 (1936). Brandeis expressed his high regard for TVA by telling

Frankfurter that "Arthur Morgan & Dave Lilienthal [directors of TVA] have
gotten the most alluring job in the Gvt." Brandeis to Frankfurter, 13 June 1933,
FP, box 28.

[50]297 U.S. 288 (1936).

[51]Brandeis to Frankfurter, 16 February 1936, FP, box 28.

[52]Brandeis, *The Curse of Bigness*, p. 41.

[53]Paul A. Freund, "Mr. Justice Brandeis," *Harvard Law Review* 70 (1957):
786.

[54]Holmes to Laski, 5 February 1923.

[55]Melvin I. Urofsky, *A Mind of One Piece: Brandeis and American Reform*
(New York: Charles Scribner's Sons, 1971).

[56]Roosevelt and the New Deal have undergone a similar historiographic
reevaluation. See Jerold S. Auerbach, "New Deal, Old Deal, or Raw Deal: Some
Thoughts on New Left Historiography," *Journal of Southern History* 35 (1969):
18–30.

[57]Melvin I. Urofsky, "The Conservatism of Mr. Justice Brandeis," *Modern
Age: A Quarterly Review* 23 (1979): 47.

[58]Ibid. The Brandeis philosophy, with its paradoxical mixture of dissimilar
elements, was criticized by both liberals and conservatives. See below, pp.
33-35.
[59]This will become even clearer when we discuss Brandeis's New Deal
recovery program later in this chapter.

[60]Frankfurter to Arthur M. Schlesinger, Jr., 18 June 1963, FP, box 101.

[61]Frankfurter to Walter Lippmann, 11 March 1933, FP, box 78.

[62]Frankfurter to Raymond Moley, 16 November 1935, FP, box 84.

[63]Frankfurter to Brandeis, 17 November 1934, G, box 9, folder 2.

[64]Frankfurter to Brandeis, undated, FP, box 28.

[65]Frankfurter to Brandeis, 9 December 1933, G, box 9, folder 2. Frankfurter
also shared Brandeis's attitude toward bankers. In an article on the Federal
Securities Act, he asserted that banks have "no justification except as the
conservative reservoir of savings." Felix Frankfurter, "The Federal Securities
Act," *Fortune Magazine*, August 1933, p. 109.

[66]The phrase is the title of a volume in the "Strangers and Brothers" novel sequence by C. P. Snow.

[67]Frankfurter to Brandeis, 23 September 1933, G, box 9, folder 2. Frankfurter exclaimed: "They are so greedy, our rich!"

[68]Frankfurter to Norman Hapgood, 30 November 1931, FP, box 65.

[69]Frankfurter to Arthur Schlesinger, Jr., 18 June 1963, FP, box 101.

[70]Frankfurter to Roosevelt, 16 November 1936, FDRL.

[71]Frankfurter to Harlan Stone, 25 March 1933, FP, box 105.

[72]Frankfurter to Brandeis, 23 September 1933, G, box 9, folder 2.

[73]Frankfurter to Roosevelt, 1 October 1933, FP, box 97.

[74]Frankfurter to Brandeis, 6 May 1935, G, box 9 folder 2.

[75]Ibid.

[76]Felix Frankfurter, "Social Issues Before the Supreme Court," *Yale Review*, n.s. 22 (1933): 490–94.

[77]Ibid.

[78]Frankfurter to Brandeis, 21 April 1935, G, box 9, folder 2.

[79]Archibald MacLeish and E. F. Prichard, eds., *Law and Politics: Occasional Papers of Felix Frankfurter, 1913–1938* (New York: Capricorn Books, 1962), p. 209.

[80]Felix Frankfurter, *The Public & Its Government* (New Haven: Yale University Press, 1930), pp. 60-80, passim.

[81]Felix Frankfurter, "Democracy and the Expert," *Atlantic Monthly*, November 1930, p. 650.

[82]Ibid.

[83]MacLeish and Prichard, *Law and Politics*, p. 234.

[84]Frankfurter, "Democracy and the Expert," p. 660.

[85]Frankfurter, *The Public & Its Government*, p. 158.

[86]Ibid., p. 159.

[87] Ibid.

[88] Frankfurter to Roosevelt, 18 January 1937, FP, box 98.

[89] Frankfurter to Roosevelt, 23 May 1934, FDRL.

[90] Frankfurter to Roosevelt, 18 January 1937, FP, box 98.

[91] Felix Frankfurter, "The Supreme Court and the Public," *Forum*, June 1930, p. 333.

[92] Frankfurter to John Clarke, 24 February 1938, Clarke Papers, Library of Congress. Quoted by Carl Wittke, "Mr. Justice Clarke—A Supreme Court Judge in Retirement," *Mississippi Valley Historical Review* 36 (1949): 33.

[93] 341 U.S. 552 (1951).

[94] Frankfurter, "The Supreme Court and the Public," p. 334.

[95] Felix Frankfurter, "Can the Supreme Court Guarantee Toleration?" *New Republic*, 17 June 1925, p. 178.

[96] Felix Frankfurter, "The United States Supreme Court Molding the Constitution," *Current History*, May 1930, p. 240.

[97] Brandeis to Elizabeth Brandeis Raushenbush, 19 November 1933, EBRP, quoted in Urofsky and Levy, *Letters*, 5:527. Brandeis reinforced this curse of bigness theme by observing: "If the Lord had intended things to be big, he would have made man bigger—in brains and character." Theologians would have some difficulty with this inverted argument from design!

[98] Journal of David E. Lilienthal, 13 October 1932, DELP. Brandeis had discussed his recovery program in a meeting with Lilienthal.

[99] Ibid., 3 June 1933.

[100] Brandeis to Frankfurter, 5 February 1933, FP, box 28.

[101] Burton K. Wheeler to Frankfurter, 30 March 1932, FP, box 111.

[102] Frankfurter to Wheeler, 4 April 1932, FP, box 111.

[103] Journal of David E. Lilienthal, 3 June 1933, DELP; Brandeis to Elizabeth Brandeis Raushenbush, 19 November 1933, EBRP, in Urofsky and Levy, *Letters*, 5:527.

[104] Brandeis to Frankfurter, 31 January 1933, FP, box 28.

[105] Ibid.

[106] Ibid.

[107] Ibid.

[108] Brandeis to Frankfurter, 5 February 1933, FP, box 28.

[109] Ibid.

[110] Felix Frankfurter, "What We Confront in American Life," *Survey Graphic*, March 1933, pp. 133-36. Sen. Robert F. Wagner sponsored a bill calling for an expenditure of two billion dollars for public works. See J. Joseph Huthmacher, *Senator Robert F. Wagner and the Rise of Urban Liberalism* (New York: Atheneum, 1968), pp. 89-90. Brandeis and Frankfurter were soon to call for twice this amount.

[111] Roy F. Harrod, *The Life of John Maynard Keynes* (New York: Augustus M. Kelly, 1969), p. 290. In the spring and summer of 1919, Brandeis travelled to Europe and Palestine to deal with Zionist matters. He conferred with Wilson, Colonel House, and Balfour at the conference. Mason, *A Free Man's Life*, pp. 456-58.

[112] Harrod, *Keynes*, p. 290.

[113] Brandeis to Frankfurter, 11 June 1931, FP, box 28.

[114] Brandeis to Frankfurter, 28 September 1931, FP, box 28.

[115] Brandeis to Frankfurter, 23 January 1932, FP, box 28.

[116] Brandeis to Frankfurter, 18 December 1932, FP, box 28.

[117] Frankfurter to Keynes, 19 December 1933, FP, box 272.

[118] Brandeis to Frankfurter, 30 December 1933, FP, box 28.

[119] Riesman to Frankfurter, 22 May 1936, FP, box 127. The *Nation* supported national economic planning.

[120] Max Lerner, New York *Herald Tribune*, 3 March 1935.

[121] There is little point in dealing with the conservative criticism which lumped Brandeis in with all the other dangerous radicals, or with the leftist position which depicted him as another reactionary committed to saving capitalism. On the whole, only his fellow liberals dealt with the distinctive features of his thought. The Marxist Herbert Aptheker recalled that Brandeis

told him "that the central social problem did not arise from class differences or from socio-economic arrangements per se but rather from 'bigness,' from the intense growth in the size of everything and in complexity." Aptheker to author, 14 June 1973.

[122]Laski to Homes, 3 January 1935. There were anachronistic elements in Brandeis's thought. Nathan Nathanson, one of Brandeis's law clerks, recalled that he disapproved of farm machinery and automobiles. See "Mr. Justice Brandeis: A Law Clerk's Recollections of the October Term, 1934," *American Jewish Archives* 15 (1963):12. Brandeis wrote Frankfurter: "If you produce a man who can write the story of what the automobile has done to the U. S.—and get it published—let me know." Brandeis to Frankfurter, 1 March 1935, FP, box 28. In the light of recent developments (e.g. air pollution and the energy crisis), one wonders if Brandeis was being prophetic rather than anachronistic.

[123]Berle to Roosevelt, 23 April 1934, PPF, 1306. Berle acknowledged in retrospect that "in general" he "was a pupil of Brandeis in trying to introduce the relevant social and economic material" ("Reminiscences" COHC, p. 149). This agreement at a rarified level did not extend to details.

[124]A. A. Berle, Jr., "Revenue and Progress," *Survey Graphic*, October 1935, p. 471.

[125]A. A. Berle and Gardiner Means, *The Modern Corporation and Private Property* (New York: The Macmillan Company, 1934), p. viii. Berle, in writing an article on the occasion of Brandeis's eightieth birthday, did not miss the opportunity to criticize "the would-be Brandeis follower of today" for being "impractical" and willing to engage in "mere punitive expeditions." A. A. Berle, "The Way of an American," *Survey Graphic*, November 1936, p. 597.

[126]Tugwell referred to "the malevolence of old Justice Brandeis. The old justice had a gentle manner . . . but no harder character ever played a part in the nation's public life." Rexford G. Tugwell, *The Democratic Roosevelt: A Biography of FDR* (New York: Doubleday & Company, 1957), p. 545. Not even Aaron Burr?

[127]See below, pp. 40-42.

[128]Rexford G. Tugwell, "Roosevelt and Frankfurter: An Essay Review," *Western Political Quarterly* 5 (1952): 109.

[129]Rexford G. Tugwell, *The Brains Trust* (New York: Viking Press, 1968), p. 100.

[130]Ibid., p. 60.

[131]Tugwell, *Democratic Roosevelt*, p. 220.

[132]Raymond Moley, *After Seven Years* (New York: Harper & Brothers, 1939), p. 24.

[133]Rexford G. Tugwell, "The Rise of Business, Part I," *Western Political Quarterly* 5 (1952): 274–89. Tugwell assumed that efficency increases as size increases. Brandeis, however, was more cautious: "Very often a business grows in efficiency as it grows from a small business to a large business . . . a business may be too large to be efficient as well as too small" (*The Curse of Bigness*, p. 109).

[134]An effort will be made to discuss Brandeis's philosophy in the light of recent thought, but it seems appropriate to defer this analysis until the conclusion of this study.

[135]Raymond Moley, *The First New Deal* (New York: Harcourt, Brace & World, 1966), p. 275. His contemporary work, *The First Seven Years* (1939), does not mention Brandeis's recovery program.

[136]See below, pp. 173-76. Historians dealing with Brandeis likewise pass over the recovery program while focusing on the curse of bigness. See the appendix for a historiographical survey. The silence of the Brain Trusters is not easy to explain. Perhaps they all felt some sympathy for Brandeis's recovery program (though not his general philosophy) at the time, and therefore had no reason to attack it.

CHAPTER III
The Interregnum

[1]Brandeis to Frankfurter, 31 July 1932; Brandeis to Frankfurter, 16 September 1932; Frankfurter's memo of a telephone call, 5 July 1932—all in FP, box 97.

[2]Frankfurter to Roosevelt, 6 September 1932, FDRL; Roosevelt to Frankfurter, 14 September 1932, FDRL.

[3]Frankfurter to Roosevelt, 12 October 1932, FP, box 97.

[4]See James A. Farley, *Jim Farley's Story, the Roosevelt Years* (New York: McGraw-Hill Co., 1948); Alfred Rollins, *Roosevelt and Howe* (New York: Alfred A. Knopf, 1962); Edward Flynn, *You're the Boss* (New York: Viking Press, 1947).

[5]Raymond Moley, *The First New Deal* (New York: Harcourt, Brace & World, 1966); Rexford G. Tugwell, *The Brains Trust* (New York: Viking Press, 1968); and A. A. Berle, *Navigating the Rapids, 1918-1971: From the Papers of Adolf A. Berle* (New York: Harcourt Brace Jovanovich, 1973).

[6]Frankfurter to Brandeis, 18 July 1933, G, box 9, folder 2; Frankfurter to Brandeis, 31 October 1933, G, box 9, folder 2.

[7]A. A. Berle, "Reminiscences," COHC, pp. 22-23.

[8]John McCarter, "Atlas with Ideas," *New Yorker*, 18 January 1943, p. 23. See also Richard S. Kirkendall, "A. A. Berle, Jr., Student of the Corporation, 1917-1932," *Business History Review* 35 (1961): 43-58.

[9]Frankfurter to Max Lerner, 20 March 1953, FP, box 76.

[10]Rexford G. Tugwell, "Notes for a New Deal Diary," RTP, p. 13. Tugwell harped constantly on Brandeis's age, referring to him with such phrases as "one old man." This tactic, while more subtle, is morally indistinguishable from that of the Liberty Leaguers who spoke contemptuously of Roosevelt as "that cripple in the White House."

[11]Brandeis to Frankfurter, 17 July 1933, FP, box 28.

[12]Frankfurter to Brandeis, 8 February 1934, FP, box 116.

[13]Elliot A. Rosen, *Hoover, Roosevelt, and the Brains Trust: From Depression to New Deal* (New York: Columbia University Press, 1977), p. 140. Rosen calls this memorandum "the single most important document of the New Deal era" (p. 140), but he describes Brandeis's philosophy without showing any knowledge of his recovery program or of the possibility that Moley's memorandum could have resulted, at least in part, from Brandeis's influence. He does stress correctly Moley's close relationship with Frankfurter in the early days of the New Deal. Although Moley himself has minimized his cooperation with Brandeis and Frankfurter, the evidence suggests that, despite occasional disagreements, the relationship was productive, at least into 1934. The later estrangement reflects Moley's growing conservativism.

[14]Rexford G. Tugwell, "New Deal Diary, " 30 December 1932, RTP.

[15]Brandeis to Frankfurter, 31 January 1933, FP, box 28.

[16]Frankfurter to Moley, 9 February 1933, FP, box 84.

[17]Frankfurter continued to urge Moley to meet with Brandeis. The meeting occurred in April. Brandeis to Frankfurter, 12 April 1933, FP, box 28.

[18]Corcoran to Frankfurter, 22 April 1934, FP, box 116.

[19]Corcoran to Frankfurter, 11 May 1934, FP, box 116.

[20]Frankfurter to Brandeis, 4 August 1934, G, box 9, folder 2.

[21]Moley, *First New Deal*, p. 386.

[22]Frankfurter to Brandeis, 7 August 1932, G, box 9, folder 2.

[23]Max Lowenthal, a New York lawyer, was a 1911 graduate of the Harvard Law School. He wrote *The Investor Pays* (New York: Alfred A. Knopf, 1933), the story of the reorganization of the St. Louis Railroad by Kuhn, Loeb and Company. William O. Douglas praised it as "the most valuable contribution to the literature of corporation finance since Louis D. Brandeis' *Other People's Money*" (*Saturday Review*, 22 July 1933, p. 1). Frankfurter praised Lowenthal as "one of the acutest lawyers I know." Frankfurter to Harold Stephens, 21 November 1933, FP, box 118.

[24]Joseph Eastman, transportation expert, served on the Interstate Commerce Commission from 1919 to 1944 and was federal coordinator of transportation from 1933 to 1936. See Claude M. Fuess, *Joseph B. Eastman, Servant of the People* (New York: Columbia University Press, 1952). Bernard Flexner was a 1898 graduate of the University of Louisville Law School, and served on a variety of governmental commissions. He was for a time general counsel for Middle West Utilities, a part of Samuel Insull's empire. For Richberg, see below, pp. 66-67.

[25]Tugwell, "Notes for a New Deal Diary," p. 13.

[26]Ibid.

[27]Berle to Frankfurter, 6 August 1932, FP, box 164.

[28]Frankfurter to Berle, 8 August 1932, FP, box 164. The dates indicate that Lowenthal's appearance was attributable to Frankfurter's conference with Roosevelt shortly before. This incident probably explains why Lowenthal was not accepted. Brain Trust opposition made the appointment impractical.

[29]Rexford G. Tugwell, *The Democratic Roosevelt: A Biography of FDR* (New York: Doubleday & Company, 1957), p. 215.

[30]Ibid. The speech was delivered on 22 May 1932. See *PPA*, 1:639-40.

[31]*PPA*, 1:669-83.

[32]Tugwell, *Brains Trust*, p. 462.

[33]Ibid.

[34]Frankfurter to Roosevelt, 10 September 1932, FP, box 97. Frankfurter sent Roosevelt an article arguing the underconsumptionist thesis of the depression which fitted in with Brandeis's program for recovery.

[35]Arthur Schlesinger, Jr., *The Crisis of the Old Order* (Boston: Houghton-Mifflin, 1957), pp. 441-42.

[36]Ibid. See also Benjamin Rhoads, "Herbert Hoover and the War Debts, 1919-1933," *Prologue* 6 (1974): 130-44.

[37]Schlesinger, *Crisis*, p. 442.

[38]Ibid., p. 445.

[39]Henry L. Stimson and McGeorge Bundy, *On Active Service in Peace and War* (New York: Harper and Brothers, 1947), p. 289.

[40]Ibid., pp. 290-91. Stimson told Mills and Hoover how much he appreciated Frankfurter's "personal devotion." Herbert Feis was an economist who graduated from Harvard with a Ph.D. in 1921. In 1931 he went to the State Department and served as chief technical adviser for the American delegation at the Economic London Conference. Feis was one of the few men Frankfurter had succeeded in placing in government in the last days of Republican ascendency. Stimson thanked Frankfurter for his help in securing Feis, telling him "with what eminent satisfaction he has performed the difficult duties of the past year and a half." Stimson to Frankfurter, 5 January 1933, FP, box 103.

[41]Herbert Feis, *1933: Characters in Crisis* (Boston: Little, Brown, and Company, 1966), p. 53.

[42]Stimson and Bundy, *On Active Service*, p. 291.

[43]Moley, *First New Deal*, p. 42.

[44]Tugwell, "Diary," 30 December 1932, RTP. Moley, however, recalled later that Frankfurter acted "possibly without knowing of the difficulties Tugwell and I were having or the concentrated effort of [Norman] Davis and Stimson to sway the mind and policies of Roosevelt." Moley, *First New Deal*, p. 47. Davis, an internationalist-minded businessman, began his career in Cuba in 1902 and served in a variety of posts with the departments of State and Treasury. He was chairman of the American delegation to the London Naval Conference in 1933.

[45]Stimson and Bundy, *On Active Service*, p. 291.

[46]Ibid., pp. 291-92.

[47]Felix Frankfurter, "Memorandum on the Mediation," 4 January 1933, FP, box 97.

48 Stimson and Bundy, *On Active Service*, p. 292.

49 Ibid., pp. 293–94.

50 Brandeis to Frankfurter, 9 November 1932, FP, box 98.

51 Brandeis to Frankfurter, 24 November 1932, FP, box 98.

52 Ibid.

53 Huston Thompson to Roosevelt, 25 November 1932, PPF, 1933. Thompson began his law practice in Colorado and served as assistant attorney general for the state, 1913–18. He was appointed to the Federal Trade Commission in 1918 and served as chairman in 1920–21 and 1923–24.

54 Brandeis to Frankfurter, 21 January 1933, FP, box 28.

55 Frankfurter to Moley, 10 February 1933, FP, box 84. James Rosenberg suggested that the RFC be made an administrative agency which would not be confined to self-liquidating requirements for loans to public bodies for construction projects. Rosenberg, a lawyer who graduated from the Columbia Law School, was active in Jewish affairs.

56 Frankfurter to Moley, 27 February 1933, FP, box 84. Nicholas Kelley graduated from the Harvard Law School in 1909, served in various posts in the Treasury Department in the 1920s, and was on the Automobile Labor Board in 1934–35.

57 Frankfurter to Moley, 28 February 1933, FP, box 84. Milo R. Matbie was a public utility expert who served on the U.S. Shipping Board and the War Industries Board in 1917–18. Frank McNinch, a lawyer, had served as a member of the Federal Power Commission since 1930 and as chairman since 1933. For David Lilienthal, see below, pp. 82-83.

CHAPTER IV
Launching the New Deal: Recruitment and Personnel

1 Felix Frankfurter, Memorandum about the Solicitor Generalship, 15 March 1933, FP, box 97.

2 Ibid. Roosevelt overstated Cummings's regard for Frankfurter. When Frankfurter sent Cummings a telegram congratulating him on becoming attorney general, it took Cummings a month to dispatch a perfunctory response. Their correspondence quickly ended. Cummings later turned down two men (William A. Sutherland and Dean Acheson) for the Justice Department for

whom Frankfurter had high regard. Frankfurter to Cummings, 18 April 1933, FP, box 149; Cummings to Frankfurter, 18 May 1933, FP, box 184.

[3]Frankfurter, "Memorandum about the Solicitor Generalship."

[4]Frankfurter to Roosevelt, 14 March 1933, FP, box 97.

[5]Roosevelt to Frankfurter, 5 April 1933, FP, box 97.

[6]Frankfurter, "Memorandum about the Solicitor Generalship."

[7]Frankfurter to Roosevelt, 23 February 1933, FP, box 97. Roosevelt had trouble finding someone for the Interior, but both Frankfurter and Brandeis were pleased with Ickes. Brandeis also was cheered by the Cabinet selections. He observed: "The reported Cabinet is, on the whole, reassuring; & there are some appointments which we may well be happy over." Brandeis to Frankfurter, 23 February 1933, FP, box 28.

[8]See below, pp. 54-57.

[9]Frankfurter to Ickes, 7 March 1933, FP, box 149; Ickes to Frankfurter, 8 March 1933, FP, box 149.

[10]Harold L. Ickes, *The Secret Diary of Harold L. Ickes* (New York: Simon and Schuster, 1953), 10 March 1933.

[11]Brandeis to Frankfurter, 13 March 1933, FP, box 28. Margold graduated from the Harvard Law School in 1932, and at the time of his appointment to Interior was serving as special counsel for the National Association for the Advancement of Colored People. Ickes noted that he appointed Margold "after advising with Dr. Felix Frankfurter and Mr. Justice Brandeis." Ickes, *Diary*, 23 March 1933.

[12]Frankfurter to Ickes, 16 March 1933, FP, box 149. As early as 1931 Frankfurter had recommended Margold to Frank McNinch, who was then with the Federal Power Commission. Frankfurter to McNinch, 15 July 1931, FP, box 135.

[13]Frankfurter to Ickes, 23 March 1933, FP, box 149. Although Frankfurter did not mention Brandeis, the justice had known Glavis ever since the Ballinger-Pinchot controversy during Taft's administration, when they both had sided with Pinchot.

[14]Ickes to Frankfurter, 25 March 1933, FP, box 149.

[15]Margold to Frankfurter, 27 March 1933, FP, box 149.

[16]Ibid.

[17] Brandeis to Frankfurter, 28 March 1933, FP, box 28. Henry Slattery served as personal assistant to Ickes from 1933 to 1938, and as undersecretary of the department from 1938 to 1939. Gardner "Pat" Jackson was a Boston journalist whom Frankfurter and Brandeis had known since the Sacco-Vanzetti case. He went to Washington in 1930 and was recruited by Frankfurter in 1933. Gardner Jackson, "Reminiscences," COHC, pp. 221–29. See also Murray Kempton, *Part of Our Time, Some Ruins and Monuments of the Thirties* (New York: Simon and Schuster, 1955), pp. 51–55.

[18] Frankfurter to Margold, 30 March 1933, FP, box 149.

[19] Frankfurter to Margold, 3 April 1933, FP, box 149. Griswold eventually got a position in the solicitor general's office. Much later he became solicitor general, and was dismissed from the post in 1972.

[20] Margold to Frankfurter, 3 April 1933, FP, box 149.

[21] Frankfurter to Margold, 11 April 1933, FP, box 149; Frankfurter to Margold, 11 May 1933, FP, box 149.

[22] Ickes to McCarran, 22 December 1947, FP, box 149.

[23] Frankfurter to Ickes, 10 July 1933, FP, box 149.

[24] Livia Baker, *Felix Frankfurter* (New York: Coward-McCann, 1969), p. 36. Although Brandeis expressed hope at Ickes's appointment, it was too early to tell how he would handle the public works issue. Brandeis to Frankfurter, 14 July 1933, FP, box 28.

[25] Ickes to Frankfurter, 14 July 1933, FP, box 149.

[26] Ickes, *Diary*, 17 May 1933.

[27] Brandeis to Frankfurter, 28 September 1933, FP, box 28.

[28] Whether Ickes would ever have resigned had he not received encouragement from Frankfurter, Brandeis, and Corcoran is uncertain. It is clear, however, that these men meant much to him. Frankfurter and Corcoran had direct roles. Brandeis was more distant, but his influence was important. Ickes noted proudly that Brandeis had told Slattery that he was "doing the best job in Washington" (*Diary*, 17 December 1934). Brandeis and Frankfurter did not always approve of Ickes. Frankfurter noted that Ickes was under attack both for his honesty and because he was "devoid of tact" and possessed a "needless bitterness of thought." Frankfurter to Brandeis, 2 February 1935, G, box 9, folder 2. Ickes, for his part, resented Brandeis's actions during the Court fight and came close to breaking with him completely.

[29] Frankfurter to Perkins, 18 July 1932, FP, box 164.

[30]Frankfurter to Perkins, 9 February 1933, FP, box 164.

[31]Brandeis to Frankfurter, 23 February 1933, FP, box 28.

[32]Frankfurter to Perkins, 11 March 1933, FP, box 150. The wording of the letter indicates that Perkins had not mentioned any concern to Frankfurter. The posts in question were solicitor, director of publicity, and head of the Immigration Bureau.

[33]Perkins to Frankfurter, 14 March 1933, FP, box 150.

[34]Frankfurter to Perkins, 16 March 1933, FP, box 150. This was the kind of industrial reform which Frankfurter and Brandeis preferred over what they considered to be the administrative monstrosity of the National Recovery Administration.

[35]Perkins to Frankfurter, 18 March 1933, FP, box 150.

[36]Frankfurter to Perkins, 20 March 1933, FP, box 150.

[37]Brandeis to Frankfurter, 22 March 1933, FP, box 28. Freund had been one of Brandeis's law clerks. Brandeis to Frankfurter, 25 March 1933, FP, box 28. Stevens graduated from the Harvard Law School in 1899. He served in Congress for one term (1913–15), and in 1933 he was appointed to the Federal Trade Commission.

[38]Frankfurter to Perkins, 27 March 1933, FP, box 150.

[39]Frankfurter to Perkins, 4 April 1933, FP, box 150.

[40]Perkins to Frankfurter, 5 April 1933, FP, box 150. Brandeis, unfortunately, did not discuss his conference with Perkins in his correspondence with Frankfurter.

[41]Frankfurter to Perkins, 11 April 1933, FP, box 150. Freund and Stevens were no longer being considered. Freund later turned down the assistant counselship of the Railroad Retirement Board and took a position in the Justice Department. Frankfurter to Brandeis, 4 August 1934, G, box 9, folder 2. Wyzanski was a 1930 graduate of the Harvard Law School who had served in 1932 as the secretary of the distinguished jurist Learned Hand.

[42]Brandeis to Frankfurter, 18 April 1933, FP, box 28.

[43]Frankfurter to Wyzanski, 24 April 1933, FP, box 113.

[44]Brandeis to Frankfurter, 26 April 1933, FP, box 28. Although the details of the interview are not known, Wyzanski had been impressed with the justice, for Frankfurter replied to one of his letters by saying: "Yes, you caught some of the

essential ingredients in the blend that makes Mr. Justice Brandeis one of the truly great." Frankfurter to Wyzanski, 27 April 1933, FP, box 150.

[45]Frankfurter to Perkins, 2 May 1933, FP, box 150.

[46]Frankfurter to Robert Wagner, 8 May 1933, FP, box 150; Wagner to Frankfurter, 9 May 1933, FP, box 150.

[47]Donald Richberg, memorandum, 1933, Folder 1933, DRP.

[48]Frankfurter to Brandeis, 18 May 1933, FP, box 150.

[49]Brandeis to Frankfurter, 14 May 1933, FP, box 28. The Black bill was an inflexible approach to industrial planning introduced by Sen. Hugo Black of Alabama, which would have created a thirty-hour workweek and banned from interstate commerce articles produced in plants which exceeded this limit.

[50]Frankfurter to Perkins, 2 May 1933, FP, box 150.

[51]Ibid.

[52]Brandeis to Frankfurter, 23 May 1933, FP, box 28.

[53]Frankfurter to Brandeis, 8 February 1934, G, box 9, folder 2.

[54]Frankfurter to Brandeis, 22 May 1935, G, box 9, folder 2.

[55]Things in Labor did not always go the way Frankfurter wanted. John G. Winant, former governor of New Hampshire, was his candidate for head of the Labor Board, but Perkins appointed Francis Biddle instead. Frankfurter observed to Wyzanski that there was "a la de da quality to Biddle, which is not merely sartorial but psychic." Frankfurter to Wyzanski, 22 October 1934, FP, box 113. In the summer of 1938 Frankfurter observed that he had come to distrust "Frances Perkins' Pets." Frankfurter to Brandeis, 19 July 1938, SC, box 22, folder 2. There is, however, no evidence of a break in relations.

[56]Frankfurter to Wyzanski, 15 July 1933, FP, box 113.

[57]Frankfurter to Wyzanski, 18 July 1933, FP, box 113.

[58]Frankfurter to Wyzanski, 1 December 1933, FP, box 113. Wyzanski's response is not in the Frankfurter papers.

[59]Frankfurter to Wyzanski, 6 February 1934, FP, box 113. Frankfurter suggested a tax on bigness instead.

[60]Frankfurter to Wyzanski, 30 October 1935, FP, box 113.

[61]Stephens to Frankfurter, 26 July 1933, G, box 6, folder 2. Occasionally Frankfurter correspondence appears in the Brandeis papers—evidence that Frankfurter passed interesting items on to him.

[62]Brandeis to Frankfurter, 22 May 1933, FP, box 28.

[63]Frankfurter to Roosevelt, 17 May 1933, FDRL. Stone had written: "I wonder if the President realizes how important the efficiency of that office is going to be to his program." Stone to Frankfurter, 15 May 1933, FP, box 105.

[64]Brandeis to Frankfurter, 13 June 1933, FP, box 28.

[65]Cummings had not been Roosevelt's first choice. The president had originally selected Thomas Walsh, senator from Montana. After he died, Roosevelt turned to Cummings whose appointment was politically motivated.

[66]Brandeis to Frankfurter, 13 March 1933, FP, box 28. Acheson "yearned" to become solicitor general. Dean Acheson, *Morning and Noon* (Boston: Houghton Mifflin, 1965), p. 161. After Biggs was appointed, Brandeis suggested that Acheson could become assistant secretary of state, and Frankfurter passed this suggestion on to William Phillips, under secretary of state, and Moley. Brandeis to Frankfurter, 2 April 1933, FP, box 28; Frankfurter to Phillips, 10 March 1933, FP, box 183; Frankfurter to Moley, 25 March 1933, FP, box 84.

[67]Acheson, *Morning and Noon*, pp. 161-62. Acheson said that Cummings bore him a personal grudge because his father, the Episcopal bishop of Connecticut, had disapproved of Cummings's multiple marriages and "forbade complicity by the Episcopal Church."

[68]Acheson finally became an under secretary in the Treasury Department in May 1933. Brandeis and Frankfurter were not directly involved in this appointment. Acheson, *Morning and Noon*, p. 162.

[69]Brandeis to Frankfurter, 28 May 1933, FP, box 28. Sutherland graduated from the Harvard Law School in 1917 and served as Brandeis's secretary from 1917 to 1919. He practiced law in Atlanta from 1921 until 1933.

[70]Sutherland to Frankfurter, 2 July 1933, G, box 9, folder 2. Speaking of Corcoran, Sutherland wrote: "It may be that I should know Mr. Corcoran, but I cannot place him. I suppose that the recommendation came through you."

[71]Ibid.

[72]Frankfurter to Roosevelt, 10 July 1933, FP, box 97. Frankfurter and Brandeis's anxiety about the Justice Department was sharpened by Sutherland's

complaints about Biggs's ignorance of tax matters. Sutherland to Frankfurter, 7 July 1933, G, box 9, folder 2.

[73] Cummings to Roosevelt, 14 July 1933, FDRL. Robert N. Miller, an attorney from Louisville, favored bringing Sutherland into the department, but he said nothing for fear his support would have an adverse effect. Miller to Brandeis, 1 June 1933, G, box 9, folder 2.

[74] Ibid.

[75] Sutherland to Frankfurter, 19 July 1933, G, box 9, folder 2. Sutherland's source was Frank Wideman, an assistant attorney general.

[76] Stephens to Frankfurter, 26 July 1933, G, box 9, folder 2. Harold Stephens had been one of Frankfurter's students who graduated in 1913. Frankfurter had a modest estimate of his ability, informing Learned Hand that he was a "c man." Frankfurter to Hand, 4 December 1939, FP, box 64.

[77] Stephens to Frankfurter, 16 September 1933, FP, box 149.

[78] Ickes, *Diary*, 11 December 1934.

[79] Ibid., 17 December 1934.

[80] Frankfurter to Brandeis, 20 December 1934, G, box 9, folder 2. Reed had gone to Washington to work for Hoover's Farm Board and served as general counsel for the Reconstruction Finance Corporation.

[81] Frankfurter to Brandeis, 15 March 1935, G, box 9, folder 2.

[82] Brandeis to Frankfurter, 28 September 1933, FP, box 115.

[83] Frankfurter to Brandeis, 9 December 1933, G, box 9, folder 2.

[84] Frankfurter to Brandeis, 7 January 1934, G, box 9, folder 2.

[85] Frankfurter to Brandeis, 14 February 1934, G, box 9, folder 2.

[86] Corcoran to Frankfurter, 11 December 1933, FP, box 116. See also James E. Sargent, "FDR and Lewis W. Douglas: Budget Balancing and the Early New Deal," *Prologue* 6 (1974): 33–43.

[87] Arthur M. Schlesinger, Jr., *The Coming of the New Deal* (Boston: Houghton Mifflin Company, 1958), pp. 292-93.

[88] Frankfurter to Brandeis, 4 December 1933 and 28 November 1934, G, box 9, folder 2. Oliphant got his J. D. from the University, of Chicago, taught at

Columbia University, and served as general counsel for the Farm Credit Administration until 1933 when he joined the Treasury Department.

[89]Frankfurter to Brandeis, 4 December 1933, G, box 9, folder 2. Magill was a law professor who taught for a time at Harvard.

[90]Frankfurter and Brandeis regarded this approach with something akin to horror.

[91]Corcoran to Frankfurter, 30 December 1933, FP, box 49.

[92]Ibid.

[93]Ibid.

[94]Ibid.

[95]Frankfurter to Brandeis, 22 August 1933, G, box 9, folder 2.

[96]Frankfurter to Brandeis, 9 December 1933, G, box 9, folder 2. Frankfurter predicted that Oliphant and Morgenthau, being "very small minded people," will want "everybody of Dean's crowd out."

[97]Lowenthal to Brandeis, 17 March 1933, SC, box 13, folder 1. The "larger steps" were the proposals for tax reform and public works. The close relationship between William Woodin and Hoover's Treasury people is stressed by Susan Eastabrooke Kennedy in *The Banking Crisis of 1933* (Lexington: The University Press of Kentucky, 1973).

[98]Frankfurter to Roosevelt, 23 February 1933, FP, box 97. Woodin argued against gold buying. Frankfurter to Brandeis, 9 December 1933, G, box 9, folder 2.

[99]Frankfurter to Brandeis, 28 November 1934, G, box 9, folder 2.

[100]Brandeis to Frankfurter, 10 January 1934, FP, box 28.

[101]Dickinson complained to Frankfurter about James Landis of the Securities and Exchange Commission. Dickinson to Frankfurter, 1 August 1933, FP, box 131.

[102]William D. Reeves, "PWA and Competitive Administration in the New Deal," *Journal of American History* 60 (1973): 360.

[103]Frankfurter to Roosevelt, 1 July 1935, FP, box 98.

[104]Arthur Krock interpreted Dickinson's transfer from Commerce to Justice

over Frankfurter's objections as evidence that Frankfurter's own stock had fallen ("In Washington," *New York Times*, 26 July 1936).

[105]The relationship of Frankfurter and Brandeis to the Department of Agriculture is linked to the Agricultural Adjustment Administration. See below, pp. 70-78.

CHAPTER V
Launching the New Deal:
Legislation and the Administrative Agencies

[1]Susan Eastabrooke Kennedy, *The Banking Crisis of 1933* (Lexington: The University Press of Kentucky, 1973), pp. 177-79.

[2]Brandeis to Frankfurter, 3 March 1933, FP, box 28.

[3]Ibid., Brandeis to Frankfurter, 17 March 1933, FP, box 28.

[4]Brandeis to Frankfurter, 22 May 1933, FP, box 28.

[5]Brandeis to Frankfurter, 23 August 1933, FP, box 28.

[6]Frankfurter to Costigan, 31 March 1933, FP, box 49.

[7]Harry Shulman, "Memorandum of a talk with Brandeis," 8 December 1933, FP, box 28. Shulman was a former student of Frankfurter's and later a professor at Yale. He collaborated with Frankfurter on *Cases on Federal Jurisdiction and Procedure* in 1937.

[8]Emmanuel A. Goldenweiser, "Visit with Brandeis," 23 February 1934, EGP, box 7. Goldenweiser, an economist, was born in Kiev and became an American citizen in 1907. He became director of the Federal Reserve Board in 1926.

[9]This act, though of a later date, belongs logically in this context.

[10]Marriner S. Eccles, *Beckoning Frontiers* (New York: Alfred A. Knopf, 1951), p. 174.

[11]Ibid.

[12]Emmanuel A. Goldenweiser, "Visit with Brandeis," 19 May 1935, EGP, box 7.

[13]Frankfurter to Roosevelt, 10 July 1935, FP, box 244.

[14]Brandeis to Frankfurter, 19 March 1937, FP, box 28.

[15]Raymond Moley, *After Seven Years* (New York: Harper & Brothers, 1939), p. 194. It has become almost a reflex for some writers to refer to Brandeis's philosophy as "atomistic," which seems to be only a sophisticated sort of name-calling.

[16]Rexford G. Tugwell, "Notes for a New Deal Diary," RTP, p. 14.

[17]Donald Richberg, *My Hero, The Indiscreet Memoirs of an Eventful but Unheroic Life* (New York: G. P. Putnam & Sons, 1954), pp. 164–65.

[18]Hugh S. Johnson, *The Blue Eagle from Egg to Earth* (New York: Doubleday, Doran & Company, 1935), p. 205.

[19]Frankfurter to Alfred Cohn, 30 October 1935, FP, box 97.

[20]Ibid.

[21]Frankfurter to Johnson, 18 May 1933, FP, box 131.

[22]Johnson to Frankfurter, 26 June 1933, FP, box 131.

[23]Frankfurter to Johnson, 6 July 1933, FP, box 131; Frankfurter to Johnson, 9 July 1933, FP, box 131. Brandeis was also interested in obtaining NRA material. He wanted it for the University of Louisville library. Brandeis to Fanny Brandeis, M, box 4, folder 5.

[24]James P. Johnson, "Drafting the NRA Code of Fair Competition for the Bituminous Coal Industry," *Journal of American History* 53 (1966): 537. The telegram is quoted from the NRA records at the National Archives.

[25]Frankfurter to James Landis, 17 March 1934, FP, box 117. Frankfurter commented: "I echo all your sentiments regarding the place of NRA in the Administration's program and especially do I agree with what you say about the romantic simplicity of some of our friends, particularly among the younger lawyers, in their view of a 'partnership with industry.' And they are all so bitten with a touching confidence in regulation, and with a strange inability to understand the difficulty of regulating powerful forces."

[26]Frankfurter to Brandeis, 15 August 1933, FP, box 28.

[27]Brandeis to Frankfurter, 25 July 1933, FP, box 28.

[28]Frankfurter to Brandeis, 20 October 1933, G, box 9, folder 2.

[29]Felix Frankfurter, "NRA Memorandum," NRA folder, FP, box 159.

Frankfurter's name does not appear on the memorandum, but he did include such unsigned items of his own in his papers. Copies of this memorandum were sent to Richberg, Wagner, and Perkins.

[30]Frankfurter to Richberg, 7 June 1933, DRP, general correspondence, box 1.

[31]Frankfurter, "NRA Memorandum."

[32]Brandeis to Frankfurter, 14 August 1933, FP, box 28.

[33]Ibid.

[34]Brandeis to Frankfurter, 21 February and 27 February 1934, FP, box 28.

[35]Brandeis to Frankfurter, 14 September 1934, FP, box 28.

[36]Brandeis to Frankfurter, 22 September 1934, FP, box 28.

[37]Ibid.

[38]Frankfurter to Roosevelt, 20 September 1934, FP, box 97; Brandeis to Frankfurter, 23 September 1934, FP, box 28.

[39]Brandeis to Frankfurter, 29 September 1934, FP, box 28.

[40]Thomas E. Vadney, *The Wayward Liberal: A Political Biography of Donald Richberg* (Lexington: University Press of Kentucky, 1970), pp. 172-73.

[41]Richberg, *My Hero*, pp. 126-27. Lilienthal's career will discussed in connection with the TVA.

[42]Journal of David E. Lilienthal, 13 October 1932, DELP.

[43]It is almost nonexistent after the fall of 1933. DRP, general correspondence, 1903-33, box 1, folder 1933.

[44]Alice Brandeis to Richberg, 10 July 1933, DRP, general correspondence, 1903-33, box 1, folder 1933.

[45]Brandeis to Richberg, 18 August 1933, DRP, general correspondence, 1903-33, box 1, folder 1933.

[46]Filene to Richberg, 5 September 1933, DRP, general correspondence, 1903-33, box 1, folder 1933.

[47]Richberg to Brandeis, 1 January 1934, G, box 9, folder 2.

[48]Frankfurter to Brandeis, 19 February 1934, G, box 9, folder 2.

[49] Frankfurter to Brandeis, 2 October 1934 G, box 9, folder 2; 21 November 1934, G, box 9, folder 2.

[50] Frankfurter to Brandeis, 28 November 1934, G, box 9, folder 2. In 1936 Brandeis observed that there was an "alarming resurgence of Donald Richberg." Brandeis to Frankfurter, 18 March 1936, FP, box 28. Lilienthal recalled seeing Richberg and hearing him mention clients "who talk about retainers of a size large enough to build a house with" (Journal, 29 December 1939, DELP).

[51] Richberg to Roosevelt, 26 April 1935, DRP, NRA folder, box 45.

[52] Frankfurter to Roosevelt, 31 August 1934, FP, box 97.

[53] Thomas G. Corcoron, "Memorandum on a Meeting with Brandeis (at his request) with Tom Corcoran and Benjamin V. Cohen after the May 27, 1935 decisions," FP, box 28. The question of Brandeis, Frankfurter, and the Court will be dealt with later. Here the matter is mentioned only to illuminate the NRA discussion.

[54] The National Industrial Recovery Act was due to expire in June 1935.

[55] Arthur M. Schlesinger, Jr., *The Politics of Upheaval*, 1935-36 (Boston: Houghton Mifflin Company, 1960), p. 276.

[56] "Memorandum on the Belcher case," undated, FP, box 98. The memorandum was probably sent in March 1935. *U.S.* v. *Belcher*, 294 U.S. 736 (1935), involved the lumber code which had interstate implications. Several peculiarities of the code made it seem risky to base the government's stand on it, however, and the case was dismissed. Paul Murphy, *The Constitution in Crisis Times, 1918-1969* (New York: Harper & Row, 1972), pp. 138-39.

[57] Schlesinger, *Politics of Upheaval*, p. 277.

[58] Corcoran to Roosevelt, 4 April 1935, FP, box 98.

[59] Max Freedman, ed., *Roosevelt and Frankfurter, Their Correspondence, 1928-1945* (Boston: Little, Brown, and Company, 1967), pp. 259-60.

[60] Frankfurter to Roosevelt, 30 May 1935, FP, box 98.

[61] Frankfurter to Roosevelt, 30 May 1935, FP, box 98. The Webb-Kenyon Interstate Liquor Act (1913), passed over Taft's veto, had enhanced the police power of the states by forbidding interstate shipment of liquor into states where sale was illegal.

[62] Felix Frankfurter, "Memorandum to Roosevelt," 28 December 1935, printed in Freedman, *Roosevelt and Frankfurter*, p. 297.

[63] Ibid.

[64] Frankfurter to Roosevelt, 29 May 1935, FP, box 98.

[65] It seems likely that this letter was written by Frankfurter without consulting Brandeis. It was unlikely that Brandeis would have approved, even as a rhetorical device, of the idea of assaulting the Court with legislation—even legislation he favored. Brandeis's reverence for the Court precluded his wishing to see it criticized, even in a good cause.

[66] The reform legislation of 1935 will be discussed below, pp. 101-23.

[67] Frankfurter to Roosevelt, 18 March 1933, FP, box 97.

[68] Frankfurter to Thomas, 27 March 1935, cited by M. S. Venkataramani in "Norman Thomas, Arkansas Sharecroppers, and the Roosevelt Agricultural Problems, 1933–1937," *Mississippi Valley Historical Review* 47 (1960): 236–37.

[69] Frankfurter to Roosevelt, 8 June 1937, FP, box 98. Frankfurter referred to himself as one "who don't know what 'winter wheat' is! So you say!"

[70] Brandeis to Alfred Brandeis, 31 October 1921, M, box 4, folder 4.

[71] Brandeis to Alfred Brandeis, 5 November 1921, M, box 4, folder 4.

[72] Brandeis to Alfred Brandeis, 3 October 1924, M, box 4, folder 4.

[73] Brandeis to Alfred Brandeis, 2 June 1927, M, box 4, folder 4.

[74] Howe to Brandeis, 21 August 1933, G, box 6, folder 1.

[75] Lilienthal to Brandeis, 5 June 1936, SC, box 6, folder 2.

[76] Donald H. Grubbs, *Cry from the Cotton: The Southern Tenant Farmer's Union and the New Deal* (Chapel Hill: University of North Carolina, 1971), pp. 72-73.

[77] Gardner Jackson, "Reminiscences," COHC, 1959, p. 651.

[78] Philip Broughton to Brandeis, 22 January 1936, G, box 12, folder 1. Broughton worked for the Resettlement Administration and was introduced to Brandeis in 1934 by Jackson as "one of the most thoughtful fellows I have encountered within the New Deal." Jackson to Brandeis, 1 November 1934, G, box 8, folder 1.

[79] Grubbs, *Cry from the Cotton*, p. 75. Grubbs cites interviews he had with Jackson in 1961 and 1962. Jackson reported to Brandeis on the progress of his work. Jackson to Brandeis, 23 August 1936, SC, box 16, folder 2.

[80] Jackson, "Reminiscences," pp. 651–53.

[81] Grubbs, *Cry from the Cotton*, pp. 150–51.

[82] Jackson, "Reminiscences," p. 417.

[83] Ibid., p. 418.

[84] Ibid., p. 418–19.

[85] Brandeis to Frankfurter, 1 August 1933, FP, box 28.

[86] Brandeis to Frankfurter, 24 February 1935, FP, box 28.

[87] Brandeis to Frankfurter, 27 February 1935, FP, box 28.

[88] Milo Perkins, memorandum, 5 June 1935, RTP.

[89] Frankfurter to Roosevelt, 15 November 1935, FP, box 28.

[90] Ibid.

[91] Moley, *After Seven Years*, pp. 306–07; Raymond Moley, *The First New Deal*, (New York: Harcourt, Bruce & World, 1966) p. 157. Unfortunately Frankfurter did not express an opinion about the AAA in his correspondence with Brandeis.

[92] See above, pp. 70-71.

[93] Villard to Frankfurter, 5 February 1936, FP, box 115.

[94] Frankfurter to Villard, 24 February 1936, FP, box 115.

[95] In March 1933 Frankfurter wrote to Tugwell: "I don't know when I took such a quick and deep liking at first sight to a man as I did Wallace." Frankfurter to Tugwell, 11 March 1933, FP, box 125. Brandeis also expressed approval of Wallace and his book *New Frontiers* (New York: Reynal, 1934). Brandeis to Frankfurter, 7 October 1934, FP, box 28.

[96] Frankfurter to Tugwell, 11 March 1933, FP, box 125.

[97] Ibid; Frankfurter to Tugwell, 15 March 1933, FP, box 125. None of these men obtained a position with the agency.

[98] George N. Peek, "In and Out: The Experiences of the First AAA Administrator," *The Saturday Evening Post*, 16 May 1936, p. 7.

[99]Ernst K. Lindley and Jay Franklin, *The New Dealers* (New York: Simon and Schuster, 1934), pp. 92–95; Ezekiel to Brandeis, 13 November 1936, SC, box 17, folder 2.

[100]Cohen to Frankfurter, 23 February 1933, FP, box 180; Louis B. Wehle to Brandeis, 16 August 1932, G, box 5, folder 2. In 1935 Means wrote Brandeis a long letter, summarizing some research which he thought showed that large businesses were surviving the depression better than small firms. He concluded: "This data seems to be quite contrary to your suggestion that the development since 1929 has been in the direction of smaller enterprises." Means to Brandeis, 15 February 1935, G, box 7, folder 2.

[101]Jerome Frank, "Reminiscences," COHC, pp. 13–14. Frank assumed that Frankfurter had talked to Roosevelt.

[102]Stephens to Frankfurter, 26 July 1933, G, box 6, folder 2.

[103]Russell Lord, *The Wallaces of Iowa* (Boston: Houghton Mifflin Company, 1947), p. 346. Frankfurter wished to use Frank as a means of getting other people into the AAA. He wrote to Frank that he had "asked Tom Corcoran to talk with you about matters of personnel. He is a shrewd fellow generally and knows a good deal about Washington ways." Frankfurter to Frank, 24 April 1935, FP, box 125. Frank recalled that he received many personnel suggestions from Frankfurter by means of Corcoran, but added that Frankfurter "pretty much recommended men without regard to their ideologies, but primarily from the point of view of their competence as legal technicians...." Frank, "Reminiscences," pp. 130–31.

[104]James M. Landis to Frankfurter, 1 June 1932, JMLP, general correspondence, container 5; Murray Kempton, *Part of Our Time, Some Ruins and Monuments of the Thirties* (New York: Simon and Schuster, 1955), p. 52.

[105]Nathan Witt to Frankfurter, 14 June 1932, JMLP, general correspondence, container 5.

[106]Ibid.

[107]Kempton, *Part of Our Time*, pp. 51–53; Jackson, "Reminiscences," COHC, pp. 412–13, 417.

[108]Frankfurter to Margold, 30 March 1933, FP, box 149.

[109]Brandeis to Frankfurter, 28 March 1933, FP, box 28.

[110]William Leuchtenberg, *Franklin D. Roosevelt and the New Deal* (New York: Harper & Row, 1963), pp. 76. 139. Margold reported to Frankfurter that Ickes was "non-committal for the present" about Jackson's working in the Interior Department. Margold to Frankfurter, 3 April 1933, FP, box 149.

[111] Kempton, *Part of Our Time*, pp. 51–53.

[112] Frankfurter to Margold, 11 March 1933, FP, box 149.

[113] Much later during the Hiss-Chambers affair, Frankfurter denied having recommended Lee Pressman. Allen Weinstein, *Perjury: The Hiss-Chambers Case* (New York: Alfred A. Knopf, 1978), p. 447.

[114] Jackson, "Reminiscences," p. 651.

[115] Arthur M. Schlesinger, Jr., *The Coming of the New Deal* (Boston: Houghton Mifflin Company, 1958), pp. 74–75.

[116] Ibid., pp. 76–77. Schlesinger's source is an interview with Gardner Jackson. Jackson discussed Wallace in his article "Henry Wallace: A Divided Mind," *Atlantic Monthly*, August 1948, pp. 27–33.

[117] Jackson to Brandeis, 21 December 1934, G, box 8, folder 1.

[118] Schlesinger, *Coming of the New Deal*, pp. 78–79.

[119] Ibid., p. 80.

[120] Brandeis to Frankfurter, 7 February 1935, FP, box 28.

[121] Frankfurter to Brandeis, 19 February and 15 March 1934, G, box 9, folder 2.

[122] Jackson saw Brandeis at least four times and Frankfurter once in the period from 1933 to 1935, in addition to correspondence.

[123] Frankfurter to Brandeis, 9 February 1935, G, box 9, folder 2.

[124] Ibid. Frank recalled having difficulties with Corcoran which undoubtedly further strained his relationship with Frankfurter. Frank, "Reminiscences," p. 166.

[125] Frankfurter to Frank, 10 June 1935, FP, box 55.

[126] Frankfurter to Frank, 27 November 1935, FP, box 181. For a discussion of legal realism, see Edward A. Purcell, *The Crisis of Democratic Theory: Scientific Naturalism and the Problem of Value* (Lexington: University Press of Kentucky, 1973), pp. 74–94.

[127] Frankfurter to Frank, 6 and 11 December 1935, FP, box 181.

[128] Michael E. Parrish, *Securities Regulation and the New Deal* (New Haven: Yale University Press, 1970), pp. 44–46. Thompson had already been involved

in this field, having submitted to Louis Howe a memorandum dealing with securities, holding companies, and anti-trust laws. Huston Thompson to Roosevelt, 25 November 1932, PPF 1333.

[129] James M. Landis, "The Legislative History of the Securities Act of 1933," *George Washington Law Review* 28 (1959): 31-32.

[130] James M. Landis, "Reminiscences," COHC, p. 158.

[131] Parrish, *Securities Regulation*, pp. 52-55.

[132] Moley, *First New Deal*, p. 310. Felix Frankfurter, "Memorandum," 11 May 1933, JMLP, general correspondence, box 7.

[133] Frankfurter, "Memorandum" 11 May 1933; Landis, "Reminiscences," pp. 158-60.

[134] Landis, "Legislative History," p. 34; Landis, "Reminiscences," p. 160.

[135] Landis, "Legislative History," pp. 34-35.

[136] Ibid., p. 36.

[137] Ibid., pp. 38-39; Landis, "Reminiscences," p. 204.

[138] Frankfurter to Roosevelt, 17 April 1933, FDRL.

[139] Frankfurter to Roosevelt, 8 May 1933, FDRL.

[140] Thompson to Brandeis, 17 May 1933, SC, box 13, folder 1.

[141] Parrish, *Securities Regulation*, pp. 69-70. When the measure passed, Frankfurter wrote to Roosevelt that passage "again vindicates your leadership." Frankfurter to Roosevelt, 24 May 1933, FDRL.

[142] Cohen to Landis, 17 June 1933, JMLP, general correspondence, box 4, folder "C."

[143] Felix Frankfurter, "The Securities Act," *Fortune Magazine*, August 1933, pp. 53-54.

[144] Stimson to Frankfurter, 5 December 1933 and 26 January 1934, FP, box 103.

[145] Frankfurter to Stimson, 20 February 1934, FP, box 103.

[146] It is impossible to say how much personal consultation occurred which left no record in the correspondence. Frankfurter's days in Washington in April

1933 were hectic. "Everyone has been after me," he wrote his wife, "as tho I could move mountains." Frankfurter to Marion Frankfurter, 8 April 1933, FP, box 14.

[147] Brandeis to Frankfurter, 17 April 1933, FP, box 28.

[148] Brandeis to Frankfurter, 26 April 1933, FP, box 28.

[149] Brandeis to Frankfurter, 5 August 1933, FP, box 28.

[150] The TVA owed its existence primarily to the determination of Sen. George W. Norris of Nebraska. See Richard Lowitt, *George W. Norris: The Persistence of a Progressive, 1913-1933* (Urbana, Illinois: University Press of Illinois, 1971).

[151] Samuel Konefsky, *The Legacy of Holmes and Brandeis: A Study in the Influence of Ideas* (New York: The Macmillan Company, 1956), p. 173. The quotation is based on Konefsky's interview with Hurst, 14 September 1951.

[152] Brandeis to Frankfurter, 13 June and 3 August 1933, FP, box 28.

[153] Thomas K. McGraw, *Morgan vs. Lilienthal* (Chicago: Loyola University Press, 1970), p. 19; Richberg, *My Hero*, pp. 126-27.

[154] Brandeis to Frankfurter, 24 February 1933, FP, box 28.

[155] Box 59, DELP.

[156] McGraw, *Morgan vs. Lilienthal*, p. 19. Lilienthal reported that Senator Norris told him he had seen Roosevelt in late May and that the president had told him he was going to get Lilienthal for the TVA, saying: "If we could get Lilienthal, it would be a ten strike." Journal, 22 June 1933, DELP. Undoubtedly Frankfurter used his influence in this matter also.

[157] Frankfurter to Roosevelt, 10 June 1933, G, box 9, folder 2. Moley, who was in a position to know, observed that "there is also no doubt that Frankfurter had a decisive hand in commending Lilienthal to Roosevelt." Moley, *First New Deal*, p. 333.

[158] Frankfurter to Brandeis, 12 August 1933, G, box 9, folder 2. The "other Morgan" was Harcourt Morgan, who had been president of the University of Tennessee and was deeply committed to reform.

[159] Brandeis to Frankfurter, 24 August 1933, FP, box 28.

[160] Arthur Morgan's side of the story is told in his *The Making of the TVA* (Buffalo: Prometheus, 1974).

[161] It is sobering to realize how easily the victories of one generation can be

undone in the next. The TVA has evolved from a reforming agency into a typical
power company which buys vast quantities of strip-mined coal, and is deeply
implicated in the destruction of Appalachia. Harry M. Caudill, *Night Comes to
the Cumberlands: A Biography of a Depressed Area* (Boston: Little, Brown,
1963), pp. 319–24.

CHAPTER VI
The New Deal in the Doldrums

[1]Elmus Wicker, "Roosevelt's 1933 Monetary Experiment," *Journal of
American History* 57 (1971): 864–79. Wicker argues that monetary tinkering
was opposed by most of Roosevelt's advisers, and that his experimentation was
politically motivated.

[2]Arthur M. Schlesinger, Jr., *The Coming of the New Deal* (Boston: Houghton
Mifflin Company, 1958), p. 200; James R. Moore, "Sources of New Deal
Economic Policy: The International Dimension," *Journal of American History*
61 (1974): 730.

[3]Schlesinger, *Coming of the New Deal*, p. 203; Moore, "Sources," 730–33.

[4]The Brain Trust had resented Frankfurter's mediation during the
interregnum, fearing that Roosevelt might get involved in internationalist
schemes. See above, pp. 42-44.

[5]Moore, "Sources," 737.

[6]Frank Friedel, *Franklin D. Roosevelt: Launching the New Deal* (Boston:
Little, Brown, and Company, 1973), pp. 458–62; Schlesinger, *Coming of the New
Deal*, p. 209.

[7]Feis to Frankfurter, 4 April 1933, FP, box 54. Feis discussed the
misunderstanding that existed between Hull and Moley, reporting that Moley
"still seems to move in a honeymoon of irresponsibility." It was Feis who
proposed a program of internationally coordinated public works financed by
governmental borrowing. See Moore, "Sources," 731. Although this proposal
was not discussed in the Feis-Frankfurter correspondence, it is an internationalist application of the Brandeis-Frankfurter program for recovery.

[8]Frankfurter to Brandeis, 12 June 1933, G, box 9, folder 2.

[9]Freidel, *Launching the New Deal*, pp. 477–78.

[10]*PPA*, 2:264. Schlesinger characterized the tone as "stern and con-
temptuous." See *Coming of the New Deal*, p. 222.

[11] Schlesinger, *Coming of the New Deal*, pp. 223–24.

[12] Frankfurter to Brandeis, 6 July 1933, FP, box 28.

[13] Frankfurter to Brandeis, 11 and 14 July 1933, FP, box 28.

[14] Frankfurter to Roosevelt, 6 July 1933, FP, box 97.

[15] Brandeis to Frankfurter, 8 July 1933, FP, box 28.

[16] John M. Blum, ed., *From the Morgenthau Diaries* (Boston: Houghton Mifflin, 1959), p. 61.

[17] Ibid., pp. 65–67.

[18] Brandeis to Frankfurter, 13 June 1933, FP, box 28.

[19] Frankfurter to Brandeis, 14 June 1933, G, box 9, folder 2.

[20] Brandeis to Frankfurter, 26 April 1933, FP, box 28.

[21] Dean Acheson, *Morning and Noon* (Boston: Houghton Mifflin, 1965), pp. 174–75.

[22] Corcoran to Frankfurter, 30 December 1933, FP, box 49.

[23] Acheson, *Morning and Noon*, pp. 180–81.

[24] Frankfurter to Brandeis, 18 July 1933, G, box 9, folder 2.

[25] Schlesinger, *Coming of the New Deal*, p. 239.

[26] Acheson, *Morning and Noon*, p. 188. Stanley Reed supported gold buying and rebuked Acheson for being so indifferent to his career as to oppose it.

[27] Brandeis to Frankfurter, 30 October 1933, FP, box 115.

[28] Frankfurter to Brandeis, 7 November 1933, G, box 9, folder 2.

[29] Frankfurter to Brandeis, 17 November 1933, G, box 9, folder 2.

[30] Frankfurter to Roosevelt, 23 November 1933, FP, box 97. Frankfurter did not claim that these economists agreed with gold buying.

[31] Frankfurter to Roosevelt, 12 December 1933, FP, box 97.

[32] Max Freedman, ed., *Roosevelt and Frankfurter, Their Correspondence, 1928–1945* (Boston: Little, Brown, and Company, 1967), pp. 176–77.

[33]Frankfurter to Brandeis, 23 November 1933, G, box 9, folder 2. Sprague resigned on 21 November warning of a "drift into unrestrained inflation" and a collapse of the government's credit. Schlesinger, *Coming of the New Deal*, pp. 244–45.

[34]Frankfurter to Brandeis, 9 December 1933, G, box 9, folder 2.

[35]Frankfurter to Brandeis, 18 December 1933, G, box 9, folder 2.

[36]Frankfurter to Brandeis, 17 January 1934, G, box 9, folder 2.

[37]Schlesinger, *Coming of the New Deal*, p. 246; Broaddus Mitchell, *Depression Decade: From New Era through New Deal, 1929-1941* (New York: Harper Torchbooks, 1969), p. 153.

[38]Sen. William Borah of Idaho observed that they "were deeply moved" about the Constitution of the United States" since they "had just discovered it." Schlesinger, *Coming of the New Deal*, p. 489.

[39]Brandeis to Frankfurter, 3 August 1933, FP, box 28. Frankfurter replied: "Your debit & credit of administration to date hits exactly my own feelings." Frankfurter to Brandeis, 8 August 1933, G, box 9, folder 2.

[40]Brandeis to Frankfurter, 5 August 1933, FP, box 28. Frankfurter's reply is not in the correspondence.

[41]Ibid. Vincent Astor, wealthy scion of a prominent family, had supported Roosevelt. Brandeis, however, remained suspicious.

[42]Brandeis to Frankfurter, 14 August 1933, FP, box 28.

[43]Frankfurter to Brandeis, 16 August 1933, FP, box 28.

[44]Brandeis to Frankfurter, 10 September 1933, FP, box 28. Rosenman wrote to Brandeis later: "I hope that the other matters we discussed at Chatham result in as speedy action." Rosenman to Brandeis, 20 October 1933, G, box 5, folder 3. Roosevelt had moved to regulate excessively high corporate salaries by directing the Federal Trade Commission to investigate them.

[45]Brandeis to Frankfurter, 20 September 1933, FP, box 28. Unfortunately Brandeis did not discuss the specific proposals.

[46]Moley to Brandeis, 18 September 1933, G, box 5, folder 3.

[47]Brandeis to Frankfurter, 28 September 1933, FP, box 115.

[48]Frankfurter to Brandeis, 31 October 1933, G, box 9, folder 2.

[49]Frankfurter to Brandeis, 7 November 1933, G, box 9, folder 2.

[50]Brandeis to Frankfurter, 9 November 1933, FP, box 115. There is a special bitterness in this ironic reference to a quality for which Brandeis had high regard.

[51]Brandeis to Frankfurter, 6 November 1933, FP, box 115. About a week later, Brandeis commented: "My main grief is in the loss of F.D. as an instrument of advanced political action." Brandeis to Frankfurter, 24 November 1933, FP, box 115.

[52]Ibid.

[53]Frankfurter to Brandeis, 3 December 1933, G, box 9, folder 2.

[54]Frankfurter to Roosevelt, 1 October 1933, FP, box 97.

[55]Frankfurter to Roosevelt, 29 October 1933, FP, box 97.

[56]Frankfurter to Roosevelt, 9 November 1933, FP, box 97.

[57]The CWA, established on 8 November 1933, was an emergency unemployment relief program which lasted until March 1934. It spent $933 million on 180,000 projects for four million persons. It was a useful temporary expedient, but fell far short of the commitment Brandeis and Frankfurter desired.

[58]Brandeis to Frankfurter, 25 January 1934, FP, box 115.

[59]Frankfurter to Brandeis, 8 February 1934, G, box 9, folder 2.

[60]Frankfurter to Brandeis, 7 November 1933, G, box 9, folder 2.

[61]Roosevelt to Frankfurter, 12 December 1933, FP, box 97.

[62]Brandeis to Frankfurter, 25 and 30 January 1933, FP, box 28. In his budget message of 3 January 1934, Roosevelt stated that the government "should plan to have a definitely balanced budget for the third year of recovery and from that time on seek a continuing reduction of the national debt." *PPA*, 3:20.

[63]Brandeis to Frankfurter, 7 December 1933, FP, box 115.

[64]Brandeis to Frankfurter, 11 February and 4 March 1934, FP, box 115.

[65]Brandeis to Frankfurter, 11 August 1928, FP, box 28.

[66]Frankfurter to Roosevelt, 29 May 1933, FP, box 97.

[67] Frankfurter to Roosevelt, 29 January 1934, FP, box 97.

[68] Frankfurter to Brandeis, 2 February 1934, G, box 9, folder 2. Despite these efforts, the abolition of contingent fees had not been accomplished by early 1936. Frankfurter to Roosevelt, 19 February 1936, FP, box 98.

[69] Eugene Meyer was a banker and newspaper publisher who after a year at the RFC became publisher of the *Washington Post*. He was instrumental in the formation of the RFC. He drafted the bill creating the corporation and "almost singlehandedly put the new agency into operation." Gerald D. Nash, "Herbert Hoover and the Origins of the Reconstruction Finance Corporation," *Mississippi Valley Historical Review* 46 (1959): 458.

[70] Brandeis to Frankfurter, 14 May 1933, FP, box 28. There is an earlier reference to the "bill drafters." Brandeis was discussing the Securities Act and so he was probably referring to Landis and Cohen. Brandeis to Frankfurter, 26 April 1933, FP, box 28.

[71] Brandeis to Frankfurter, 24 November, 7 and 17 December 1933, FP, box 28.

[72] Frankfurter to Moley, 16 June 1933, FP, box 84.

[73] Frankfurter to Brandeis, 18 July 1933, G, box 9, folder 2.

[74] Frankfurter to Brandeis, 28 July 1933, G, box 9, folder 2. Frankfurter also said that he had Corcoran "reverse the charges in phoning me." Since Frankfurter was a man of modest means, it is possible that Brandeis was helping with the expenses of this "public purpose."

[75] Frankfurter to Missy LeHand, 23 September 1933, FP, box 97.

[76] Corcoran to Frankfurter, 10 October 1933, FP, box 115. "Le bon Dieu" is an ironic reference to Mrs. Brandeis, who carefully guarded her husband's health by protecting him from many visitors, particularly at night.

[77] Corcoran to Frankfurter, 11 December 1933, FP, box 115.

[78] Moley to Frankfurter, 16 December 1933, FP, box 117.

[79] Frankfurter to Brandeis, 31 October 1933, G, box 9, folder 2.

[80] Corcoran to Frankfurter, 30 December 1933, FP, box 49.

[81] Brandeis to Frankfurter, 30 December 1933 and 10 January 1934, FP, box 28.

[82]They accepted his judgments about others. Brandeis to Frankfurter, 5 February 1934, FP, box 28.

[83]Corcoran to Frankfurter, 30 December 1933, FP, box 49.

[84]Brandeis to Frankfurter, 21 February 1934, FP, box 28.

[85]Brandeis to Frankfurter, 25 January 1934, FP, box 28.

[86]Frankfurter to Brandeis, 29 July 1934, G, box 9, folder 2; Brandeis to Frankfurter, 1 August 1934 FP, box 28.

[87]Frankfurter to Brandeis, 4 August 1933, G, box 9, folder 2.

[88]Brandeis to Frankfurter, 3 August 1934, FP, box 28. Moley's growing estrangement from Roosevelt made the plan less and less desirable. By this time a year had passed since Moley left the administration, and he had been drifting steadily away from Roosevelt despite his good work on the securities exchange reform. By October Brandeis was wondering if he was "spurlos versunkt." Brandeis to Frankfurter, 24 October 1934, FP, box 28. He did not, however, openly break with Roosevelt until 1936. Elliot A. Rosen, "Roosevelt and the Brains Trust: An Historiographical Overview," *Political Science Quarterly* 87 (1972): 541.

[89]Frankfurter to Roosevelt, 10 March 1935, FP, box 97.

[90]Ibid.

[91]Frankfurter to Missy LeHand, 24 March 1935, FP, box 244.

[92]Corcoran got into the swing of things quickly. On 4 April he sent Roosevelt a confidential telegram about the dismissal of the *Belcher* case.

[93]James M. Landis, "The Legislative History of the Securities Act of 1933," *George Washington Law Review* 28 (1959): 29-49. Landis recalled that Cohen "had been summoned by Frankfurter from the ranks of active practitioners" (p. 33).

[94]Cohen had difficulty finding his niche, and effort was necessary to keep him in public service. For a time in the fall of 1933, it appeared as though he would return to private practice. By November, however, Judge Mack reported to Brandeis that Cohen was "doing very important work and seems to be more cheerful." Mack to Brandeis, 23 November 1933, FP, box 115. Cohen continued, however, to have recurrent bouts of discontent. Frankfurter wrote to Brandeis in the summer of 1934 that he had had a visit from Cohen "whom it will require a new endeavor to keep in Washington." Frankfurter to Brandeis,

29 August 1934, G, box 9, folder 2. Cohen may have been suffering a letdown following the passage of the Securities Exchange Act in June.

[95]Frankfurter to Brandeis, 28 December 1933, G, box 9, folder 2.

[96]Frankfurter to Brandeis, 20 December 1934 and 4 April 1935, G, box 9, folder 2.

[97]He was consulted, along with Corcoran, by Morgenthau and Oliphant of the Treasury Department on tax matters. See Frankfurter to Brandeis, 20 December 1934 and 22 May 1935, G, box 9, folder 2.

[98]Both Corcoran and Cohen received considerable attention in the press: Max Stern, "The Little Red House," *Today Magazine*, 19 May 1934, p. 5; "Twins: New Deal's Legislative Architects, Corcoran and Cohen," *Newsweek*, 13 July 1935, pp. 24–25; "The Janizariat," *Time*, 12 September 1938, pp. 22–24; Walter Davenport, "It Seems There Were Two Irishmen," *Collier's*, 10 September 1938, pp. 14, 76–79. An embittered "expose" of Corcoran is Alva Johnston's "White House Tommy," *Saturday Evening Post*, 31 July 1937, p. 5. This article prompted Brandeis's puzzled query to Frankfurter: "Who is Alva Johnston?" Brandeis to Frankfurter, 30 July 1937, FP, box 29.

[99]Yet for all his many contributions, Cohen never seemed happy anywhere. Frankfurter reported that when Joseph P. Kennedy, head of the SEC, asked Cohen to become the agency's chief counsel, he got into "a silly snarl over salary . . . with Jim Landis and declined." Frankfurter concluded with a touch of despair that it was "too bad about Ben." Frankfurter to Brandeis, 18 July 1934, G, box 9, folder 2. Landis later recalled simply that Kennedy did not want Cohen. James M. Landis, "Reminiscences," COHC, p. 260–61. Yet Cohen continued in public service for many years, after a lapse due to ill health. During and after the war he worked primarily on diplomatic affairs.

[100]Michael E. Parrish, *Securities Regulation and the New Deal* (New Haven: Yale University Press, 1970), pp. 113–15.

[101]Schlesinger, *Coming of the New Deal*, pp. 456–57. Landis later recalled that Cohen did "all the work" on the SEC bill ("Reminiscences," COHC, p. 261).

[102]Corcoran to Frankfurter, 13 October, 11 December 1933, FP, box 116.

[103]Parrish, *Securities Regulation*, pp. 113–15.

[104]Frankfurter to Landis, 20 December 1933, FP, box 117.

[105]Lowenthal to Frankfurter, 26 October 1933, FP, box 117.

[106]Corcoran to Frankfurter, 16 November 1933, FP, box 116.

[107]Corcoran to Frankfurter, 30 December 1933, FP, box 116. Brandeis told Frankfurter in mid-December that Corcoran had "been in several times. Doubtless he is keeping you fully informed." Brandeis to Frankfurter, 17 December 1933, FP, box 115.

[108]Corcoran assured Frankfurter that they were "working . . . for all L.D.B.'s ideas, and the Stock Exchange regulation." Like Landis, Corcoran reported that Cohen was the key draftsman, though he and Landis helped. Corcoran once referred simply to "Ben's exchange bill." Corcoran to Frankfurter, 11 February 1934, FP, box 116.

[109]Parrish, *Securities Regulations*, p. 121.

[110]Corcoran to Frankfurter, 11 February 1934, FP, box 116.

[111]Frankfurter to Roosevelt, 5 February 1934, FP, box 244.

[112]Frankfurter to Roosevelt, 14 February 1934, FP, box 244.

[113]Frankfurter to Roosevelt, 22 February 1934, FP, box 244.

[114]Schlesinger, *Coming of the New Deal*, pp. 466-67.

[115]Frankfurter to Roosevelt, 8 May 1934, FP, box 97.

[116]Frankfurter to Roosevelt, 8 June 1934, FP, box 97.

CHAPTER VII
A New Beginning

[1]Arthur M. Schlesinger, Jr., *The Politics of Upheaval, 1935-1936* (Boston: Houghton Mifflin Company, 1960), pp. 291, 393.

[2]See the appendix.

[3]Brandeis's relationship with Roosevelt, never very close despite Tugwell's assertions, cooled temporarily after the "Black Monday" decisions of 27 May 1935. But his influence in administration circles remained strong. See below, pp. 144-53.

[4]Even Corcoran prior to his appointment as a presidential aide in March 1935 was more of a scout spying out the terrain than a decision maker.

[5]They were close to only a handful of progressive senators such as Edward Costigan, George Norris, and Robert LaFollette.

[6]Frankfurter to Brandeis, 1 and 19 May 1934, G, box 9, folder 2.

[7]The three had obviously talked over the situation among themselves. Cohen in his letter said that Corcoran "placed the situation regarding your return very fairly." Cohen to Frankfurter, 11 May 1934, FP, box 115. Corcoran said that Brandeis thought he should return quickly. Corcoran to Frankfurter, 11 May 1934, FP. box 116.

[8]Brandeis to Frankfurter, 11 May 1934, FP, box 115. Brandeis said that Frankfurter should not ask Roosevelt if he wanted his advice before September because he might say no, and "he needs you—as does the country—very much."

[9]Corcoran to Frankfurter, 11 May 1934, FP, box 116. Moley had spoken "a little sharply about the three of us pushing reforms too hard and too fast."

[10]Cohen to Frankfurter, 11 May 1934, FP, box 115.

[11]Brandeis to Frankfurter, 7 June 1934, FP, box 28.

[12]Brandeis to Frankfurter, 1 July 1934, FP, box 28. The main topic of the meeting was social security, a subject of great importance to Brandeis. This explains the presence of Brandeis's daughter. Both she and her husband Paul taught at the University of Wisconsin, and both were active in reform, particularly the fight for unemployment compensation.

[13]Frankfurter to Brandeis, 20 July 1934, G, box 9, folder 2. While still a good source of information, Moley was drifting away from Brandeis and Frankfurter. Corcoran reported that he was "vacillating considerably toward the right." Corcoran to Frankfurter, 18 June 1934, FP, box 115. It is interesting that Frankfurter felt he had to be caught up on "the personal relations." The blunt term for this is gossip, but gossip is, in fact, the indispensable tool of the political strategist. Without gossip, without a sense of how people reacted, Frankfurter would have been without a sense of direction. A historian disparaged the Brandeis-Frankfurter correspondence in a letter to the author by characterizing it as gossip, but this is one reason why the correspondence is so valuable. Leo C. Rosten has aptly observed that gossip "is a guide to the whole drama of personal relationships which is, at bottom, the administrative and bureaucratic machine of government" (*The Washington Correspondents* [New York: Harcourt, Brace, and Company, 1937], pp. 14-16).

[14]Frankfurter to Brandeis, 31 August 1934, G, box 9, folder 2.

[15]Brandeis to Frankfurter, 3 August 1934, FP, box 28.

[16]Frankfurter to Brandeis, 31 August 1934, G, box 9, folder 2.

[17]Ibid. Congress established the Federal Housing Administration on 28 June

1934, but Brandeis and Frankfurter believed that the housing program had been inadequate.

[18]Ibid.

[19]Louis D. Brandeis, "Memo of Mr. Brandeis on Irregular Employment, June 1911," FP, box 226, pp. 1-3. Arthur M. Schlesinger, Jr., asserted that the Wisconsin plan of unemployment compensation was developed by John R. Commons in 1921 and revised in the early 1930s by Harold R. Groves and Paul A. Raushenbush, Brandeis's son-in-law (*The Coming of the New Deal* [Boston: Houghton Mifflin Company, 1958] p. 301). The memorandum shows that Brandeis had suggested the basis of social security legislation at least a decade earlier.

[20]Brandeis to Paul Kellogg, 11 March 1928, printed in Melvin I. Urofsky and David W. Levy, *The Letters of Louis D. Brandeis*, 7 vols. (Albany: State University of New York Press, 1922), 5:329.

[21]Paul A. Raushenbush, "Starting Unemployment Compensation in Wisconsin," *Unemployment Insurance Review* 4 (1967); 17-18.

[22]Brandeis to Morris L. Cooke, 10 February 1930, MLCP, box 54. Paul Douglas, *In the Fullness of Time: The Memoirs of Paul H. Douglas* (New York: Harcourt, Brace, Javanovich, 1971), pp. 70-71. In 1930 Douglas was an economics professor at the University of Chicago.

[23]Brandeis to Cooke, 18 April 1930, MLCP, box 54. The institute failed in 1931 due to lack of support. Brandeis to Cooke, 8 October 1931, MLCP, box 54.

[24]Raushenbush, "Starting Unemployment Compensation in Wisconsin," pp. 18-20; Elizabeth Brandeis Raushenbush, "Wisconsin Tackles Job Security," *The Survey*, 15 December 1931, pp. 295-96. Harold Groves was a colleague of the Raushenbushs at the University of Wisconsin who was elected to the legislature in 1930.

[25]Brandeis to Laski, 28 February 1932, M, box 18, folder 3.

[26]Daniel Nelson, *Unemployment Insurance: The American Experience* (Madison: University of Wisconsin Press, 1969), pp. 194-96.

[27]Abraham Epstein, "Enemies of Unemployment Insurance," *New Republic*, 6 September 1933, pp. 94-96.

[28]Elizabeth Brandeis Raushenbush, "Employment Reserves vs. Insurance," *New Republic*, 28 September 1933, pp. 177-78.

[29]Elizabeth Brandeis Raushenbush, "Security for Americans," *New Republic*, 5 December 1934, p. 95.

[30]The idea of a tax incentive had been used by Sen. Robert Wagner and Rep. David Lewis in their bill which had died during the 1934 congressional session. J. Joseph Huthmacher, *Senator Robert P. Wagner and the Rise of Urban Liberalism* (New York: Atheneum, 1968), pp. 174-75.

[31]Raushenbush, "Starting Unemployment Compensation in Wisconsin," p. 22.

[32]Brandeis to Elizabeth Brandeis Raushenbush, 10 September 1933, Urofsky and Levy, *Letters*, 5:520.

[33]Elizabeth Brandeis Raushenbush to Brandeis, 20 September 1933, G, box 7, folder 1.

[34]Elizabeth Brandeis Raushenbush to Brandeis, 24 September 1933, G, box 7, folder 1. Isador Lubin was commissioner of labor statistics from 1934 to 1946.

[35]Brandeis to Elizabeth Brandeis Raushenbush, 30 September 1933, Urofsky and Levy, *Letters*, 5:523. Although Brandeis and Lubin corresponded occasionally, they did not exchange letters on employment compensation.

[36]Raushenbush, "Starting Unemployment Compensation in Wisconsin," pp. 22-23. Elizabeth Brandeis Raushenbush to Brandeis, 8 January 1934, G, box 11, folder 3. Brandeis alluded to this Christmas meeting, saying that "there may be some results of national significance." Brandeis to Alice P. Goldmark, 11 January 1934, Urofsky and Levy, *Letters*, 5:530-31. Also see Charles Wyzanski, "Brandeis," *Atlantic Monthly*, November 1956, p. 69. Wyzanski, who seemed to locate the meeting in Brandeis's apartment, said that his role was "obscure though decisive." Lincoln Filene was a liberal merchant from Boston who was active in many reform groups, including the Savings Bank Insurance League.

[37]Elizabeth Brandeis Raushenbush to Brandeis, 8 January 1934, G, box 11, folder 3. As early as March 1933, Frankfurter was trying to bring Raushenbush to the attention of such people as Perkins. Frankfurter to Perkins, 23 March 1933, FP, box 150.

[38]Raushenbush, "Starting Unemployment Compensation in Wisconsin," p. 23.

[39]Brandeis to Frankfurter, 10 January 1934, FP, box 28.

[40]Frankfurter to Brandeis, 8 February 1934, G, box 9, folder 2.

[41]Franklin D. Roosevelt, "Memo from the President to the Assistant Secretary of Agriculture," 28 February 1934, PSF, Agriculture Department, Tugwell File. Tugwell was opposed to the Wagner-Lewis bill because of its Brandeisian approach. See Rexford G. Tugwell, "New Deal Diary," 6 June, 22 September, and 17 December 1934, RTP.

[42]Elizabeth Brandeis Raushenbush to Brandeis, 12 February 1934, G, box 7, folder 1.

[43]Elizabeth Brandeis Raushenbush to Brandeis, 15 February 1934, G, box 7, folder 1.

[44]*PPA*, 3:162.

[45]Perkins told Roosevelt in April that everybody assumed his support on the basis of his letter to Doughton, and warned that this was "our only chance in twenty-five years to get a bill like this." Quoted in Nelson, *Unemployment Insurance*, p. 204.

[46]*PPA*, 3:162-63, 321-22.

[47]Edwin Witte, *The Development of the Social Security Act* (Madison: University of Wisconsin Press, 1963), p. 201.

[48]Douglas, *In the Fullness of Time*, p. 75. Douglas complained that the people Perkins called on to help with the planning were supporters of the Wisconsin approach.

[49]Corcoran to Frankfurter, 18 June 1934, FP, box 149.

[50]Brandeis to Elizabeth Brandeis Raushenbush, 8 June 1934, Urofsky and Levy, *Letters*, 5:539-40.

[51]Brandeis to Frankfurter, 7 July 1934, FP, box 28.

[52]Schlesinger, *Coming of the New Deal*, p. 305.

[53]Frankfurter to Brandeis, 18 July 1934, G, box 9, folder 2.

[54]Frankfurter to Brandeis, 20 July 1934, G, box 9, folder 2.

[55]Brandeis to Frankfurter, 26 July 1934, G, box 9, folder 2.

[56]Brandeis to Frankfurter, 8 August 1934, FP, box 28.

[57]Ibid.

[58]Frankfurter to Brandeis, 31 August 1934, FP, box 28.

[59]Ibid.

[60]Frankfurter to Roosevelt, undated, FP, box 244. The letter was written after Frankfurter returned from England in the first week of July, and before Roosevelt gave his Wisconsin speech on 9 August.

[61]Ibid.

[62]Frankfurter to Brandeis, 9 August 1934, G, box 9, folder 2. Frankfurter did not know the content of the Wisconsin speech. He wrote to Brandeis: "F.D. has made his Wisconsin speech, but I shall have to wait until tomorrow to know what he said." Roosevelt did not mention the Wisconsin plan in the speech. 3:370-75.

[63]Frankfurter to Brandeis, 17 September 1934, G, box 9, folder 2.

[64]Brandeis to Frankfurter, 28 October 1934, FP, box 28.

[65]Schlesinger, *Coming of the New Deal*, p. 306. Roosevelt was being pressured by the advocates of the nationalist approach. Tugwell noted that he and Hopkins had argued with the president over the Labor Day weekend "against unemployment and for a guarantee of jobs on public works." Tugwell, "Diary," 22 September 1934, RTP.

[66]Nelson, *Employment Insurance*, p. 209. PPA, 3:452-55.

[67]Frances Perkins, *The Roosevelt I Knew* (New York: The Viking Press, 1946), p. 292.

[68]Ibid., pp. 292-93.

[69]Nelson, *Unemployment Insurance*, p. 211.

[70]Frankfurter to Brandeis, 4 January 1935, G, box 9, folder 2.

[71]Tugwell, "Diary," 28 December 1934, RTP. Tugwell did not say who did the rewriting. Hopkins's own power would expand as a result of adopting Tugwell's position, and this may account for his opposition to the Wisconsin approach.

[72]Brandeis to Frankfurter, 31 December 1934, FP, box 28.

[73]Brandeis to Frankfurter, 23 January 1935, FP, box 28.

[74]Frankfurter to Brandeis, 18 January 1935, G, box 9, folder 2.

[75]Wyzanski to Frankfurter, 24 January 1935, FP, box 113.

[76]Frankfurter to Brandeis, 22 January 1935, G, box 9, folder 2.

[77]Schlesinger, *Coming of the New Deal*, pp. 312-13.

[78]Brandeis to Frankfurter, 25 March 1935, FP, box 28.

[79]Frankfurter was in Washington often during the summer of 1935, and had ample opportunity to congratulate him in person.

[80]U.S., *Statutes at Large*, vol. 49, p. 620ff; Schlesinger, *Coming of the New Deal*, p. 313.

[81]Brandeis to Frankfurter, 6 February 1937, FP, box 28.

[82]Brandeis to Elizabeth Brandeis Raushenbush, 14 October 1939, Urofsky and Levy, *Letters*, 5:625.

[83]Schlesinger, *Coming of the New Deal*, p. 306.

[84]Brandeis to Frankfurter, 25 January 1934, FP, box 28.

[85]Frankfurter to Brandeis, 8 February 1934, G, box 9, folder 2.

[86]Frankfurter to Roosevelt, 25 October 1934, FP, box 97. Unfortunately Frankfurter did not write to Brandeis about the details of the meeting.

[87]Frankfurter to Roosevelt, 16 October 1934, FP, box 97.

[88]Frankfurter to Roosevelt, 21 November 1934, FP, box 97. Frankfurter evidently thought highly of this effort. He sent a copy of the letter to Brandeis. Frankfurter to Brandeis, 21 November 1934, G, box 9, folder 2.

[89]Frankfurter to Roosevelt, 26 November 1934, FDRL. Four days earlier, Brandeis had written to Frankfurter advocating greater housing construction. Brandeis to Frankfurter, 22 November 1934, FP, box 28. Five billion dollars was probably Brandeis's figure.

[90]Harold L. Ickes, *The Secret of Harold L. Ickes* (New York: Simon and Schuster, 1953), 5 September, 7 December 1934.

[91]Frankfurter to Roosevelt, 29 April 1935, FP, box 98.

[92]Brandeis to Frankfurter, 16 April 1935, FP, box 28.

[93]William Leuchtenburg, *Franklin D. Roosevelt and the New Deal* (New York: Harper & Row, 1963), p. 125.

[94]Ibid. Roosevelt did not think such a sustained effort possible. He denied that he could borrow three billion dollars a year for ten years. Evidently Brandeis had suggested something like this. Frankfurter to Roosevelt, 31 August 1934, FP, box 97.

[95]Ibid.

[96]Hopkins preferred work relief to direct relief even though it was more expensive because it "preserves a man's morale. It saves his skill. It gives him a chance to do something socially useful" (*Vital Speeches of the Day*, 31 December

1934, p. 211). He did not link work relief to recovery as did Frankfurter and Brandeis.

[97] Brandeis to Frankfurter, 24 November 1932, FP, box 28.

[98] Brandeis to Frankfurter, 28 May 1933 and 11 May 1934, FP, box 28.

[99] Brandeis to Frankfurter, 29 September 1934, FP, box 28.

[100] Frankfurter to Brandeis, 20 December 1934, G, box 9, folder 2.

[101] Schlesinger argued that the program "proceeded from Morgenthau's own mistrust of large concentrations of economic power as well as from the views of his exceedingly able general counsel, Herman Oliphant, a quiet but radical member of the neo-Brandeisian group" (*Coming of the New Deal* p. 325). This statement is incomplete. Frankfurter and Brandeis had been consistently urging tax reform on Roosevelt. Roosevelt requested the Treasury to cooperate with Frankfurter. Morgenthau, however, represented the program as a departmental creation. He mentioned Frankfurter briefly in connection with the intercorporate dividend tax. John M. Blum, ed., *From the Morgenthau Diaries* (Boston: Houghton Mifflin, 1959), pp. 298–300.

[102] *PPA*, 4:36. By January 1935 three aspects of Brandeis's reform program had been accepted by Roosevelt and passed on to Morgenthau: a limitation on contingent fees in government claims, excise taxes on "tramp corporations" (corporations organized in states in which they do not do a substantial amount of their business), and excise taxes on insiders' transactions. Max Freedman, ed., *Roosevelt and Frankfurter, Their Correspondence, 1928–1945* (Boston: Little, Brown, and Company, 1967), pp. 250–51. These proposals, though desirable, were limited and did not constitute a major shift in policy.

[103] Raymond Moley, *The First New Deal* (New York: Harcourt, Brace & World, 1966), p. 531.

[104] Schlesinger, *Politics of Upheaval*, p. 326.

[105] Brandeis to Frankfurter, 24 February 1935, FP, box 28.

[106] Brandeis to Frankfurter, 12 March 1935, FP, box 28.

[107] Niles to Frankfurter, 22 April 1935, quoted in Freedman, *Roosevelt and Frankfurter*, pp. 260–61. Niles, a Bostonian, was director of the Ford Hall Forum. He later became an assistant to Harry Hopkins. Ickes referred to him as a "Progressive from Boston" (*Diary*, 15 May 1935).

[108] Frankfurter to LeHand, 22 April 1935, FP, box 98; Roosevelt to Frankfurter, 20 April 1935, and Frankfurter to Roosevelt, 30 April 1935, FP, box 98.

[109]Frankfurter to Brandeis, 3 April 1935, FP, box 98.

[110]Frankfurter to Roosevelt, 3 May 1935, FP, box 98. All had supported Roosevelt in 1932, though only Costigan and Wheeler were Democrats.

[111]Frankfurter to Roosevelt, 16 May 1935, FP, box 98.

[112]Ickes, *Diary*, 15 May 1935.

[113]Frankfurter to Roosevelt, 16 May 1935, FP, box 98. On 19 May Brandeis wrote to Frankfurter asking for information about the conference. This was three days after his eyes were supposedly shining with warm satisfaction.

[114]Frankfurter to Brandeis, 21 and 22 May 1935, G, box 9, folder 2.

[115]Frankfurter to Brandeis, 21 July 1935, G, box 9, folder 2.

[116]Ickes, *Diary*, 10 August 1935. In November 1935 Frankfurter wrote to Richberg: "You know how relatively rare my visits in Washington have been since March, 1933." Frankfurter to Richberg, 19 November 1935, FP, box 159. The truth was that Frankfurter saw a great deal of Roosevelt in 1935 (particularly in the summer) despite such disclaimers—which probably did not fool any knowledgeable observers. Acheson recalled that in 1939 a security guard at the White House admitted Frankfurter even though he was not on the visitor list because he was such "a constant caller." Dean Acheson, *Morning and Noon* (Boston: Houghton Mifflin, 1965), p. 211.

[117]Frankfurter to Brandeis, 24 May 1935, G, box 9, folder 2.

[118]Frankfurter to Brandeis, 14 June 1935, G, box 9, folder 2. Frankfurter, Corcoran, and Cohen were all involved in drafting. Working productively with the Treasury Department was a new experience for Frankfurter.

[119]Moley, *First New Deal*, p. 531.

[120]*PPA*, 4:270–76.

[121]Schlesinger, *Politics of Upheaval*, p. 328.

[122]Brandeis to Frankfurter, 20 June 1935, FP, box 28.

[123]Schlesinger, *Politics of Upheaval*, p. 328.

[124]Frankfurter to Brandeis, 10 July 1935, G, box 9, folder 2; Brandeis to Frankfurter, 19 July 1935, FP, box 28.

[125]Frankfurter to Brandeis, 21 July 1935, G, box 9, folder 2.

126U.S., Congress, Senate, *Congressional Record*, 74th Cong., 1st Sess., 1935, 79, 9657-59, quoted in Eugene Gerhart, *America's Advocate: Robert H. Jackson* (Indianapolis: Bobbs-Merrill, 1958), p. 71.

127Brandeis to Frankfurter, 9 August 1935, FP, box 28; Frankfurter to Brandeis, 15 August 1935, G, box 9, folder 2.

128Sidney Ratner, *American Taxation* (New York: W. W. Norton Company, 1942), pp. 469-72.

129*U.S., Statutes at Large*, vol. 49, p. 1014.

130Brandeis to Frankfurter, 30 August 1935, FP, box 28.

131William Randolph Hearst characterized Roosevelt's tax program as "essentially communism." Schlesinger, *Politics of Upheaval*, p. 329.

132Brandeis, "The Case Against the Holding Company," 23 November 1931, memorandum in Pinchot Papers, box 2029, quoted in Philip J. Funigiello, *Toward a National Power Policy: The New Deal and the Electric Utility Industry, 1933-1941* (Pittsburgh: University of Pittsburgh, 1973), p. 21. Funigiello says that all opponents of the holding company "drew from a common intellectual source, Justice Louis D. Brandeis."

133Frankfurter to Brandeis, 7 August 1932, G, box 9, folder 2.

134Frankfurter to Moley, 28 February 1933, FP, box 84.

135Funigiello, *Toward a National Power Policy*, p. 40.

136Ibid., p. 42. Morris Cooke, a friend of Brandeis, was a consulting engineer active in various aspects of government power policy.

137Ibid., p. 50.

138Ibid., p. 52.

139Ibid., pp. 64-65.

140Michael E. Parrish, *Securities Regulation and the New Deal* (New Haven: Yale University Press, 1970), p. 156. The quote is from Stimson's diary, 10 February 1935.

141Frankfurter to Brandeis, 20 December 1934, 22 January 1935, G, box 9, folder 2.

142Funigiello, *Toward a National Power Policy*, p. 65.

[143]Schlesinger, *Politics of Upheaval*, pp. 305–6. Schlesinger cited a letter he received from Corcoran in 1958. Frankfurter continued to argue for a more flexible approach. He wrote to Roosevelt that holding companies had no ultimate justification and that the national interest demanded their elimination, but he cautioned that "they can not be eliminated overnight." Frankfurter to Roosevelt, 21 January 1935, FP, box 98.

[144]Funigiello, *Toward a National Power Policy*, p. 66.

[145]Schlesinger, *Politics of Upheaval*, p. 311.

[146]*PPA*, 4:98–102.

[147]Brandeis to Frankfurter, 25 March 1935, FP, box 28.

[148]Frankfurter to Brandeis, 15 March 1935, G, box 9, folder 2.

[149]Moley, *First New Deal*, p. 158. A study of Frankfurter's appointments, culled from his correspondence, also indicates that he spent a good deal of time with Roosevelt during this period.

[150]Frankfurter to Brandeis, 13 April 1935, G, box 9, folder 2.

[151]Frankfurter to Wheeler, 3 May 1935, FP, box 111.

[152]Schlesinger, *Politics of Upheaval*, p. 313; Frankfurter to Wheeler, 12 June 1935, FP, box 111. He also expressed the appreciation of Cohen and Corcoran for "the generosity and graciousness with which you have treated them throughout this fight."

[153]Frankfurter to Brandeis, 14 June 1935, G, box 9, folder 2.

[154]Brandeis to Frankfurter, 20 June 1935, FP, box 28.

[155]Funigiello, *Toward a National Power Policy*, pp. 67–69.

[156]Ibid., pp. 94–95.

[157]Moley, *First New Deal*, p. 158; Parrish, *Securities Regulation*, p. 116. Holding companies were permitted to control more than one integrated utility system "if the additional systems could not stand alone economically and were not so large or so scattered as to impair the advantages of localized management, efficient operation, or effective regulation." Funigiello, *Toward a National Power Policy*, p. 96.

[158]Moley, *First New Deal*, p. 158.

[159]Brandeis and Frankfurter did not comment on the final version in their correspondence.

[160]Ellis Hawley, *The New Deal and the Problem of Monopoly* (Princeton: Princeton University Press, 1966), p. 343.

[161]In 1933 Frankfurter wrote to Margold that Senators Costigan, LaFollette, Cutting, Norris, Borah, Wheeler, and Johnson could be trusted to make sound personnel recommendations. He concluded: "So far as Costigan, LaFollette, Norris, and Borah are concerned, it will, I think, do no harm to mention my name." Frankfurter to Margold, 30 March 1933, FP, box 149. Given Wagner's prominence as a liberal senator, the omission of his name is pointed.

[162]Rexford G. Tugwell, *The Democratic Roosevelt: A Biography of FDR* (New York: Doubleday & Company, 1957), pp. 219–20.

[163]Huthmacher, *Senator Robert F. Wagner*, p. 154.

[164]Frankfurter to Brandeis, 15 March 1935, G, box 9, folder 2.

[165]Frankfurter to Brandeis, 22 May 1935, G, box 9, folder 2.

[166]Brandeis to Frankfurter, 14 August 1933, FP, box 28.

[167]Roosevelt himself was not enthusiastic about the Wagner bill. Huthmacher, *Senator Robert F. Wagner*, p. 154.

[168]Cooke's letters to Brandeis do not deal with REA matters.

[169]This act established NRA-type regulations for the bituminous coal industry.

[170]See above, pp. 61-63.

CHAPTER VIII
The Supreme Court

[1]*Home Building & Loan Association* v. *Blaisdell*, 290 U.S. 398 (1934); *Nebbia* v. *New York*, 292 U.S. 571 (1934). Both cases were five-to-four decisions. George Sutherland, Willis Van Devanter, Pierce Butler, and James McReynolds (the so-called "Four Horsemen") constituted a conservative bloc.

[2]U.S., *Statutes at Large*, vol. 48, p. 195.

[3]Paul L. Murphy, *The Constitution in Crisis Times, 1918–1969* (New York:

Harper & Row, 1972), p. 136; Alfred H. Kelly and Winfred A. Harbison, *The American Constitution: Its Origins and Development* (New York: W. W. Norton Company, 1970), p. 739.

[4]*Panama Refining Company* v. *Ryan*, 293 U.S. 430 (1935). Brandeis did not comment on this case in his correspondence with Frankfurter.

[5]Freund to Frankfurter, 11 December 1934, FP, box 56.

[6]Frankfurter to Wyzanski, 22 January 1935, FP, box 118.

[7]Kelly and Harbison, *The American Constitution*, p. 740.

[8]*Gold Cases*, 294 U.S. 307 (1935).

[9]Brandeis had written an earlier decision in a case involving the government's contractual obligation. In *Lynch* v. *U.S.*, 292 U.S. 577 (1934), he acknowledged that the government could not be sued without its consent, but he also argued that valid contracts constitute property rights protected by the Fifth Amendment. When the government enters into contractual relations "its rights and duties therein are governed generally by the law applicable to contracts between individuals." Brandeis to Frankfurter, 24 February 1935, FP, box 28.

[10]*Stewart Dry Goods* v. *Lewis*, 294 U.S. 569–70 (1935).

[11]*Railroad Retirement Board* v. *Alton Railroad Company*, 295 U.S. 392 (1935). Brandeis and Frankfurter had expected Roberts to be a judicial liberal. When he was appointed, Brandeis wrote to Frankfurter that his confirmation "closes happily a worthy struggle." Brandeis to Frankfurter, 21 May 1930, FP, box 27. Frankfurter, however, called his decision in the *Railroad* case a tragedy. Frankfurter to Brandeis, 7 May 1935, G, box 9, folder 2.

[12]*Louisville Bank* v. *Radford*, 295 U.S. 601–3 (1935). This was the kind of decision Brandeis would have liked to have written in the *Gold Cases*. Frankfurter, in an undated memo to Roosevelt, (FP, box 98) advised him not to appeal the case until after the Justice Department could be reorganized. He told Roosevelt that the petition for certiorari could be withdrawn under the pretext that since the government's case had been sustained by several district courts, only an appeal to the Sixth Circuit Court was necessary. Frankfurter's advice was probably intended to prevent the administration embarrassment. Frankfurter and Brandeis had different roles in connection with Court matters, and this caused some tension from time to time.

[13]*Humphrey's Executor* v. *United States*, 295 U.S. 602 (1935). William E. Leuchtenburg, "The Case of the Contentious Commissioner," reprinted in Richard Lowitt and Joseph F. Wall, *Interpreting Twentieth Century America: A Reader* (New York: Crowell, 1973), pp. 272–80.

[14]*Myers* v. *United States*, 272 U.S. 52 (1926).

[15]Leuchtenburg, "The Contentious Commissioner," p. 280.

[16]*Humphrey's Executor* v. *United States*, 295 U.S. 602 (1935).

[17]Arthur M. Schlesinger, Jr., *The Politics of Upheaval, 1935-1936* (Boston: Houghton Mifflin Company, 1960), p. 279.

[18]*Myers* v. *United States*, 272 U.S. 52 (1926).

[19]James Landis, "Mr. Justice Brandeis: A Law Clerk's View," JMLP, article and book file, box 169.

[20]Ibid.

[21]Frankfurter to Calvert Magruder, 19 October 1933, FP, box 82.

[22]A. T. Mason, *Brandeis: A Free Man's Life* (New York: The Viking Press, 1946), p. 619. Mason says that he got his information from reporters who had had a confidential interview with Brandeis at Chatham on 23 June 1935.

[23]*Schechter* v. *United States*, 295 U.S. 528 (1935).

[24]Ibid.

[25]Schlesinger, *Politics of Upheaval*, p. 286.

[26]Ibid., p. 287. Speech writer Stanley High reported that the talk was that the NRA decision was "the worst blow the pres. ever had." High wrote that Missy LeHand told him Roosevelt was irritable and troubled the evening of 27 May. Diary of Stanley High, 20 March 1936, FDRL.

[27]Quoted in Mason, *A Free Man's Life*, p. 620.

[28]Ibid.

[29]Harry Hopkins, "Statement to Me by Thomas Corcoran Giving His Recollection of the Genesis of the Supreme Court Fight," 3 April 1939, Harry Hopkins Papers, FDRL, quoted by Schlesinger, *Politics of Upheaval*, p. 280.

[30]Ibid.

[31]He wrote to his good friend Judge Julian Mack: "I think our Court did much good for the country yesterday." Brandeis to Mack, 29 May 1935, P, box 61, folder 1.

[32]Felix Frankfurter, "Memo on the Belcher Case," undated, attached to a

letter of Paula Tully to Frankfurter dated 13 March 1935, FP, box 98. Although Roosevelt's name does not appear on the memo, its wording implies that it was sent to him. The existing NRA law was to expire in June 1935 and Frankfurter hoped that it would die. The next best thing would be for a weakened and constitutionally unobjectionable version to be passed by Congress. Schlesinger, *Politics of Upheaval*, p. 276.

[33] Murphy, *Constitution in Crisis Times*, pp. 138–39.

[34] Frankfurter, "Memo on the Belcher Case."

[35] Frankfurter to Brandeis, 4 April 1935, G, box 9, folder 2.

[36] Corcoran to Roosevelt, 4 April 1935, FP, box 98.

[37] Max Freedman, ed., *Roosevelt and Frankfurter, Their Correspondence, 1928-1945* (Boston: Little, Brown, and Company, 1967), pp. 259-60.

[38] Frankfurter to Brandeis, 13 April 1935, G, box 9, folder 2.

[39] Corcoran to Roosevelt, 4 April 1935, FP, box 98.

[40] Riesman to Frankfurter, 21 November 1935, FP, box 127.

[41] Rexford G. Tugwell, "Notes for a New Deal Diary," 31 May 1935, RTP. In his entry the day before, Tugwell indicated that "we" expected that at least Cardozo and Stone would have gone with the administration. They had given up on Brandeis.

[42] Frankfurter to Roosevelt, 29 May 1935, FP, box 98.

[43] Ibid. This warning was particularly apt in the light of Roosevelt's court plan of 1937, which did constitute such a frontal assault.

[44] Frankfurter to Roosevelt, 30 May 1935, FP, box 98.

[45] Ibid. Perkins reported that this idea originated with Frankfurter in 1932. On the last night of the 1935 session, the public contracts bill was passed by Congress. It was "an important forerunner of the Fair Labor Standards Act." Frances Perkins, *The Roosevelt I Knew* (New York: The Viking Press, 1946), pp. 253-54.

[46] Frankfurter to Roosevelt, 30 May 1935, FP, box 98.

[47] Ibid.

[48] Ibid.

[49]In any case a constitutional amendment would not be a quick solution because of the time required for ratification.

[50]Frankfurter to Brandeis, 3 June 1935, G, box 9, folder 2.

[51]Schlesinger, *Politics of Upheaval*, p. 286. The President was not, as some reported, angry or intemperate. Frankfurter wrote to Brandeis that the talk "was admirably calm and relaxed." Frankfurter to Brandeis, 3 June 1935, G, box 9, folder 2.

[52]Frankfurter to Brandeis, 3 June 1935, G, box 9, folder 2.

[53]Frankfurter to Rosenman, 27 May 1952, FP, box 99.

[54]Schlesinger, *Politics of Upheaval*, pp. 286–87.

[55]Roosevelt to Hapgood, 22 July 1935, special XGP 31, "Papers of Louis D. Brandeis," FDRL. The phrase "Cape Cod friend" alludes to Brandeis's habit of spending his summers at Chatham, Massachusetts.

[56]Harold L. Ickes, *The Secret Diary of Harold L. Ickes* (New York: Simon and Schuster, 1953), 13 November 1935.

[57]Kurland to Frankfurter, 14 December 1953, FP, box 72. Kurland quoted the passage from Ickes's *Diary*, and Frankfurter replied: "Ickes accurate! He was constitutionally unable to be so whenever his ego was involved and seldom was his ego not involved." Frankfurter criticized the gullibility of historians for "discussing the Ickes Diary without any considerations of its trustworthiness." Frankfurter to Kurland, 17 December 1953. It is not clear, however, why Ickes's ego should have been involved in this instance.

[58]Brandeis to Frankfurter, 20 September 1935, FP, box 28.

[59]*Colgate* v. *Harvey*, 296 U.S. 404 (1935); Frankfurter to Stone, 9 January 1936, FP, box 105.

[60]*United States* v. *Butler*, 297 U.S. 87 (1936).

[61]Frankfurter to Stone, 9 January 1936, FP, box 105.

[62]*Ashwander* v. *Tennessee Valley Authority*, 297 U.S. 288 (1936).

[63]Frankfurter to Clark, 18 February 1936, FP, box 44.

[64]*Carter* v. *Carter Coal Company*, 298 U.S. 238 (1936).

[65]Kelly and Harbison, *The American Constitution*, p. 752.

[66] *Carter* v. *Carter Coal Company.*

[67] Ibid.

[68] Ibid.

[69] Diary of Stanley High, 18 May 1936. "Mac" was presidential secretary Marvin McIntyre.

[70] Ibid.

[71] *Morehead* v. *New York ex. rel. Tipaldo*, 298 U.S. 587 (1936).

[72] Ibid.

[73] Murphy, *Constitution in Crisis Times*, p. 151, quoted from *Newsweek*, 13 June 1936, p. 12.

[74] Diary of Stanley High, 28 October 1936.

CHAPTER IX
The Court Fight

[1] Roosevelt to Frankfurter, 1 January 1937, FP, box 98.

[2] Frankfurter to Roosevelt, 15 January 1937, FP, box 98.

[3] U.S. 75th Cong., 1st sess., *Senate Report*, p. 711. The birth years of the justices were: Brandeis, 1856; Butler, 1866; Cardozo, 1870; Hughes, 1862; McReynolds, 1862; Roberts, 1875; Stone, 1872; Sutherland, 1862; Van Devanter, 1859.

[4] Frankfurter to Roosevelt, 7 February 1937, FP, box 98.

[5] Joseph Alsop and Turner Catledge, *168 Days* (New York: Doubleday, Doran & Company, 1938), p. 31.

[6] Ibid., pp. 33–36.

[7] Samuel I. Rosenman, *Working with Roosevelt* (New York: Harper & Brothers, 1952), p. 149.

[8] Robert Sherwood, *Roosevelt and Hopkins* (New York: Harper and Brothers, 1948), p. 90, quoted from Hopkins's "Memorandum on the Court Fight,"

written in April 1939. It is interesting that Richberg appeared in this inner circle. The eagle-eyed Brandeis wrote to Frankfurter in March 1936 that there was "an alarming resurgency of Donald Richberg." Brandeis to Frankfurter, 18 March 1936, FP, box 28.

[9]Rosenman, *Working with Roosevelt*, p. 156.

[10]Sherwood, *Roosevelt and Hopkins*, p. 90. Hopkins quoted from a statement Corcoran had made to him.

[11]Brandeis to Frankfurter, 6 February 1937, FP, box 28. Brandeis observed prophetically: "It looks as if he were inviting some pretty radical splits in the Democratic party & allies."

[12]Roosevelt to Frankfurter, 9 February 1937, FP, box 98.

[13]Frankfurter to Roosevelt, 15 February 1937, FP, box 98.

[14]Frankfurter to Roosevelt, 18 February 1937, FP, box 98.

[15]Ibid. There seems to be a trace of sophistry in these words. To paraphrase Brandeis, how would such words sound coming from Huey Long?

[16]William E. Leuchtenburg flatly says that Frankfurter "abhorred" the court plan ("Origins of the Court Fight," in Harold M. Hollingsworth and William Holmes, *Essays on the New Deal* [Austin: University of Texas Press, 1969], pp. 340-63). Liva Baker (*Felix Frankfurter* [New York: Coward-McCann, 1969], pp. 182–83) and Alsop and Catledge (*168 Days*, pp. 75–76) argue that Frankfurter opposed the plan. So close a friend as Dean Acheson had to confess that Frankfurter never expressed an opinion on the subject to him, but that he guessed that he "was dead against it" while remaining silent because of his "loyalty and devotion to the President" (*Morning and Noon* [Boston: Houghton Mifflin, 1965], p. 202). James M. Landis recalled that "Frankfurter never went along with the President on that. . . . There were a lot of guys that didn't go along with him" ("Reminiscences," COHC, p. 49).

[17]Baker, *Frankfurter*, p. 183, based on an interview with Adrian Fisher on 31 August 1967.

[18]Frankfurter, "The Supreme Court and the Public," *Forum*, June 1930, p. 334. Earlier, in 1925, Frankfurter had argued in an unsigned editorial in the *New Republic* that the "real battles of liberalism are not won in the Supreme Court" but in "the general drift of public opinion" ("Can the Supreme Court Guarantee Toleration?" *New Republic*, 17 June 1925, p. 178).

[19]Felix Frankfurter, "The Supreme Court of the United States," *Encyclopedia of the Social Sciences* (New York: Macmillan Co., 1934), vol. 45, reprinted in *Law*

and Politics; Occasional Papers of Felix Frankfurter, 1913–1938, ed. Archibald MacLeish and E. F. Prichard (New York: Capricorn Books, 1962), p. 28.

[20]Max Freedman, ed., *Roosevelt and Frankfurter, Their Correspondence, 1928–1945* (Boston: Little, Brown, and Company, 1967), p. 372.

[21]Stephen Wise to Brandeis, 1 September 1937, P, box 66, folder 2. Wise observed: "Alas, Felix is ill and he must for a time pass out of the picture." Some observers attributed this illness to the strains imposed by the fight. Matthew Josephson, "Profiles," *New Yorker*, 30 November 1937, p. 26. Frankfurter, however, described his malady as fatigue due to spinal defects aggravated by poor posture. The problem, he reported, was "all mechanical, the miserable disharmony of the bones." Frankfurter to Roosevelt, 1 September 1937, FP, box 98.

[22]Other men around the president suffered similar conflicts. Robert Jackson, drawn by Roosevelt into the inner circle, observed: "While the proposal seemed to me in many respects unsatisfactory, once the President had become committed to it, it was the only proposal that had a chance, and there was genuine need for some kind of reform in the Supreme Court." Eugene Gerhart, *America's Advocate: Robert H. Jackson* (Indianapolis: Bobbs-Merrill, 1958), p. 108. Gerhart concluded that Jackson "had committed himself to become a leading spokesman for a plan he did not formulate, for a scheme he did not personally admire as a lawyer. Such are the demands of political loyalty."

[23]Frankfurter to Brandeis, 26 March 1937, FP, box 28. Frankfurter noted on the draft that the letter was never sent.

[24]Hapgood to Frankfurter, 21 March 1937, FP, box 65.

[25]Stone to Frankfurter, 10 March 1937, FP, box 105.

[26]Burlingham to Frankfurter, 7 February 1937, FP, box 34.

[27]Frankfurter to Burlingham, 16 March 1937, FP, box 34. The temptation he felt to become solicitor general was much less than "terrific."

[28]Frankfurter to G. Root, 4 March 1937, FP, box 34.

[29]There is no evidence that they saw each other during this period.

[30]Charles B. Hughes, "Biographical Notes," pp. 20–21, HP.

[31]Ibid.

[32]A. T. Mason, *Brandeis: A Free Man's Life* (New York: The Viking Press, 1946, p. 626. The source for this statement is an interview Mason had with Wheeler on 25 February 1944.

[33]Ibid.

[34]Alsop and Catledge, *168 Days*, pp. 125–26.

[35]Hughes's letter was a detailed defense of the Court's efficiency. He argued that the Court was "fully abreast" of its work and that "this gratifying condition has obtained for several years." Hughes further stated that an increase in the number of justices would impair the Court's efficiency. Hughes, "Biographical Notes," pp. 22–23.

[36]Frankfurter to Brandeis, 26 March 1937, FP, box 28. This was not one of Frankfurter's most persuasive arguments. He narrowed the question to suit his own convenience. For Brandeis, tampering with the Court clearly was a matter of basic policy.

[37]Ibid.

[38]Frankfurter to Brandeis, 31 March 1937, FP, box 28. Ironically, Brandeis had written earlier: "Overruling Atkins case must give you some satisfaction." Brandeis to Frankfurter, 29 March 1937, FP, box 28.

[39]*Morehead* v. *New York ex rel. Tipaldo*, 298 U.S. 587 (1936).

[40]*West Coast Hotel Co.* v. *Parrish*, 300 U.S. 379 (1937).

[41]Frankfurter to Brandeis, 31 March 1937, FP, box 28. Frankfurter later changed his opinion of Roberts's role in the case. See above, pp.

[42]Ibid. Stone also resented the way Hughes handled the letter. He wrote to Frankfurter that he did not approve of "such an extra-official expression on a constitutional question by the Court or its members," and said that Cardozo agreed with him. He rebutted Hughes's claim that there was not enough time to consult the other justices by observing that every one was in town and "could have been brought together for a conference on an hour's telephone notice or less." Stone to Frankfurter, 21 December 1939, FP, box 105.

[43]Frankfurter to Roosevelt, 30 March 1937, FP, box 98.

[44]Brandeis to Frankfurter, 5 April 1937, FP, box 28.

[45]Brandeis to Frankfurter, 25 April 1937, FP, box 28. Brandeis commented that "it was fine to see you again."

[46]Freedman, *Roosevelt and Frankfurter*, p. 396.

[47]Frankfurter was equally reticent.

[48]Brandeis to Frankfurter, 26 May 1937, FP, box 28.

⁴⁹Brandeis to Frankfurter, 5 January 1938, FP, box 28.

⁵⁰James M. Burns, *Roosevelt: The Lion and the Fox* (New York: Harcourt, Brace and Company, 1956), pp. 300–302. Louis W. Koenig asserts that Corcoran was opposed to the plan but went along with it out of loyalty to Roosevelt (*The Invisible Presidency* [New York: Holt, Rinehart and Winston, 1960], p. 345). Harold L. Ickes depicted Corcoran as consistently optimistic about the outcome of the struggle (*The Secret Diary of Harold L. Ickes* [New York: Simon and Schuster, 1953], 25 April 1937). In early May Ickes reported Corcoran's reaction to those senators who objected to Roosevelt's appointing so many men by saying that it reminded him of the story of the man who was told not to worry about his new wife being pregnant when he married her because "she is only a little bit pregnant" (*Diary*, 3 May 1937). When Van Devanter resigned, Corcoran assumed that it was done to embarrass Roosevelt and, significantly enough, believed that Brandeis had been in on the plot (*Diary*, 15 June 1937). Cohen's attitude to the plan was ambivalent. He believed that something was needed to bring the Court into line, but he did not specifically endorse the president's plan. Cohen to Frankfurter, 9 July 1937, FP, box 45.

⁵¹Burns, *Lion and the Fox*, p. 302.

⁵²*National Labor Relations Board* v. *Jones & Laughlin Steel Corporation*, 301 U.S. 1 (1937).

⁵³Frankfurter to Roosevelt, 12 April 1937, FP, box 98.

⁵⁴Roosevelt to Frankfurter, 5 April 1937, FP, box 98.

⁵⁵Frankfurter to Roosevelt, 21 April 1937, FP, box 98. The juxaposition of "the Good Lord" and "the principle of luck" is theological eclecticism of a high order!

⁵⁶Burlingham to Roosevelt, 25 May 1937. See Freedman, *Roosevelt and Frankfurter*, p. 399. Burlingham added that the other recommendations "should of course, be fully discussed and decided on their merits."

⁵⁷Ibid. p. 400. Freedman does not provide documentation for this assertion. He must have gotten this information from Frankfurter himself.

⁵⁸Burns, *Lion and the Fox*, pp. 306–8.

⁵⁹Frankfurter to Brandeis, 15 July 1937, FP, box 28. While Frankfurter and Wheeler had never been close, they had cooperated on the holding company bill and had carried on a pleasant correspondence. Their correspondence ended 14 December 1936, and was not resumed until 1957. FP, box 111.

⁶⁰Ibid.

[61]Brandeis to Frankfurter, 30 July 1937, FP, box 28.

[62]Frankfurter to Roosevelt, 20 July 1937, FP, box 98. Assuming that Lehman's action was the expression of an honest conviction, it is difficult to see why it should have been so bitterly resented.

[63]Burns, *Lion and the Fox*, p. 315.

[64]Felix Frankfurter, "Notes for an Address on the State of the Union," FP, box 98.

[65]Ibid.

[66]Frankfurter employed a similar tactic in connection with the invalidation of the NRA. Roosevelt thanked Frankfurter for his suggestions. Roosevelt to Frankfurter, 12 August 1937, FP, box 98.

[67]Raymond Moley, *The First New Deal* (New York: Harcourt, Brace & World, 1966), p. 386. Moley saw something of a "corrupt bargin" involved in Frankfurter's stance during the Court fight. He said that Frankfurter knew Roosevelt was considering him for the Court and that his refusal to denounce the president's plan was explicable only in this context. This opinion, expressed to Frankfurter during the struggle, led to the final break between them. After that Moley "had no more letters or telegrams. And when I wrote congratulating him on his appointment there was no reply."

[68]Cohen to Frankfurter, 11 October 1937, FP, box 45.

[69]Brandeis to Frankfurter, 14 November 1937, FP, box 28. Corcoran had written to Brandeis in June about the business details of an effort by Sherman Mittel of the National Home Library Foundation to publish a book by David Cushman Coyle entitled *Why Pay Taxes?* The letter is crisp and businesslike. Corcoran to Brandeis, 26 June 1937, M, box 12, folder 2.

[70]Brandeis to Frankfurter, 30 January 1938, FP, box 28.

[71]Brandeis to Frankfurter, 11 February 1938, FP, box 28. See also a memo written by Wehle, 31 December 1937, PPF 2335, box 1; Wehle to Roosevelt, 31 December 1937, and Roosevelt to McIntyre, 4 January 1938, PPF 693.

[72]Frankfurter to Brandeis, 12 July 1938, FP, box 28.

[73]Felix Frankfurter, "Mr. Justice Roberts," *University of Pennsylvania Law Review* 104 (1955): 313.

[74]Frankfurter to Roosevelt, 30 March 1937, FP, box 98.

CHAPTER X
The Later New Deal

[1]William E. Leuchtenburg, *Franklin D. Roosevelt and the New Deal* (New York: Harper & Row, 1963). The Court fight hurt Roosevelt, but it is certainly not a complete explanation. James T. Patterson argues that an essentially rural-based conservative coalition would have emerged in Congress during Roosevelt's second term even if the Court fight had never occurred (*Congressional Conservatism and the New Deal* [Lexington: University Press of Kentucky, 1967], pp. 128, 330-31).

[2]Brandeis to Frankfurter, 3 December 1935, FP, box 28.

[3]Frankfurter to Roosevelt, 30 January 1936, FP, box 97.

[4]Frankfurter to Roosevelt, 19 February 1936, FP, box 97. In early March Frankfurter warned Roosevelt that some lawyers were confident that they could "kill any such 'outrageous attempts' to restrict free pursuit of profit by the great leaders of the bar!" Frankfurter to Roosevelt, 4 March 1936, FP, box 97.

[5]Brandeis to Frankfurter, 15 December 1935, FP, box 28. Early in 1936 Brandeis sent Frankfurter some figures on insurance companies' earnings, criticizing specifically the Equitable Insurance Company. Brandeis to Frankfurter, 9 and 26 February 1936, FP, box 28.

[6]Frankfurter to Roosevelt, 4 March 1936, FP, box 97; *PPA*, 6:102-7.

[7]Brandeis to Frankfurter, 5 April 1936, FP, box 28. The Revenue Act of 1936 was not a draconian measure. It left the rates on individual income taxes, estate taxes, and gift taxes practically the same as before. The innovation was a new surtax designed to force corporations to distribute their profits. The tax rates "were graduated according to the ratio of undistributed profits to adjusted net income." Sidney Ratner, *American Taxation* (New York: W. W. Norton Company, 1942), p. 473. Brandeis called for increases in corporation and estate taxes.

[8]The dispute was discussed in the Roosevelt-Frankfurter correspondence of February 1936, FP, box 97.

[9]Brandeis to Frankfurter, 15 December 1935, 9 and 27 February 1936, FP, box 28.

[10]Frankfurter's suggestions were not always welcome. He tried to discourage Eleanor Roosevelt from appearing on the same platform with the British pacifist George Lansbury by expressing concern to Missy LeHand. Mrs. Roosevelt was "furious" and dispatched Frankfurter a curt note. Joseph Lash, *Eleanor and*

Franklin (New York: W. W. Norton Company, 1971), pp. 562-63. The letters dealing with Palestinian matters are in P, box 63, folder 1.

[11]Frankfurter to Roosevelt, 13 June 1936, FP, box 97.

[12]Max Freedman, ed., *Roosevelt and Frankfurter, Their Correspondence, 1928-1945* (Boston: Little, Brown, and Company, 1967), pp. 347-49.

[13]Ibid., pp. 350-51.

[14]Ibid., pp. 351-52.

[15]Ibid., p. 347. A comparison of Frankfurter's draft with the platform adopted by the convention shows some resemblances, particularly in the opening sections which chronicle Republican failure and New Deal achievement. See Henry S. Commager, ed., *Documents of American History*, 2 vols. (New York: F. S. Crofts, 1944), 2:538-41.

[16]Brandeis to Frankfurter, 29 September 1936, FP, box 28.

[17]Brandeis to Frankfurter, 4 November 1936, FP, box 28.

[18]*PPA*, 6:302-3.

[19]Ibid.

[20]Frankfurter to Roosevelt, 24 May 1936, FP, box 97; Freedman, *Roosevelt and Frankfurter*, p. 424.

[21]Freedman, *Roosevelt and Frankfurter*, p. 425.

[22]Brandeis did applaud Sen. Robert LaFollete's expose of the violence used by employers. Brandeis to Frankfurter, 7 May 1937, FP, box 28.

[23]Roosevelt to Frankfurter, 25 June 1937, FP, box 98

[24]On 26 August 1937, Congress passed the Revenue Act of 1937 which attempted to close loopholes in the existing laws. Although it was strongly opposed by business interests, many loopholes remained in effect. Sidney Ratner, *American Taxation* (New York: W. W. Norton Company, 1942), pp. 477-78.

[25]Frankfurter to Roosevelt, 31 October 1937, FP, box 28.

[26]Freedman, *Roosevelt and Frankfurter*, pp. 430-31. Holmes wrote to Laski at the time: "I . . . regretted very much the decision as to stock dividends but that also couldn't be helped." Holmes to Laski, 11 March 1920.

[27]Ibid.

[28]Ibid.

[29]Ibid. Frankfurter cited pages 102-3 of Brandeis's *Other People's Money* to show that new enterprises "have never found it very easy to obtain money through ordinary investment banking channels."

[30]Freedman, *Roosevelt and Frankfurter*, pp. 434–36. Frankfurter went over old ground in arguing for the importance of small business and the danger of monopoly.

[31]William E. Leuchtenburg, *Franklin D. Roosevelt and the New Deal* (New York: Harper & Row, 1963), p. 244.

[32]Ibid., p. 245. Leuchtenburg lists such men as Eccles, Louis Bean, Mordecai Ezekiel, Lauchlin Currie, Hopkins, and Aubrey Williams. Also included were men closer to Brandeis and Frankfurter such as Isador Lubin, William Douglas, and Jerome Frank.

[33]Samuel Lubell, "The Daring Young Man on the Flying Pri-cees," *Saturday Evening Post*, 13 September 1941, p. 84. In October 1937 Brandeis wrote to Frankfurter: "I understand Leon Henderson is trying to make F.D. realize the danger of high prices." Brandeis to Frankfurter, 17 October 1937, FP, box 28.

[34]Brandeis criticized Roosevelt for opposing the Miller-Tydings Enabling Act which buttressed the "fair trade" laws. He also strongly opposed the reorganization bill. Brandeis to Frankfurter, 21 August 1937, FP, box 28; and 18 March 1938, FP, box 29.

[35]Ratner, *American Taxation*, pp. 478–82.

[36]Magill to Roosevelt, 14 May 1938, PPF 1820, box 4, quoted in Leuchtenburg, *Roosevelt and the New Deal*, p. 260. There is an irony in Magill's reforming role. Frankfurter had earlier described him as "bland" and "fundamentally a conventional conservative." Frankfurter to Brandeis, 4 December 1933, G, box 9, folder 2.

[37]Leuchtenburg, *Roosevelt and the New Deal*, p. 260.

[38]Frances Perkins, *The Roosevelt I Knew* (New York: The Viking Press, 1946), pp. 253–54.

[39]Frankfurter had suggested this step to Roosevelt earlier.

[40]Harold L. Ickes, *The Secret Diary of Harold L. Ickes* (New York: Simon and Schuster, 1953), is an excellent source for this campaign.

[41]Brandeis to Frankfurter, 14 November 1937, FP, box 28. In *Smyth* v. *Ames*, 169 U.S. 466 (1898), the Court voided an attempt by a state to set railroad rates.

The appointment of Thurman Arnold as assistant attorney general in charge of the antitrust division came at the end of 1938. Although Arnold had attracted Brandeis's attention in 1936 (Brandeis to Frankfurter, 5 and 27 November 1936, FP, box 28), he never commented on Arnold's trust-busting activities. Arnold did not believe big business had to be destroyed; he was content to enforce existing laws. See Gene M. Gressley, "Thurman Arnold, Antitrust, and the New Deal," *Business History Review* 38 (1964): 214–31.

[42]Frankfurter to Brandeis, 24 June 1938, SC, box 22, folder 2.

[43]Brandeis to Frankfurter, 28 July 1938, FP, box 28.

[45]Brandeis to Frankfurter, 7 April and 4 December 1938, FP, box 28. Brandeis was interested in getting some publicity for this view and asked Frankfurter if the *New York Times* and the *New York Herald Tribune* and other publications could "be induced to take up the subject wholly on economic-employment lines?"

[46]Alban W. Barkley, *That Reminds Me* (New York: Doubleday & Company, 1954), p. 96.

[47]Brandeis to Frankfurter, 30 July 1937, FP, box 28.

[48]Brandeis to Frankfurter, 11 February 1938, FP, box 28.

[49]Frankfurter to Brandeis, 26 July 1938, SC, box 22, folder 2; Brandeis to Frankfurter, 30 August 1938, FP, box 28. For a discussion of the final stages of the struggle, see Thomas McGraw, *Morgan* v. *Lilienthal* (Chicago: Loyola University Press, 1970). Arthur E. Morgan's side of the struggle is found in his *Making of the TVA* (Buffalo: Prometheus Books, 1974), pp. 164–85.

[50]Frankfurter to Brandeis, 19 July 1938, SC, box 22, folder 2.

[51]Frankfurter to Brandeis, 20 August 1938, SC, box 22, folder 2.

[52]Cohen to Frankfurter, 11 October 1937, FP, box 29.

[53]Ickes, *Diary*, 16 July 1938.

[54]Leonard Baker, *Back to Back* (New York: The Macmillan Company, 1967), p. 249. Baker quotes from the Morgenthau diaries, FDRL, book 69, p. 30,809.

[55]Freedman, *Roosevelt and Frankfurter*, p. 481.

[56]Brandeis to Frankfurter, 30 September 1938, FP, box 28; Freedman, *Roosevelt and Frankfurter*, p. 481.

[57]Ickes, *Diary*, 18 September 1938. Ickes observed that if Brandeis did not resign until after Roosevelt left office and a conservative was appointed, he "will have something to answer for to the liberals of the country."

[58]James Farley, *Jim Farley's Story: The Roosevelt Years* (New York: McGraw-Hill Book Company, 1948), pp. 161–62.

[59]Eugene Gerhart, *America's Advocate: Robert H. Jackson* (Indianapolis: Bobbs-Merrill, 1958), p. 166, quoted from Jackson's autobiographical notes.

[60]Ickes, *Diary*, 2 January 1939. Norris wrote a "long and persuasive letter" urging Frankfurter's appointment. See Freedman, *Roosevelt and Frankfurter*, p. 481.

[61]Roosevelt to Frankfurter, 4 January 1939, FP, box 98.

[62]Ickes, *Diary*, 15 January 1939.

[63]Acheson to Frankfurter, 26 April 1938, FP, box 19.

[64]Ickes, *Diary*, 15 January 1939.

[65]Ibid., 4 February 1939.

[66]Frankfurter to Brandeis, 13 February 1939, FP, box 28.

[67]Fanny Brandeis, memorandum, May 1940, M, box 18, folder 1.

[68]Brandeis to Frankfurter, 25 July 1940, FP, box 28.

[69]Brandeis to Frankfurter, 8 September 1940, FP, box 28.

[70]Brandeis to Frankfurter, 24 August 1941, FP, box 28.

[71]Brandeis to Roosevelt, 25 April 1941, PPF 2335. Roosevelt assured Brandeis that he had passed his suggestion along to the British. Roosevelt to Brandeis, 5 May 1941, PPF 2335.

[72]Frankfurter to Roosevelt, 14 October 1941, FP, box 98. Freedman, *Roosevelt and Frankfurter*, p. 618.

[73]Freedman, *Roosevelt and Frankfurter*, p. 744.

APPENDIX:
Brandeis's Recovery Program and the Historians

[1]See above, pp. 33-35.

[2]A. T. Mason, *Brandeis: A Free Man's Life* (New York: The Viking Press, 1946), pp. 613–27.

[3]James M. Burns, *Roosevelt: The Lion and the Fox* (New York: Harcourt, Brace and Company, 1956), p. 155.

[4]Arthur M. Schlesinger, Jr., *The Politics of Upheaval, 1935–1936* (Boston: Houghton Mifflin Company, 1960), p. 220.

[5]Ibid., p. 221.

[6]Ibid., p. 235.

[7]Ibid., p. 237.

[8]William E. Leuchtenburg, *Franklin D. Roosevelt and the New Deal* (New York: Harper & Row, 1963), pp. 163–64.

[9]Ibid., pp. 152, 260.

[10]Ellis Hawley, *The New Deal and the Problem of Monopoly* (Princeton: Princeton University Press, 1966), pp. 286–87

[11]Ibid., p. 287.

[12]Ibid., p. 344.

[13]Otis Graham, *Encore for Reform: The Old Progressives and the New Deal* (New York: Oxford University Press, 1967), p. 76.

[14]Ibid.

[15]Ibid., p. 125.

[16]Frank Freidel, *Franklin D. Roosevelt: Launching the New Deal* (Boston: Little, Brown, and Company, 1973), p. 340.

[17]Ibid., p. 345. Freidel argues that Landis, Corcoran, and Cohen were more advanced in their thinking than Brandeis. They were "all three . . . of the Brandeis-Wilson tradition, but ready to move well beyond the New Freedom" (p. 345). The truth is that Brandeis was never confined to the limitations of the New Freedom.

[18]Elliot A. Rosen, *Hoover, Roosevelt, and the Brains Trust: From Depression to New Deal* (New York: Columbia University Press, 1977), p. 205.

[19]Ibid., pp. 202–3, 244–45, 304.

BIBLIOGRAPHY

Manuscript and Oral History Sources

Adolf A. Berle, Jr., "Reminiscences," COHC, 1974.
Louis D. Brandeis Papers, University of Louisville.
Charles C. Burlingham, "Reminiscences," COHC, 1961.
Morris L. Cooke Papers, FDRL.
Mordecai Ezekiel, "Reminiscences," COHC, 1957.
Jerome N. Frank, "Reminiscences," COHC, 1960.
Felix Frankfurter Papers, Library of Congress.
Emmanuel A. Goldenweiser Papers, Library of Congress.
Stanley High Papers, FDRL.
Charles E. Hughes Papers, Library of Congress.
Gardner Jackson, "Reminiscences," COHC, 1959.
James M. Landis, "Reminiscences," COHC, 1964.
James M. Landis Papers, Library of Congress.
David E. Lilienthal Papers, Princeton University.
Herbert S. Marks Papers, FDRL.
Frances Perkins, "Reminiscences," COHC, 1976.
Lee Pressman, "Reminiscences," COHC, 1958.
Donald Richberg Papers, Library of Congress.
Samuel I. Rosenman Papers, FDRL.
Rexford Tugwell, "Reminiscences," COHC, 1972.
Rexford Tugwell Papers, FDRL.

Books

Acheson, Dean. *Morning and Noon.* Boston: Houghton Mifflin, 1965.

Alsop, Joseph, and Turner Catledge. *The 168 Days.* New York: Doubleday, Doran & Company, 1938.

Alsop, Joseph, and Robert Kintner. *Men Around the President.* New York: Doubleday, Doran & Company, 1939.

Baker, Leonard. *Back to Back: The Duel between FDR and the Supreme Court.* New York: The Macmillan Company, 1967.

Baker, Liva. *Felix Frankfurter,* New York: Coward-McCann, 1969,

Barkley, Alban W. *That Reminds Me.* New York: Doubleday & Company, 1954.

Bellush, Bernard. *The Failure of the NRA.* New York: Norton, 1975.

Berle, Adolf A., and Gardiner Means. *The Mordern Corporation and Private Property.* New York: The Macmillan Company, 1934.

Berle, Beatrice B., and Travis B. Jacobs. *Navigating the Rapids, 1918–1971: From the Papers of Adolf A. Berle.* New York: Harcourt Brace Jovanovich, 1973.

Biddle, Francis. *In Brief Authority.* Garden City: Doubleday and Company, 1962.

Blum, John M., ed., *From the Morgenthau Diaries.* Boston: Houghton Mifflin, 1959.

Brandeis, Louis D. *Business—A Profession.* Boston: Small, Maynard & Company, 1914.

———. *The Curse of Bigness and Miscellaneous Papers.* New York: Viking Press, 1934.

———. *Other People's Money—and How the Bankers Use It.* New York: Frederick A. Stokes Company, 1914.

Burns, James M. *Roosevelt: The Lion and the Fox.* New York: Harcourt, Brace and Company, 1956.

Byrnes, James F. *Speaking Frankly.* New York: Harper & Brothers, 1947.

Carosso, Vincent. *Investment Banking in America: A History.* Cambridge: Harvard University Press, 1970.

Childs, Marquis. *I Write From Washington.* New York: Harper & Row, 1942.

Clapper, Raymond. *Watching the World.* Edited by Mrs. Raymond Clapper. New York: McGraw-Hill, 1944.

Conrad, David E. *The Forgotten Farmers: The Story of Sharecroppers in the New Deal.* Urbana: University of Illinois Press, 1965.

Curtis, Charles P. *Lions under the Throne.* Boston: Houghton Mifflin Company, 1947.

Daniels, Jonathan. *Frontier on the Potomac*. New York: The Macmillan Company, 1946.

―――. *The Man of Independence*. New York: J. B. Lippincott Company, 1950.

Davis, Kenneth. *Franklin D. Roosevelt: The Beckoning of Destiny, 1882-1928*. New York: G. P. Putnam's Sons, 1972.

DeBedts, Ralph F. *The New Deal's SEC: The Formative Years*. New York: Columbia University Press, 1964.

Douglas, Paul H. *In the Fullness of Time: The Memoirs of Paul H. Douglas*. New York: Harcourt Brace Jovanovich, 1971.

Douglas, William O. *Go East, Young Man: The Early Years*. New York: Random House, 1974.

Eccles, Marriner S. *Beckoning Frontiers*. New York: Alfred A. Knopf, 1951.

Farley, James A. *Jim Farley's Story, the Roosevelt Years*. New York: McGraw-Hill, 1948.

Feis, Herbert. *1933: Characters in Crisis*. Boston: Little, Brown, and Company, 1966.

Flexner, Bernard. *Mr. Justice Brandeis and the University of Louisville*. Louisville: University of Louisville, 1938.

Flynn, Edward J. *You're the Boss*. New York: Viking Press, 1947.

Frankfurter, Felix. *The Business of the Supreme Court; A Study in the Federal Judicial System*. New York: The Macmillan Company, 1923.

―――. *Felix Frankfurter on the Supreme Court, Extrajudicial Essays on the Court and the Constitution*. Edited by Philip B. Kurland. Cambridge: Harvard University Press, 1970.

―――. *Law and Politics; Occasional Papers of Felix Frankfurter, 1913-1938*. Edited by Archibald MacLeish and E. F. Prichard. New York: Capricorn Books, 1962.

―――. *Mr. Justice Brandeis*. New Haven: Yale University Press, 1932.

―――. *Mr. Justice Holmes and the Supreme Court*. Cambridge: Harvard University Press, 1938.

―――. *Of Law and Life & Other Things That Matter; Papers and Addresses of Felix Frankfurter, 1956-1963*. Edited by Philip B. Kurland. Cambridge: Harvard University Press, 1965.

―――. *Of Law and Men; Papers and Addresses, 1939-1956*. Edited by Philip Elman. New York: Harcourt, Brace, 1956.

―――. *The Public & Its Government*. New Haven: Yale University Press, 1930.

Freedman, Max, ed. *Roosevelt and Frankfurter, Their Correspondence, 1928-1945*. Boston: Little, Brown, and Company, 1967.

Freidel, Frank. *Franklin D. Roosevelt: Launching the New Deal*. Boston: Little, Brown, and Company, 1973.

————. *Franklin D. Roosevelt: The Triumph.* Boston: Little, Brown, and Company, 1956.

Fuess, Claude M. *Joseph B. Eastman: Servant of the People.* New York: Columbia University Press, 1952.

Funigiello, Philip J. *Toward a National Power Policy: The New Deal and the Electric Utility Industry, 1933-1941.* Pittsburgh: University of Pittsburgh, 1973.

Fusfeld, Daniel R. *The Economic Thought of Franklin D. Roosevelt.* New York: Columbia University Press, 1956.

Gerhart, Eugene. *America's Advocate: Robert H. Jackson.* Indianapolis: Bobbs-Merrill, 1958.

Goldman, Solomon, ed. *The Words of Justice Brandeis.* New York: H. Schuman, 1953.

Graham, Otis. *Encore for Reform: The Old Progressives and the New Deal.* New York: Oxford University Press, 1967.

————. *Toward a Planned Society: From Roosevelt to Nixon.* New York: Oxford University Press, 1976.

Grubbs, Donald H. *Cry From the Cotton: The Southern Tenant Farmer's Union and the New Deal.* Chapel Hill: University of North Carolina, 1971.

Hapgood, Norman. *The Changing Years.* New York: Farrar & Reinhart, 1930

Harrod, Roy F. *The Life of John Maynard Keynes.* New York: Augustus M. Kelley, 1969.

Hawley, Ellis. *The New Deal and the Problem of Monopoly.* Princeton: Princeton University Press, 1966.

Hendel, Samuel. *Charles Evans Hughes and the Supreme Court.* New York: King's Crown Press, 1951.

Himmelberg, Robert F. *The Origins of the NRA.* New York: Fordham University Press, 1976.

Hollingsworth, Harold M., and William Holmes. *Essays on the New Deal.* Austin: University of Texas Press, 1969.

Howe, Mark DeWolfe, ed. *The Holmes-Laski Letters.* 2 vols. New York: Atheneum, 1963.

Hurd, Charles. *When the New Deal Was Young and Gay.* New York: Hawthorn Books, 1965.

Huthmacher, J. Joseph. *Senator Robert F. Wagner and the Rise of Urban Liberalism.* New York: Atheneum, 1968.

Ickes, Harold L. *The Secret Diary of Harold L. Ickes.* 2 vols. New York: Simon and Schuster, 1953.

Janeway, Eliot. *The Struggle for Survival: A Chronicle of Economic Mobilization in World War II.* New Haven: Yale University Press, 1951.

Johnson, Hugh S. *The Blue Eagle From Egg to Earth.* New York: Doubleday, Doran & Company, 1935.

Jones, Jesse, and Edward Araly. *Fifty Billion Dollars: My Thirteen Years with the RFC, 1932-1945.* New York: The Macmillan Company, 1951.

Kelly, Alfred H., and Winifred A. Harbison, *The American Constitution: Its Origins and Development.* New York: Norton, 1970.

Kempton, Murray. *Part of Our Time, Some Ruins and Monuments of the Thirties.* New York: Simon and Schuster, 1955.

Kennedy, Susan Eastabrooke. *The Banking Crisis of 1933.* Lexington: The University Press of Kentucky, 1973.

Kimmel, Lewis H. *Federal Budget and Fiscal Policy, 1789-1958.* Washington, D.C.: Brookings Institute, 1959.

Kirkendall, Richard S. *Social Scientists and Farm Politics in the Age of Roosevelt.* Columbia: University of Missouri Press, 1966.

Koenig, Louis W. *The Invisible Presidency.* New York: Holt, Rinehart, and Winston, 1960.

Konefsky, Samuel Joseph. *The Legacy of Holmes and Brandeis: A Study in the Influence of Ideas.* New York: The Macmillan Company, 1956.

Krock, Arthur. *Memoirs: Sixty Years on the Firing Line.* New York: Popular Library, 1968.

Kurland, Philip B. *Mr. Justice Frankfurter and the Constitution.* Chicago: Chicago University Press, 1971.

Lash, Joseph P. *Eleanor and Franklin.* New York: W. W. Norton Company, 1971.

_____. *From the Diaries of Felix Frankfurter.* New York: Norton, 1975.

Lerner, Max. *Ideas Are Weapons: The History and Uses of Ideas.* New York: The Viking Press, 1940.

Leuchtenburg, William E. *Franklin D. Roosevelt and the New Deal.* New York: Harper & Row, 1963.

Lief, Alfred. *The Brandeis Guide to the Modern World.* Boston: Little, Brown and Company, 1941.

_____. *Brandeis: The Personal History of an American Ideal.* New York: Stackpole Sons, 1936.

_____. *The Social and Economic Views of Mr. Justice Brandeis.* New York: The Vanguard Press, 1930.

Lilienthal, David E. *The Journals of David E. Lilienthal.* vol 1. *The TVA Years, 1939-1945, Including a Selection of Journal Entries from the 1917-1939 Period.* New York: Harper & Row, 1964.

Lindley, Ernst K., and Jay Franklin. *The New Dealers.* New York: Simon and Schuster, 1934.

Lord, Russell. *The Wallaces of Iowa.* Boston: Houghton Mifflin Company, 1947.

Lowitt, Richard. *George W. Norris: Persistence of a Progressive 1913-1933*. Urbana: University of Illinois Press, 1971.

———. *George W. Norris: The Triumph of a Progressive, 1933-1944*. Champaign: University of Illinois Press, 1978.

Lubove, Roy. *The Struggle for Social Security, 1900-1935*. Cambridge: Harvard University Press, 1968.

Lynch, David. *The Concentration of Economic Power*. New York: Columbia University Press, 1946.

McCune, Wesley. *The Nine Young Men*. New York: Harper & Brothers, 1947.

McGraw, Thomas K. *Morgan v. Lilienthal*. Chicago: Loyola University Press, 1970.

———. *TVA and the Power Fight, 1933-1939*. New York: J. B. Lippincott Company, 1971.

Mason, Alpheus T. *Brandeis A Free Man's Life*. New York: The Viking Press, 1946.

———. *Brandeis, Lawyer and Judge in the Modern State*. Princeton: Princeton University Press, 1933.

———. *The Brandeis Way: A Case Study in the Workings of Democracy*. Princeton: Princeton University Press, 1938.

———. *Harlan Fiske Stone: Pillar of the Law*. New York: Viking Press, 1956.

Mendelson, Wallace. *Felix Frankfurter: A Tribute*. New York: Reynal and Company, 1964.

Mersky, Roy. *Louis Dembitz Brandeis, 1856-1941: A Bibliography*. New Haven: Yale Law School, 1958.

Michelson, Charles. *The Ghost Talks*. New York: G. P. Putnam's Sons, 1944.

Mitchell, Broaddus. *Depression Decade: From New Era through New Deal, 1929-1941*. New York: Harper Torchbooks, 1969.

Moley, Raymond. *After Seven Years*. New York: Harper & Brothers, 1939.

———. *The First New Deal*. New York: Harcourt, Brace & World, 1966.

———. *27 Masters of Politics*. New York: Funk and Wagnalls, 1949.

Morgan, Arthur E. *The Making of the TVA*. Buffalo: Prometheus, 1974.

Morgenthau, Henry, Jr. *From the Morgenthau Diaries*. Edited by John M. Blum. Houghton Mifflin, 1959.

Morison, Elting E. *Turmoil and Tradition: A Study of the Life and Times of Henry L. Stimson*. Boston: Houghton Mifflin Company, 1960.

Murphy, Paul L. *The Constitution in Crisis Times: 1918-1939*. New York: Harper & Row, 1972.

Nelson, Daniel. *Unemployment Insurance: The American Experience, 1915-1935*. Madison: University of Wisconsin Press, 1969.

Nixon, Edgar B. *Franklin D. Roosevelt and Conservation.* Hyde Park: Franklin D. Roosevelt Library, 1957.

Parrish, Michael E. *Securities Regulation and the New Deal.* New Haven: Yale University Press, 1970.

Paschal, Joel Francis. *Mr. Justice Sutherland, A Man Against the State.* Princeton: Princeton University Press, 1951.

Patterson, James T. *Congressional Conservatism and the New Deal.* Lexington: University Press of Kentucky, 1967.

Peare, Catherine Owens. *The Louis D. Brandeis Story.* New York: Crowell, 1970.

Pearson, Drew, and Robert S. Allen. *Nine Old Men.* Garden City: Doubleday, Doran, 1937.

Pecora, Ferdinand. *Wall Street under Oath.* New York: Simon and Schuster, 1939.

Perkins, Frances. *The Roosevelt I Knew.* New York: The Viking Press, 1946.

Perkins, Van L. *Crisis in Agriculture: The Agricultural Adjustment Administration and the New Deal, 1933.* Berkeley: University of California Press, 1969.

Phillips, Harlan B., ed. *Felix Frankfurter Reminisces.* New York: Reynal & Company, 1960.

Pusey, Merlo J. *Charles Evans Hughes.* New York: The Macmillan Company, 1951.

———. *The Supreme Court Crisis.* New York: The Macmillan Company, 1937.

Rabinowitz, Ezekiel. *Justice Louis D. Brandeis: The Zionist Chapter of His Life.* New York: Philosophical Library, 1968.

Ratner, Sidney. *American Taxation.* New York: W. W. Norton Company, 1942.

Richberg, Donald R. *My Hero, The Indiscreet Memoirs of an Eventful but Unheroic Life.* New York: G. P. Putnam's Sons, 1954.

Robinson, Edgar Eugene. *The Roosevelt Leadership, 1933-1945.* Philadelphia: J. B. Lippincott Company, 1955.

Rollins, Alfred B. *Roosevelt and Howe.* New York: Alfred A. Knopf, 1962.

Roosevelt, Eleanor. *This I Remember.* New York: Harper & Brothers, 1949.

Roosevelt, Elliot, ed. *F.D.R. His Personal Letters.* 4 vols. New York: Duell, Sloan and Pearce, 1950.

Rosen, Elliot A. *Hoover, Roosevelt, and the Brains Trust: From Depression to New Deal.* New York: Columbia University Press, 1977.

Rosenman, Samuel I. *Working with Roosevelt.* New York: Harper & Brothers, 1952.

Rosten, Leo C. *Washington Correspondents*. New York: Harcourt, Brace and Company, 1937.

Salmond, John A. *The Civilian Conservation Corps, 1933–1942: A New Deal Case Study.* Durham: Duke University Press, 1967.

Schlesinger, Arthur M., Jr. *The Coming of the New Deal.* Boston: Houghton Mifflin Company, 1958.

————. *The Crisis of the Old Order, 1919–1933.* Boston: Houghton Mifflin Company, 1957.

————. *The Politics of Upheaval, 1935–1936.* Boston: Houghton Mifflin Company, 1960.

Selznich, Philip. *TVA and the Grass Roots.* Berkeley: University of California Press, 1949.

Sherwood, Robert E. *Roosevelt and Hopkins.* New York: Harper & Brothers, 1948.

Sternsher, Bernard. *Rexford Tugwell and the New Deal.* New Brunswick: Rutgers University Press, 1964.

Stimson, Henry S., and McGeorge Bundy. *On Active Service in Peace and War.* New York: Harper & Brothers, 1947.

Thomas, Helen Shirley. *Felix Frankfurter: Scholar on the Bench.* Baltimore: The Johns Hopkins Press, 1960.

Todd, Alden. *Justice on Trial: The Case of Louis D. Brandeis.* New York: McGraw-Hill, 1964.

Trombley, Kenneth E. *The Life and Times of a Happy Liberal.* New York: Harper & Brothers, 1954.

Tugwell, Rexford G. *The Brains Trust.* New York: Viking Press, 1968.

————. *The Democratic Roosevelt: A Biography of FDR.* New York: Doubleday & Company, 1957.

Tully, Grace. *F.D.R., My Boss.* New York: Charles Scribner's Sons, 1949.

Urofsky, Melvin I. *A Mind of One Piece: Brandeis and American Reform.* New York: Charles Scribner's Sons, 1971.

————, and David Levy. *The Letters of Louis D. Brandeis.* 5 vols. Albany: State University of New York Press, 1972–78.

Vadney, Thomas E. *The Wayward Liberal: A Political Biography of Donald Richberg.* Lexington: University Press of Kentucky, 1970.

Wallace, Henry. *New Frontiers.* New York: Reynal, 1934.

Wehle, Louis B. *Hidden Threads of History: Wilson Through Roosevelt.* New York: The Macmillan Company, 1953.

Whitman, William. *David Lilienthal.* New York: Henry Holt and Company, 1948.

Witte, Edwin E. *The Development of the Social Security Act.* Madison: University of Wisconsin Press, 1963.

Journal and Magazine Articles

Abrahams, Paul P. "Brandeis and Lamont on Finance Capitalism."
    Business History Review 47 (1973) 72–94.
Acheson, Dean "Felix Frankfurter." *Harvard Law Review* 76 (1962):
    14–16.
_____. "Mr. Justice Brandeis." *Harvard Law Review* 55 (1941):
    191–92.
Alsop, Joseph, and Robert S. Kintner. "Trust-buster—the Folklore of
    Thurman Arnold." *Saturday Evening Post*, 12 August 1939, pp.
    5–11.
_____. "We Shall Make America Over. The Birth of the Brain Trust."
    Saturday Evening Post, 29 October 1938, pp. 5–7, 74–80.
_____. "We Shall Make America Over: The New Dealers in Action."
    Saturday Evening Post, 19 November 1938, pp. 14–15, 85–92.
Amidon, Beulah. "Other People's Insurance: The Social Invention of
    Louis D. Brandeis." *Survey Graphic*, November 1936, pp. 598–602,
    638–40.
Auerbach, Jerold S. "New Deal, Old Deal, or Raw Deal: Some Thoughts
    on New Left Historiography," *Journal of Southern History* 35
    (1969): 18–30.
_____. "Southern Tenant Farmers: Socialist Critics of the New Deal."
    Labor History 7 (1966): 3–18.
Beard, Charles A. "America Must Stay Big." *Today*, 14 September 1935,
    pp. 3–4, 21.
Belair, Felix. "Two of the Selfless Six." *The Nation's Business*, July
    1937, pp. 25–26, 90–93.
"Benjamin V. Cohen: Utility Act and Its Author Have Their Day in
    Court." *Newsweek*, 21 February 1938, pp. 13–14.
Benston, George J. "Required Disclosure and the Stock Market: An
    Evaluation of the Securities Exchange Act of 1934." *American
    Economic Review* 68 (1973): 132–55.
Berle, Adolf A. "A High Road for Business." *Scribner's Magazine*, June
    1933, pp. 325–32.
_____. "Revenue and Progress." *Survey Graphic*, October 1935, pp.
    469–73, 512.
_____. "The Way of an American." *Survey Graphic*, November 1936,
    p. 597.
Bickel, Alexander M. "Felix Frankfurter," *Harvard Law Review* 78
    (1935): 1527–28.

———. "Frankfurter and Friend." *New Republic*, 3 February 1968, pp. 27–31.

———. "Passion and Passion: Centennial Year Thoughts on the Brandeis Way." *New Republic*, 12 November 1956, pp. 15–17.

Bloom, Solomon F. "The Liberalism of Louis D. Brandeis: The Father of the New Deal." *Commentary*, 10 June 1948, pp. 313–21.

Bolles, Blair. "Cohen and Corcoran: Brain Twins." *American Mercury*, January 1938, pp. 38–45.

———. "Prose and Politics: Writers in the New Deal." *Saturday Review of Literature*, 30 March 1940, pp. 3–4, 17.

"Boomerang and Blackjack." *Time Magazine*, 22 July 1935, pp. 14–15.

Braemer, John. "The New Deal and the 'Broker State': A Review of the Recent Scholarly Literature." *Business History Review* 46 (1972): 409–29.

"Brain Rivalry: Growing Influence of Frankfurter and Harvard." *Business Week*, 24 May 1933, pp. 14–15.

Bremer, William W. "Along the 'American Way': The New Deal's Work Relief Programs for the Unemployed." *Journal of American History* 42 (1975): 636–53.

Bunting, David. "Interlocking Directorates." *Business History Review* 45 (1971): 317–35.

Carosso, Vincent. "Washington and Wall Street: The New Deal and Investment Bankers, 1933–1940." *Business History Review* 44 (1970): 425–45.

Carter, John F. "Big Bad Wolves vs Little Hot Dogs." *Today*, 2 November 1935, pp. 5, 20–22.

Childs, Marquis W. "Robert H. Jackson, the Man Who Has Always Been a New Dealer." *Forum and Century*, March 1940, pp. 148–54.

———. "The Supreme Court Today." *Harper's Magazine*, May 1938, pp. 581–88.

Clapper, Raymond. "Felix Frankfurter's Young Men." *Review of Reviews*, January 1936, pp. 27–29, 57.

———. "Top Sergeants of the New Deal." *Review of Reviews*, August 1933, pp. 19–23.

———. "What Will the Supreme Court Say?" *Review of Reviews*, January 1935, pp. 37–40, 72.

Coyle, David C. "Decentralize Industry." *Virginia Quarterly Review*, July 1935, pp. 321–38.

———. "The Twilight of National Planning." *Harper's Magazine*, October 1935, pp. 562–67.

Creel, George W. "Young Man Went East." *Collier's Magazine*, 9 May 1936, pp. 9, 95.

Davenport, Walter. "It Seems There Were Two Irishmen." *Collier's Magazine*, 10 September 1938, pp. 14, 76–79.

Dilliard, Irving. "Memoir Off The Record." *Saturday Review*, 9 July 1960, pp. 14–15.

Epstein, Abraham. "Enemies of Unemployment Insurance." *New Republic*, 16 September 1933, pp. 94–96.

Flexner, Bernard. "The Fight on the Securities Act." *Atlantic Monthly*, February 1934, pp. 232–50.

Flynn, John T. "Other People's Money." *New Republic*, 18 August 1937, p. 46.

Frankfurter, Felix. "Bankers and the Conspiracy Law." *New Republic*, 21 January 1925, pp. 218–20.

_____ "Brandeis." *New Republic*, 5 February 1916, pp. 4–6.

_____ "Can the Supreme Court Guarantee Toleration?" *New Republic*, 17 June 1925, pp. 85–87.

_____ "Democracy and the Expert." *Atlantic Monthly*, November 1930, pp. 649–60.

_____ "The Federal Securities Act." *Fortune Magazine*, August 1933, pp. 53–55, 106–11.

_____ "Herbert Croly and the American Political Opinion." *New Republic*, 16 July 1930, pp. 247–50.

_____ "Mr. Hoover on Power Control." *New Republic*, 17 October 1928, pp. 240–43.

_____ "Mr. Justice Roberts." *University of Pennsylvania Law Review* 104 (1955): 311–17.

_____ "Public Services and the Public." *Yale Review*, September 1930, pp. 1–24.

_____ "Rigid Outlook in a Dynamic World." *Survey Graphic*, January 1938, pp. 5–7.

_____ "Social Issues before the Supreme Court." *Yale Review*, March 1933, pp. 476–95.

_____ "The Supreme Court and the Public." *Forum*, June 1930, pp. 329–34.

_____ "United States Supreme Court Molding the Constitution." *Current History*, May 1930, pp. 235–40.

_____ "What Has Prohibition Done to America?" *New Republic*, 15 November 1922, pp. 305–6.

_____ "What We Confront in American Life." *Survey Graphic*, March 1933, pp. 133–36.

_____ "Why I Am for Smith." *New Republic*, 31 October 1928, pp. 292–95.

_____ "Why I Shall Vote for LaFollette." *New Republic* 22 October 1925, pp. 199–201.

————. "Young Men Go to Washington." *Fortune Magazine*, January 1936 pp. 61-63.

"Frankfurter and FDR." *Newsweek*, 15 January 1968, p. 73.

"Frankfurter Biography *Fortune Magazine*, January 1936, pp. 63, 87-90.

Freund, Paul. "The Liberalism of Louis D. Brandeis." *American Jewish Archives*, April 1958, pp. 3-11.

————. "Mr. Justice Brandeis: A Centennial Memoir." *Harvard Law Review* 70 (1957): 709-92.

Garraty, John A. "The New Deal, National Socialism, and the Great Depression." *American Historical Review* 78 (1973): 907-44.

Gressley, Gene M. "Thurman Arnold, Antitrust, and the New Deal." *Business History Review* 38 (1964): 214-31.

Hamilton, Walton N. "The Jurist's Art." *Columbia Law Review* 33 (1931): 1073-93.

Handlin, Oscar. "Reader's Choice." *Atlantic Monthly*, February 1968, pp. 138-39.

Hapgood, Norman. "Justice Brandeis: Apostle of Freedom." *Nation*, 5 October 1937, pp. 330-31.

Heffron, Paul. "Felix Frankfurter: Manuscript Historian." *Manuscripts* 23 (1971): 179-84.

Hawley, Ellis W. "Herbert Hoover, the Commerce Secretariat, and the Vision of an "Associative State," 1921-1928." *Journal of American History* 61 (1974): 116-40.

Jackson, Gardner. "Henry Wallace: A Divided Mind." *Atlantic Monthly*, August 1948, pp. 27-33.

Jaffe, Louis L. "The Constitutional Universe of Mr. Justice Frankfurter." *Harvard Law Review* 62 (1949): 357-73.

————. "Professors and Judges as Advisors to Government: Reflections on the Roosevelt-Frankfurter Relationship." *Harvard Law Review* 83 (1969): 366-75.

————. "Was Brandeis an Activist? The Search for Intermediate Premises." *Harvard Law Review* 80 (1967): 986-1003.

"The Janizariat." *Time Magazine*, 12 September 1938, pp. 22-34.

Johnson, Hughes S. "Think Fast, Captain!" *Saturday Evening Post*, 26 October 1935, pp. 5-7, 85-86.

Johnson, James E. "Drafting the NRA Code of Fair Competition for the Bituminous Coal Industry." *Journal of American History* 53 (1965): 521-41.

Johnston, Alva. "White House Tommy." *Saturday Evening Post*, 31 July 1937, pp. 5, 65-67.

Kenin, Garson. "Trips to Felix." *Atlantic Monthly*, March 1964, pp. 55-62.

Kirkendall, Richard S. "A. A. Berle, Jr., Student of the Corporation, 1917–1932." *Business History Review* 35 (1961): 43–58.

———. "Franklin D. Roosevelt and the Service Intellectual." *Mississippi Valley Historical Review* 49 (1962): 456–71.

———. "The New Deal as Watershed: The Recent Literature." *Journal of American History* 54 (1968): 839–52.

Kraines, Oscar. "Brandeis' Philosophy of Scientific Management." *Western Political Quarterly* 13 (1960): 191–201.

Landis, James M. "The Legislative History of the Securities Act of 1933." *George Washington Law Review* 28 (1959): 29–49.

Laski, Harold J. "Mr. Justice Brandeis." *Harper's Magazine*, January 1934, pp. 209–18.

———. "The Roosevelt Experiment." *Atlantic Monthly*, February 1934, pp. 143–53.

Lerner, Max. "Homage to Brandeis." *Nation*, 25 February 1939, p. 222.

Levy, David. "The Lawyer as Judge: Brandeis' Views of the Legal Profession." *Oklahoma Law Review* 22 (1969): 374–95.

Lilienthal, David E. "The TVA and Decentralization." *Survey Graphic*, June 1940, pp. 335–37, 363–67.

Lubell, Samuel. "The Daring Young Man of the Flying Pri-cees." *Saturday Evening Post*, 13 September 1941, pp. 12–13, 78–86.

McCarter, John. "Atlas with Ideas." *New Yorker*, 16 January 1943, pp. 23–30 and 23 January 1943, pp. 20–29.

McClennen, Edward F. "Louis D. Brandeis as a Lawyer." *Massachusetts Law Quarterly* 33 (1948): 1–28.

Magruder, Calvert C. "Mr. Justice Brandeis." *Harvard Law Review* 55 (1941): 193–94.

Miller, Neville. "Justice Brandeis and the University of Louisville School of Law." *The Filson Club History Quarterly* 34 (1960): 156–59.

Mitchell, J. "Brandeis' Heavenly Visitor." *New Republic*, 2 December 1936, p. 150.

Moley, Raymond. "Felix Frankfurter." *Newsweek*, 12 September 1938, p. 40.

———. "Frankfurter Rumors." *Newsweek*, 4 October 1937, p. 44.

———. "The Legend of Landis." *Fortune Magazine*, August 1934, pp. 44–47, 118–20.

———. "A Real Lawyer Clean-up." *Today*, 3 February 1934, p. 13.

———. "Regulation— The Reality or the Illusion." *Today*, 17 March 1934, p. 13.

———. "Sweet Compulsion." *Newsweek*, 12 December 1938, p. 44.

———. "There are Three Brains Trusts." *Today*, 14 April 1934, pp. 3–4, 23.

Moore, James R. "Sources of New Deal Economic Policy: The International Dimension." *Journal of American History* 61 (1974): 728-44.

Mulder, Ronald S. "The Progressive Insurgents in the United States Senate, 1935-1936: Was There a Second New Deal?" *Mid-America* 57 (1975): 106-25.

Murphy, Bruce Allen. "A Supreme Court Justice as Politician: Felix Frankfurter and Federal Court Appointments." *American Journal of Legal History* 21 (1977): 316-34.

Nash, Gerald D. "Herbert Hoover and the Origins of the Reconstruction Finance Corporation." *Mississippi Valley Historical Review* 46 (1959): 453-68.

Nathanson, Nathaniel L. "Mr. Justice Brandeis: A Law Clerk's Recollections of the October Term, 1934." *American Jewish Archives* 15 (1963) 6-13.

"Necks In: Irishman and Jew Keep Quiet Behind Today's Rooseveltian Brain Trust." *Literary Digest*, 22 May 1937, pp. 7-8.

"New Dealers Still Wanted: Reports about Corcoran and Cohen." *New Republic*, 13 January 1941, p. 40.

Nichols, Jeannette P. "Roosevelt's Monetary Diplomacy in 1933." *American Historical Review* 56 (1951): 295-317.

Peek, George N., and Samuel Crowthen. "In and Out: The Experiences of the First AAA Administrator." *Saturday Evening Post*, 16 May 1936, pp. 5-7, 105-110.

Raushenbush, Elizabeth Brandeis. "Wisconsin Tackles Job Security." *The Survey*, 15 December 1931, pp. 295-96.

———. "Employment Reserves vs. Insurance." *New Republic*, 27 May 1933, pp. 177-79.

———. "Security for Americans." *New Republic*, 5 December 1934, pp. 94-97.

Raushenbush, Paul. "Job Insurance." *Today*, 17 February 1934, pp. 6-7.

———. "Starting Unemployment Compensation in Wisconsin." *Unemployment Insurance Review* 4 (1967): 16-28.

Reeves, William D. "PWA and Competitive Administration in the New Deal." *Journal of American History* 60 (1973): 357-72.

Rhodes, Benjamin D. "Herbert Hoover and the War Debts." *Prologue* 6 (1974): 130-44.

Richberg, Donald. "The Industrial Liberalism of Justice Brandeis." *Columbia Law Review* 31 (1931): 1094-1103.

Rodell, Fred. "Felix Frankfurter, Conservative." *Harper's Magazine*, October 1941, pp. 449-59.

Roose, Kenneth D. "The Recession of 1937-38." *Journal of Political Economy* 56 (1948): 239-48.

Rosen, Elliot A. "Roosevelt and the Brains Trust: An Historiographical Overview." *Political Science Quarterly* 87 (1972): 531-57.
Rosenfarb, Joseph. "Reflections on a Visit to Mr. Justice Brandeis." *Iowa Law Review* 27 (1942): 359-66.
Rossiter, Clinton. "The Political Philosophy of Franklin D. Roosevelt." *Review of Politics* 2 (1949): 87-95.
Sargent, James E. "FDR and Lewis W. Douglas: Budget Balancing and the Early New Deal." *Prologue* 6 (1974): 33-43.
Shapiro, Edward S. "Decentralist Intellectuals and the New Deal." *Journal of American History* 58 (1972): 938-57.
Sireveg, Torbjorn. "Rooseveltian Ideas and the 1937 Court Fight: A Neglected Factor." *The Historian* 33 (1971): 578-95.
Stern, Max. "The Little Red House." *Today*, 19 May 1934, p. 5.
Tugwell, Rexford G. "The Compromising Roosevelt." *Western Political Quarterly* 6 (1953): 320-41.
———. "Roosevelt and Frankfurter: An Essay Review." *Political Science Quarterly* 85 (1970): 99-114.
———. "The Two Great Roosevelts." *Western Political Quarterly* 5 (1952): 84-93.
"Twins: New Deal's Legislative Architects, Corcoran and Cohen." *Newsweek*, 13 July 1935, pp. 24-25.
Urofsky, Melvin I. "The Conservatism of Mr. Justice Brandeis." *Modern Age: A Quarterly Review* 23 (1978): 39-48.
———. "The Lawyer-Qua-Citizen: The Relevence of Brandeis Today." *The Filson Club History Quarterly* 47 (1973): 5-13.
———. "Wilson, Brandeis and the Trust Issue." *Mid-America* 49 (1967): 3-28.
Venkataramani, M. S. "Norman Thomas, Arkansas Sharecroppers, and the Roosevelt Agricultural Problems, 1933-37." *Mississippi Valley Historical Review* 47 (1960): 225-46.
Villard, Oswald G. "Career of Brandeis." *The Nation*, 10 October 1936, p. 422.
Weiner, Stephen A. "Mr. Justice Brandeis, Competition and Smallness: A Dilemma Re-explained." *Yale Law Journal* 66 (1956-57): 69-96.
Wicker, Elmus. "Roosevelt's 1933 Monetary Experiment." *Journal of American History*, 57 (1971): 864-79.
Wilson, William. "The Two New Deals: A Valid Historical Concept?" *The Historian* 28 (1966): 268-88.
Wittke, Carl. "Mr. Justice Clarke—A Supreme Court Judge in Retirement." *Mississippi Valley Historical Review* 36 (1949): 27-50.
Wyzanski, Charles. "Brandeis." *Atlantic Monthly*, November 1956, pp. 66-72.

INDEX

Index

271

Resettlement Administation, 72, 210
Revenue Act of 1935, 117-19
Revenue Act of 1936, 245
Revenue Act of 1937, 246
Revenue Act of 1938, 161
Richberg, Donald, 39, 53, 64-68, 82, 131, 140, 208-9, 231, 240
Riesman, David, 11-12, 33, 131
Ritchie v. *Wayman* (Illinois), 180
Roberts, Owen, 15, 135, 146, 152-53, 235, 239
Robinson, Joseph, 149-50
Rogers, James Harvey, 58, 93
Roosevelt, Eleanor, 245
Roosevelt, Franklin D., ix, 5-10, 12, 22-24, 26, 31, 34, 37, 39-45, 47-48, 53, 55-56, 58, 60-62, 66-70, 73, 77-78, 80-82, 86-95, 97-103, 106-10, 114-23, 125-34, 136-37, 139-43, 145, 147-49, 151-52, 156-63, 165-67, 169-70, 174-75, 184-85, 189, 198-99, 203, 214-15, 218-19, 221, 223-24, 227-32, 235-38, 241, 243-45, 247, 249
Roosevelt, Theodore, 1, 9, 151
Root, Elihu, 3
Roper, Daniel, 59, 78, 93, 98
Rosen, Elliot A., 175-76
Rosenberg, James, 45, 198
Rosenman, Samuel I., 91, 133, 140, 218
Rural Electrification Administration, 123, 234

Sacco-Vanzetti case, 200
St. Louis Railroad, 196
Savings Bank Insurance League, 226
Schechter v. *United States*, 68-69, 129-31, 133, 135
Schlesinger, Arthur M., Jr., 21, 174
Securities and Exchange Commission, 120, 184, 205, 222
Securities Exchange Act, 94, 96-100, 170, 222
Securities Regulation, 78-81
Sedgewick, Ellery, 90
Seward, William H., 24
"Share Our Wealth," 115

Shea, Frank, 78
Sherman Act, 16, 25, 59, 69, 120, 162, 187
Shulman, Harry, 62, 206
Slattery, Henry, 50, 200
Smith, Al, 9, 37, 90, 182, 185
Smyth v. *Ames*, 162, 247
Snow, C.P., 190
Social Security, 103-12
Social Security Act, 70, 112, 132, 170
Southern Tenant Farmers' Union, 72, 77
Sprague, Oliver, 53, 88-90, 218
State Department, 60, 197
Stephens, Harold, 54, 56, 88, 204
Stevens, Raymond, 52, 201
Stewart Dry Goods v. *Lewis*, 126, 235
Stimson, Henry L., 1-3, 43-44, 81, 120, 197, 232
Stone, Harlan F., 15, 54, 127, 135-36, 143, 164, 237, 239, 242
Supreme Court, 3-6, 16, 19, 27-29, 68-70, 91, 125-37, 139-53, 159-60, 164-66, 169, 182, 186, 210, 240-43, 245
Survey Graphic, 31, 104
Sutherland, George, 19, 128, 135, 147-48, 234, 239
Sutherland, William A., 55, 198, 203-4
Swarthmore Unemployment Institute, 104, 225

Taft, William Howard, 127, 180, 209
Tammany Hall, 9
Tax policy, 29-30, 114-15, 117-19, 156, 159-61, 187
Taylor, Frederick, 7, 35, 183
Tennessee Valley Authority (TVA), 19, 55, 81-83, 90, 133, 135, 164, 189, 215-16
Texas, 79
Textile Industry, 12-13
Thayer, James B., 2, 19, 21, 27, 188
Thomas, Norman, 70, 73
Thompson, Huston, 44, 78-81, 198, 213-14
Today magazine, 39